I COULD DO
ANYTHING
IF I ONLY KNEW WHAT IT WAS

I COULD DO ANYTHING

IF I ONLY KNEW WHAT IT WAS

How to Discover What You Really Want and How to Get It

BARBARA SHER

WITH

BARBARA SMITH

DELACORTE PRESS

Published by
Delacorte Press
Bantam Doubleday Dell Publishing Group, Inc.
1540 Broadway
New York, New York 10036

LIBRARY OF CONGRESS CATALOGING IN PUBLICATION DATA

Sher, Barbara.
I could do anything if I only knew what it was : how to discover what you really want and how to get it / by Barbara Sher with Barbara Smith.
p.   cm.
ISBN 0-385-30788-8
1. Self-actualization (Psychology) 2. Career changes— Psychological aspects. 3. Goal (Psychology) I. Smith, Barbara. II. Title.
BF637.S4S518   1994
158'.1—dc20   93-14478   CIP

Manufactured in the United States of America

Published simultaneously in Canada

April 1994

10 9

BVG

To the memory of my beloved dad, Sam Sher.
He lit up our lives.

Acknowledgments

T HANKS TO the many people who gave hours to the reading and critiquing of this manuscript—there are too many to mention by name, but you know who you are and you'll find your influence in these pages. Four readers must be given special thanks: Susan Brauser, a great reader, and Julie Schonfeld, a fine writer (and Julie's dad who told her what the good life is—you'll find him quoted in the Introduction). Judith Riven went over the manuscript line by line and was a great help. The fourth reader is my wonderful mom, Nettie Sher, who was fascinated by these pages and when she finished, looked at me and said, "You should have been twins."

Kris Dahl and Leslie Schnur are my guardian angels—the agent and the editor from heaven. I thank them for a great experience. May they live long and be well.

Most of all, I want to thank my clients who have always had the courage to confront their own lives and change them into lives they love. They have inspired me year after year, and by letting me work with them they have given me a life that I love.

—B. Sher

With thanks to Jane and Elaine, and to Maura Walker, and in memory of Stella Smith.

—B. Smith

CONTENTS

FOURTEEN

Preface

NOT KNOWING what you want to do with your life is no joke. It's painful to be without direction. My first book, *Wishcraft: How To Get What You Really Want,* defines *winning* as getting what you want, and it shows step-by-step how to become a winner, how to create a life that fulfills your greatest dreams. But for years readers have been calling me, saying "I love *Wishcraft,* but I can't use it because I can't find a goal. I just don't *know* what I want."

I got curious. I wanted to know what the problem was, so I started meeting with these people who couldn't figure out what they wanted. I let them all tell their stories, and I asked some questions, and in a short time, *every time,* the same thing emerged: each of these clients was locked in an internal battle and didn't even know it.

It had never occurred to them that down deep they really knew what they wanted but their desires were masked by an inner conflict. Knowing the problem came as a great surprise—and a great relief. Now all we had to do was design a program to get around each conflict—and designing these programs turned out to be surprisingly easy. People woke up and swung into action after only one or two sessions!

This was wonderful. I decided to gather these discoveries and strategies into a book so everyone who needed help could find it.

You are now holding that book.

Are you having trouble going after what you want in life because you can't figure out what it is? *I want you to know that you are not alone.* Your problem is a common one and there is a way out. You're going to find yourself in these pages. And almost as soon as you recognize yourself, you'll be learning techniques that can help you. Don't be surprised if you find yourself in more than one chapter. Read them all. Most of us are complicated creatures with many sides, and the exercise that could create a breakthrough for you might be in any chapter.

Working your way through this book is going to be exciting, enlightening, sometimes a bit painful, and often very funny. Learning what's really going on inside you can be difficult, but it's also invigorating, and the rewards are enormous.

You *can* do anything if you only know what it is. And you're about to find out.

Introduction

THIS book is designed to help you find the good life. By that, I don't mean swimming pools, mansions, and private jets—unless those are really your big passions. But if you picked up a book called *I Could Do Anything If I Only Knew What It Was,* you're probably looking for a lot more than a swimming pool.

You want a life you will love.

A friend's father got it right when he said "The good life is when you get up in the morning and can't wait to start all over again."

Is that you? Or does his idea of the good life sound like an unreachable paradise? If you aren't the kind of person who jumps out of bed every morning excited about the day ahead, I know you desperately long to find a goal that will make you feel like my friend's father. You crave work that will spark excitement and energy; you yearn to find the place where you can make your mark. Albert Schweitzer found his place, so did Golda Meir, and so did the kid next door who practiced guitar day and night.

They knew how to live. They believed in what they were doing with all their hearts. They *knew* their work was important.

2

When you get near people who are pursuing their heart's desire, you can *see* the intensity on their faces.

Life is just too short to live without that kind of focus.

In the early 1980s, two Harvard psychologists completed a study of people who called themselves happy. And what did happy people have in common? Money? Success? Health? Love?

None of these things.

They had only two things in common: They knew exactly what they wanted and they felt they were moving toward getting it.

That's what makes life feel good: when it has direction, when you are headed straight for what you love.

And I mean *love.*

I don't mean what you're skilled at. *I don't really care what your skills are.* When I was a single working mother with two babies, you know what my skills were? I could clean house like a demon; catch a moving bus with my arms full of laundry, groceries, and kids; and squeeze a dollar until the picture of George Washington screamed for mercy.

I do not want the career that uses those skills, thank you.

I don't believe you live the good life by doing what you *can* do; you live it by doing what you *want* to do. I don't even think your greatest talents necessarily show up in your skills. All of us are good at things we're not madly in love with. *And all of us have talents we've never used.*

Relying on your skills to guide you is simply unacceptable. That's why I don't intend to give you personality tests or skills assessments to find out what you should be doing.

I *know* what you should be doing.

You should be doing what you love.

What you love is what you are gifted at. Only love will give you the drive to stick to something until you develop your gift. That's the way really big things get accomplished in this world— by people no different than you and I who know what they want and put everything they've got behind it.

If you don't know what you want, you can't get out of the

starting gate—and that's discouraging. But you're not alone. Recent figures show that as many as 98 percent of Americans are unhappy in their jobs. And it isn't only financial considerations that keep them where they are; they simply don't know what to do instead. What you may have thought was your private little nightmare turns out to be heartbreakingly common.

Well, I have a surprise for you.

You *do* know what you want.

Everybody does. That's why you feel so restless when you can't find the right track. You sense there's some particular work you are meant to be doing. And you're right. Einstein needed to formulate theories of physics, Harriet Tubman needed to guide people to freedom, and you need to follow *your* original vision. As Vartan Gregorian said, "The universe is not going to see someone like you again in the entire history of creation." Each of us is one of a kind. Every living person has a completely original way of looking at the world, and originality *always* needs to express itself.

But many of us get stopped. Every time we resolve to change our lives, every time we go to pick up the baton and get into the race, something happens. For some mysterious reason our determination melts. We look at the baton and think "This race isn't it." And we put down the baton, uneasy because time is slipping away, frightened that we'll *never* find "it."

There are two reasons for this.

One reason it's so hard to know what we want is that we have so many options. This wasn't always true. Our parents and their parents had fewer choices and clearer goals. It's a tribute to the success of our culture that so many of us have the freedom to search for our own life's work.

Freedom is glorious. But freedom also torments us because it requires us to create our own goals.

Did you know that fewer people get depressed during war than in peacetime? In a war, everything is important. Day to day, you know exactly what to do. Your life may be frightening, but the struggle to survive gives you direction and drive. You don't waste any time trying to figure out what you're worth or what you're supposed to do with your life. You just try to keep alive, save your home, help your neighbors. The reason we love to watch films about people whose lives are in danger is because every move is loaded with meaning.

When there's no emergency to rise to, we have to *create* goals that have meaning. You can create such goals if you know what your dream is—but this is a relatively new way of living. The old way to live was to let necessity create your goal; the new way is to use your dream to create your goal. We have had very little practice at this new way.

The second reason you don't know what you want is that something inside you is stopping you from knowing. Your dreams are obscured by some kind of internal conflict. It's not as easy as you might think to spot inner conflicts. Often they're disguised as self-reproach. "Maybe I have no talent," "Maybe I'm just lazy," "If I were smarter I'd have done more with my life."

If there's one thing I want you to get out of reading this book it's to know that not one of those statements is true.

The first goal of this book is to shine a spotlight on your particular inner conflict so you can see it clearly outlined. As soon as you see what's been in your way, you'll know exactly why you haven't created the life you wanted. You'll quit reproaching yourself. You'll understand that you've been unable to get moving *for a reason.*

Our culture is full of simpleminded myths of blame, such as "If you really wanted something badly enough, you'd go out and get it," and "If you're sabotaging yourself, you lack character." Nobody ever asks the obvious question: "Why would anybody want to do himself harm by sabotaging himself?" It takes curiosity to find the answer to that question, and judgmental people always lack curiosity.

In the following chapters we're going to stop all this blaming and swap it for honest, nonjudgmental curiosity. I have the deepest respect for sincere curiosity—and very little respect for self-righteousness. The useful answers, the answers that help us solve problems, are always the more forgiving ones. *They're based on a line of inquiry that assumes there is always a good reason for everything.* There is certainly a good reason you lost direction, and this book is going to help you find it.

Until then, just remember, whatever you were doing until you picked up this book, you were not being lazy or stupid or cowardly. Even self-improvement programs, no matter how helpful, are often judgmental. They are often based on the assumption that you don't have what you want because you haven't developed the right way of thinking. They assume you've got to get fixed before you can get what you want.

Well, forget that.

You don't have to become a better person or develop a different attitude to have a life you love. As you are, you are good enough. In fact, the smartest thing you can do is to go ahead and get what you want *before* you do anything to improve yourself. Getting your life on track will do wonders for your "bad" attitude.

I have no intention of suckering you into some program that tells you to stand up straight and be a different person. Life just isn't that simple, and wishful thinking won't make it so. I don't think people solve problems with positive thinking either. Propping up your thoughts, pretending to feel different than you really do, is not a sturdy enough system for the long haul. Creative visualization has its limitations too. I've met a lot of people who can't visualize, and others who feel strongly conflicted even *imagining* what they love. And "create your own reality" *sounds* empowering, but its flip side is that you can end up blaming yourself for everything that goes wrong. That's not fair. You're not big enough to take on fate single-handedly, and you don't need to.

What you *do* need is to understand why you don't know what you want. Once you begin to understand the perfectly good explanation for your confusion, you will finally be able to do something about it.

The second goal of this book is to show you how to do something about it. I've put tools and strategies in each chapter to help you extricate yourself from your internal conflicts every time you need to—now and in the future.

The first three chapters of this book are for *every reader.* They're the chapters that shine a light on your conflict and illuminate its contours for you. Once you see the general shape of your problem, you'll be able to flip to a chapter in the book that will give you strategies for doing whatever you've got to do to get past your particular kind of conflict.

It's not hard to learn what your inner conflict is about, because once you learn to listen for it, you'll notice inner conflicts make a lot of racket. One side of the conflict is arguing in favor of your getting what you want, and the other side is determined to stop you. All you have to do is listen carefully to the louder voice: It will lead you straight to the strategies that can help you.

Does your voice say something like *"I'd have to quit my job to get what I really want and I can't do that—I'd starve"*? If so, you'll want to read Chapter 4, "The Sure Thing," where you'll learn about the great risk you take when you avoid adventure.

Does your voice say *"Every time I try to go after what I want, I drop the ball and I don't know why"*? Then try Chapter 5, "Fear of Success: Leaving the Ones You Love Behind."

If your voice says *"I want to do so many things, I'll never be able to pick only one,"* Chapter 6 will show you how to have it all. (It will also show you how to focus on just one thing, if that's what you secretly wish you could do.)

Now, what if you're doing wonderfully in other people's eyes, you've got a skyrocketing career on your hands, but you're not happy? Is your voice saying *"How can I walk away from success? And what will I live on if I do"*? Take a new look at your options. Turn to Chapter 7, "On the Wrong Track, and Moving Fast."

When you think you know what you want, but your voice says *"I want something I shouldn't want—it's trivial or unworthy,"* that's Chapter 8. You might have a "tribal problem" with your family, friends, or culture: you want something that puts you in conflict with everything you were taught.

If you've just finished high school or college or a training program and your voice says *"I'm afraid to choose something. I might get trapped!"* then pick up Chapter 9, "Help! I'm Not Ready to Be Born Yet." It'll show you how to avoid being trapped and start living.

Chapter 10, "Regrouping: It's a Whole New Ball Game," will help if you've just been through a big change—if you've just retired or if the kids have just grown up and left home—in which case you probably hear a voice saying, *"I don't have Idea One what to do now."*

If your voice says *"What's the point? I'll only be disappointed. Nothing will ever match what I already had and lost,"* turn to Chapter 11, "I've Lost My Big Dream—There's Nothing Left." You'll discover that life is still worth living.

If you hear your voice saying *"I've tried so many things and nothing does it for me,"* then look at Chapter 12, "Nothing Ever Interests Me." You've probably got a case of disabled desire.

If your voice says *"It's not my fault I'm not doing what I want —the world won't give me a break!"* you need to look at Chapter 13, "A Rage Against the Ordinary."

And if you hear a voice saying *"I'm trying to go after something, but my heart's not really in it, and I don't know why,"* your situation is not as big a mystery as you may think. Look at Chapter 14, "The Red Herring, or Trying Hard to Love Something You Don't Really Want." You might discover you *really* want something you're trying to give up.

If you can't hear any voice from your conflict now, don't let it worry you. You'll hear it by the end of Chapter 3. I guarantee it.

CAREERS IN THE NINETIES

Once you begin to find your own path, you will have positioned yourself at the forefront of a massive historical change. In late twentieth-century industrial society, just about everybody— like it or not—is going to have to figure out what kind of work and life he really wants. Sooner or later *everybody* across *every age group* is going to have to ask "What do *I* want to do?"

The days are over when students took the path of least resistance to a banking career, say, or to law school and considered that one choice the end of their career planning. Last year's college graduates, according to one research firm, can expect to hold ten to twelve jobs in three to five different fields during their working lifetime. Like it or not, everybody's getting a second work life. Probably, a third life. Perhaps even more.

Corporations are continuing to downsize, and not only because of recent recessions: We're entering a new period in economic history. Global competition is forcing companies to make themselves lean and mean. Corporations are becoming about a third the size they once were, and they'll probably never get big again. Middle management is gone. Secretaries are being replaced by technology. The top twenty students from every college or business school may still get good job offers, but everyone else is on their own.

The wave of the future is clear: We're going to be a nation of experts—consultants and entrepreneurs—many of us working at home, all of us hired on a job-by-job basis according to our special talents.

And who's going to come shining through these cultural changes? Everyone who is willing to develop what he *loves* into a niche for himself—a niche where he can excel. *Never have we needed to locate our own gifts more.*

So let's get going. Let's see why you don't know what you want. And then, let's do something about it.

ONE

What Are You Supposed to Be Doing?

W^HAT are you supposed to be doing with your life?
Now that's an interesting question, isn't it? Because
even if you can't figure out what you *want* to be doing,
you probably know exactly what you're *supposed* to be doing.

I was supposed to be a housewife and mother, living next door to my parents.

Everyone I ask seems to have an answer ready for this question:

"I was supposed to be working alongside my father at the printing plant."

"I was supposed to marry old money and raise five whiz-bang children in a mansion by the sea."

"My father wanted me to be a partner in a Wall Street law firm, or president of a bank or a big corporation—*something* big."

"I was not supposed to pass up my brothers."

"I was supposed to do *something* special, but I could never figure out what that was."

Inside each of us rests a silent message about what's expected of us. We may never say it out loud, we may rebel against it, refuse to do it. But somehow we always know what it is. And it has a powerful effect on how we run our lives.

10

What about you? What are *you* supposed to be doing? You could be one of the lucky ones, like Picasso, who knew he was born to paint. Your silent "supposed-to" message could be a hot tip coming directly from your soul—or it could be a bum steer.

And if it *is* a bum steer, and you find yourself far from knowing what you really want to do, it can be truly painful to watch the Picassos of this world happily and industriously going about their lives. You wonder, how did you get so unlucky?

We're all raised in families, communities, and even entire cultures that barrage us with messages about what *they* want from us. Sometimes these messages are as blatant as billboards: "Get married," "Make money," "Buy your own home." Other times the messages are stealthy—they *sneak* in. Then they stay in. They never come out where we can get a good look at them and dismiss them or embrace them openly.

We usually forget when and how we first received these messages about what we're supposed to do with our lives, just as we forget when and how we first learned to eat with a fork, or sleep without wetting the bed. But whenever and however our particular "supposed-to" messages reached us, they are in us and we respond to them—usually without thinking. Some of us obey our instructions, some of us rebel, but all of us respond.

Take a moment to think about your life and your goals. *Are you living up to expectations?*

I was supposed to be living next door to my parents *and* be a jet-setting international journalist-spy, living days and nights of dazzling travel and dangerous intrigue. I've always had a hard time fulfilling this life plan. First, it's impossible. And second, I don't want it. I'm more adventurous than a homebody, and I'm considerably less adventurous than a spy.

But I, like you, was born into a world that bombarded me with ideas of what's right and wrong—and I wanted to do right. So, even though the instructions I got were impossible to fulfill, I spent years juggling those messages in my head, trying to figure out a way I might be able to fulfill them.

The ideas we receive may contradict each other and be wrong

for us, but they are part of our first world. *They get in deep.* They affect us. It doesn't even matter if our parents were trying with all their hearts not to influence us. Children are inevitably influenced. Children are fast learners and they are magical learners. As children, we can hear messages even when they're not spoken.

And each message we get—blatant or invisible—stays inside us, where it can sit, unexamined, throughout our adult lives, undermining our happiness. For example, even if you seem to know what you want, thrive at your work, and are fascinated by it, *you can have a nagging feeling that you're not doing what you're supposed to be doing.*

Jack M., who, at twenty-nine, was a journalist reporting from the battle lines in South Africa during the worst heat of the apartheid conflicts—and loving every minute of it—told me, "I was supposed to have been a doctor. Journalism was never good enough, somehow."

Benita B., thirty-six, a single woman making a very good salary on Wall Street, said, "I'm supposed to *marry* a successful person, not *be* one."

And Susan C., forty-seven, the author of a respected literary novel, said, "I think I was supposed to be a great beauty. Not an intellectual. I'm frumpy. You're looking at a failure."

It's easy to see how hurtful Jack's, Benita's, and Susan's "supposed-to" messages are. Unfortunately, it's not so easy to see how the same kind of expectations are hurting you.

Here's a way to start examining your own situation. Try asking one simple question:

Who says?

Who says you're not supposed to do what you're doing? For that matter, who says you *are* supposed to be doing it? Who says?

I'm inviting you to *get specific.* If you want to free yourself from the restraints of what you're supposed to be doing so you can find out what you really want, you're going to have to be precise about how messages came to you and who sent them.

Our communities and schoolmates, perhaps a teacher or a coach, each of these people fed us some ideas. But, for most of us, our earliest and most relentless message sender was our family. If you're like most people, your family's desires for your life play so steadily in the back of your mind—even today—that you've created a nonstop inner monologue to address them: You think "There, that'll show them," or "They'll love this," or "Boy, they must feel bad about what I'm doing. I'd better call and say hi." What your family wanted gave meaning—good or bad—to everything you did. *Even if you thought you really didn't care.*

Okay, what *about* your family? *How* did you get your messages from them?

Did they tell you in plain terms what was expected of you?

"You're going to be a physician. Everyone in this family becomes a physician."

"You've got to become an accountant and come into the family business. We've broken our backs to build this business and get you into college, now you owe us."

Or were they more subtle? Did they just let you know in no uncertain terms what you were *not* supposed to be doing?

John L. yearned to lead the life of a politician, but his father, who'd always complained of government intervention in his businesses, despised politicians. "Congressmen," John's father said, "they'll sell you down the river for a song."

Carol G. wanted to be an actress. On her fourteenth birthday she announced her dream at dinner, and her entire family said, "You'll never make it in acting; no one does. Forget it."

Or maybe your family didn't say anything *directly;* they made their desires very clear, instead, by talking about other people:

"Isn't it a shame Bill's wife makes so much more money than he does?" (If you're a boy that means you'd better make plenty of money. If you're a girl that means you'd better not.)

"That Smith kid showed a lot of promise, but he wound up very small-time. Now, that *Jones* kid is looking great—buying and selling buildings and driving around in a Mercedes. At twenty-seven!" (It's pretty clear what kind of kid you're supposed to be.)

Or maybe your family didn't say anything at all. Maybe the messages you got from your family were unspoken, silent ones.

You just "got the idea."

Many families say, "Do whatever you want, as long as you're happy." But if you're from the one family in a thousand who *really* means "Do what you want," I'm envious. Unlike the rest of us, you don't have to suffer from inner conflicts while you're going about the business of finding and enjoying your life's work. (If you're not sure if you're from that one family in a thousand, just try telling your folks you've become a happy striptease artist or you're happily leaving medical school, and you'll find out soon enough.)

Okay, now that you've thought about *how* you got wind of your family's wishes, take another kind of close look at that family of yours. *What* did they want from you?

Exercise 1: *What Did They Want from Me?*

Take a blank sheet of paper and jot down the names of everyone in your family and extended family. That is, write down anyone who was important to you when you were growing up, teachers, coaches, neighbors, cousins, older friends.

Under each person's name, write down what they wanted you to do with your life. If you've got your own family now, you can make this exercise even more spicy by including your present family too. Go ahead, make it a big list: everyone you lived with as a kid, everyone you live with now.

What did/do they want from you?

Don't think too much. Jot down your first feeling. You might not be absolutely sure you're right about what each person would say, but you know what you *think* is right, and *that's what counts with inner messages.* Your misinterpretations have influenced you as much as your insights.

Think about it. What *did* each of these people want you to do?

Okay, now take a look at your answer.

Chances are your paper looks something like this:

14

MY FAMILY WANTED ME TO . . .

MOM: be careful and respectable—a lawyer.
DAD: be bold and competitive—an investment banker.
BENNY: be a big hero.
KAREN: be invisible—not get so much attention.
GRANDMA: become her constant companion.

You may have started making a short list and suddenly realized all sorts of things, like George J. did.

Here's George's list:

FATHER: Had no use for me at all, but he loved opera. So I got the idea I should do something with opera: I married an opera singer—and he finally accepted me. My wife and I were badly matched and so unhappy. She wanted to leave, but I was terrified of letting her go. I never really put that together before.

MOM: She was always trying to make peace in the house. Father was silent and angry, and Mom wanted everything to *look* peaceful and okay. I must have gotten the idea I was supposed to make everything look peaceful and okay too, because I got this proper corporate job even though I hate it. Well, life is peaceful all right. And dead as dirt.

Take another good look at your list and you'll notice something else very interesting. If you're like most of us, you'll see there's a complicated twist in your instructions: you got *more* than one message, and some of the messages you got may be the *exact opposites of each other.* Remember how I was supposed to stay at home *and* be a jet-setting spy? Chances are that no person in your family wanted exactly the same thing from you that the others wanted. And chances are that at least one person wanted something with so many built-in conflicts in it that you could never understand it.

Lois M.'s mother *said* she wanted Lois to be wildly popular, even famous, but when Lois was a teenager, her mother begged Lois not to draw too much attention to herself. How does a person get famous without getting attention?

Bill R. also got conflicting messages: "I had to get married and create my own family unit *and* I had to stay with my parents forever." Don't you wonder *where* Bill was supposed to have his new family? In his parents' living room?

These messages put us in an impossible bind. We're supposed to jump right in and do things we've been told not to do. Or that we can't do. Or that we're incapable of. Meanwhile, our minds are never where they're supposed to be: on developing our own unique gifts. When we're children we have a couple of very big jobs to do. We have to find out what our people want from us and we have to find out what *we* want. *When our first job stops us from doing our second, we get lost.*

No wonder we have trouble knowing what we want out of life.

Listen, our families love us the best they can. But they were not taught to *listen* to children, they were taught to *train* them. If our families aren't listening to us, they're not likely to learn about —let alone respect—our dreams. *And our dreams are who we are.*

Almost any stranger would respect our dreams more easily than our family does. If you don't believe me try a comparison test. Next time you're with a group of strangers, tell them the most offbeat idea you can think of. Tell them your dream is to raise dalmatians in the Himalayas, but you have no contacts in Tibet. Watch their interest pick up. They'll even try to solve your problem.

Interest is the sincerest form of respect.

You don't love these strangers and they don't love you, but we are all captivated by each other's visions. It's in our nature as humans to be intrigued with any new idea—unless we have some personal reason for not doing so. Our families have plenty of personal reasons, but a stranger is a pure soul. It's possible that one stranger in twenty will react negatively to you, for his own reasons, but you'll find that the other nineteen will say something like, "Interesting idea! My cousin raises dogs!" or "My neighbor's been to Nepal! Do you want to talk to her?"

Now, to complete the comparison test, go home and tell your family the same kind of fantasy:

"I'm going to quit as CEO of International Computer Corporation and sign on as crew on one of those clam boats off Rhode Island." Or:

"I'm going to quit the clam boat crew and become the head of International Computer Corporation."

How did your family like that? Did they drop their forks before or after they scrambled to talk you out of your "folly"?

"Hold on a minute," you're probably saying right now. "Is this going to be another family bashing? Because I'm sick of that. My family was no worse than any other, and anyway that's all behind me."

Listen, I believe your family probably *was* as good as any other. And one day, no matter how mad we get, we are going to have to forgive our families and get some perspective, or we'll never be able to move forward and be free and whole.

But there's no shortcut to forgiveness. The cost of forgiving the past before you've really confronted it is that *you blame yourself for everything that happened to you.* You can't move an inch toward what you really want when you're beating up on yourself. You've got to stop blaming yourself, screw up your courage, set aside your suspicions that you're about to do some family bashing, and locate the source of your "supposed-to" problem. If you really think about it, you'll probably find the problem has been there a *long* time—which means the seeds were planted in childhood.

How can our families harm us when they love us? Very easily, unfortunately. Most of us overlook one important fact when we think love is enough: *Love and respect aren't the same thing.*

Love is *fusion.* As a baby, you belong to your parents, you're an extension of them; and fusion is good for the survival of infants. Respect is *differentiation:* you belong to yourself, and you're an extension of *no one. Differentiation is essential for the happiness of adults.*

Take just one more careful look at that list of what your family wanted from you. You've got all those messages in your head, right? Now, where on your list is the message that says you must go out and fulfill your unique identity? Who insisted that you find your own original self—whatever the cost? Very few of us ever find that message on our list. No matter how much they love us, our families rarely say "We respect you, we know you're unique, we know you want to find what you're supposed to do in this life. Go out and get what you need. We'll be here."

Parents have their own dreams—*and it's those dreams they're pushing, not yours.* In their heads, they have images of successful sons and beautiful wealthy daughters, children who are impressive—and secure. Very few parents have the luxury, the calmness of spirit, to realize that the most practical thing any child can do is to find its own vision—and follow it.

As long as you live in response to your family's messages, it's as if you had to spend your whole life dressed up as an usher for someone else's wedding. It's a rare coincidence when someone else's dream fits you, but your own will always fit like a custom-tailored suit. It's worth any effort to find your own dream.

In the meantime, while you're standing around in a life that's not really working for you, doing things that don't feel exactly right for you, don't spend much time trying to figure out how you managed to get it so wrong. *Don't blame yourself.*

Once the machinery of family messages is pointed in your direction and set in motion, nothing's your fault. We all made our big decisions about how to handle things too early, when, as children, we first received our family's messages and responded to them. *Then we dragged our child-designed solutions into adulthood, where they don't always work.* They can even result in bad marriage choices and destructive behavior.

I know a woman recently divorced from a very angry man and

she said, "I don't know how I got so stupid. You'd think I'd have known. My father was a raging bull! I hated it! So how did I walk into that mess with a raging bull husband?"

By trying to survive, that's how.

She learned as a child how to "make nice," so her father wouldn't fly off the handle, and when she went looking for a husband, these were her best skills. Naturally, she managed to find a situation where she could use them.

Mark learned the opposite from his childhood. His family's message was: It's a mad, mad, mad world and you're on your own. Mark was the fourth of five brothers and had to fight for position or get trampled. Now he's been fired from two good jobs because his automatic response to conflict is to lose his temper and start shouting.

"Why can't I just stop?" he said. "I try to forget what I learned as a kid, but the words fly out of my mouth before I can stop them."

Mark will never make those messages from family and culture disappear by pretending they aren't there. Neither will you or I. We have to take inner messages into account when we design our new lives, because they're coming along for the trip, welcome or not. In the coming pages I'll show you ways to keep those old messages quiet so they don't drown out that hot tip which, even at this very moment, is being whispered to you straight from your own soul:

What you're really supposed to be doing is whatever makes your heart sing.

It's the most practical thing you can do.

When you're doing what you *love*—mothering, designing airplanes, swimming—you're going to be really good at it. And, when you do what you love, you're going to last for the long haul in your profession (and lasting is *the* essential factor in success).

Also, if you're marching to your own drum, you may even have a jump on the trends—look at all the MBA's and lawyers who got laid off in the early 1990s. How many of them originally wanted to do something else? How often were they influenced by parents who thought lawyers were certain to be safe and prosperous? Some of them would have had more safety and prosperity as free-lancers or entrepreneurs or theatrical agents, wouldn't they?

In the next chapter I'm going to show you how to get moving toward what you want—*even before you know what that is.* But before we go further, I'd like you to create your own antidote to that nagging feeling that *you're not doing what you're supposed to be doing.*

Exercise 2: Their Impossible Dream

Draw a picture of a person who would incorporate every last thing your family wanted from you. Make it good. Use cutouts from magazines for extra fun, and then put their "perfect" child up on the wall where you can see her.

Take a look at what you're supposed to be.

"I was supposed to be smart but unaware of the ways of the world, rich but not richer than my poor dad, fattened up by Mama's cooking but slender, so I wouldn't get a heart attack like Uncle Frank." Joe laughed.

Anita cut out the picture of a designer-dressed professional, added a cloistered nun's hooded face, and put the whole thing against the background of an African village. Then she stood back and said, "There. Now *everybody's* happy."

Admit it—it's impossible. What they want can't be done. So leave that picture up there where it can remind you, and let's get you moving.

What *you* want *can* be done.

TWO

How to Get Lucky

W HEN you see people who are passionate about their work, who have found their perfect niche, the world sometimes does seem very unfair.

How did *they* get so lucky?

I'll tell you one thing they did. They got into action—and they stayed in action.

The amount of good luck that comes your way depends on your willingness to act.

Because you don't know what you want, you're probably feeling stuck. We all have a tendency to try to dope things out before we make a move, but *action is absolutely essential for people who don't know what they want.*

I can give you four good reasons:

1. Action Will Help You Think

By exposing you to real-life experiences and seeing how they feel to you, action will help you do much better thinking than you could ever hope to do sitting still and weighing all the theoretical factors. *Even action in the wrong direction is informative.*

2. Action Raises Your Self-Esteem

Most inaction isn't solely because of indecision—it's because of fear. But every time you want to do something that scares you, and you dare to do it, your self-esteem goes up a few degrees. When you're fearful but you step forward anyway, you do yourself a great service. Even if someone slams the door in your face, refuses to answer your letter, or yells at you—the worst outcome you can imagine—it doesn't matter. *You're a success every time you face down fear.* You can *feel* that success. You feel elated or determined; either way, the feeling is intoxicating.

But every time you let yourself down by *not* acting, you can feel your self-esteem drop a few degrees. Your morale sinks along with your self-esteem.

I was originally trained to work with ex-addicts in a city-run drug program. We worked in therapy-type groups, trying to create a new life for people who had actually fought their way out of addiction. But none of them had developed the skills they needed to make it in the real world. And they thought of themselves as no more than "ex-junkies."

They couldn't afford to wait until they had somehow built a good enough self-image to develop skills and find jobs, so we did what we called "acting as if." Dress as if you respect yourself, whether you do or not, we told them. Act as if you deserve that job you're trying for. Do the job as if you were first-rate.

And it worked. Because high self-esteem comes *after* action, not before.

After a while, these courageous people were doing things they had never done before, greeting people, making speeches, working in teams! How did they learn so fast?

"Do it first, learn how second," one of them said to me.

That confirms my experience: Action will raise your self-esteem better than affirmations. Telling yourself that you're a good person doesn't work for long. At least, not for me. After the second day of telling my mirror I'm wonderful, my mirror starts looking very skeptical. "Who are you trying to kid?" it seems to say. My mind doesn't like propaganda, even if it's good for me.

Acting "as if" works better than any kind of thinking, because when you've *done something,* you feel proud of yourself—even if you didn't do well.

Most of the rewarding things in life—riding a bicycle, traveling in a foreign country, or making love—begin with incompetence and embarrassment. *What will determine the course of your life more than any other one thing is whether or not you're willing to tolerate necessary discomfort.* Think back to adolescence. There's a training ground for self-protection if I ever saw one. At that age, the slightest misstep makes you want to crawl in a hole and pull it in after you. You tend to avoid potential embarrassment like the plague. Remember how uncomfortable it was when you first began dating? But aren't you glad you did it? If you become too good at avoidance, you never start living at all.

My friend Pete would never ride a horse because at the age of ten he went to a stable for lessons—and saw an eight-year-old girl riding better than he could. So he got off the horse and never got on again. No big deal? Yes, it is. "Because that's the way I lived the rest of my life," he said. An unlived life is a kind of hell.

I'm never comfortable when it's time to go on a lecture tour. After a few months at home with no lectures to perform, I'm settled in and I want to stay home, walk my dogs, buy bagels, and write at my computer. When it's time to do a workshop, I start getting tense. I groan and moan about having to find my Magic Markers, get my clothes ready, catch an early plane, wear pantyhose.

But when I get up in front of the room I have a great time and I'm glad I had to do it. And it makes me feel strong that I never considered canceling a lecture.

3. Good Luck Happens When You're in Action

I wound up a counselor, lecturer, and author in a totally slip-shod, backward way—it just happened. I called an old boyfriend on another coast to complain about my miserable life; he directed me to some great therapy groups that had helped him. I joined; the psychiatrist liked the way I did things and hired me to work for him. It led to this life I love. It was all a bunch of coincidences, happy accidents. That's how you find the best recipes and meet the best people in your life too, by accident.

I believe in planning, but the truth is that planning is mostly science fiction. There never was a plan that was more than a hopeful prediction. Even business plans are tall tales: "With this new color we expect to sell 50,000 items next year, 150,000 the year after next, and 500,000 the year after that. So we want a bank loan of two million dollars."

Pretty good story, isn't it? But with fictions like that people get loans from banks—and the best storyteller gets the biggest loan!

Perhaps the best reason to plan is that *following a plan gets you out into the world.* If you go to the library and look up articles, call people, join organizations, go to appointments, *something can happen to you.*

Try it. Set a goal, any goal, and start doing everything you can think of to achieve it. I guarantee you, your life will change. *You might not get where you thought you were going, but you could easily wind up somewhere better.* You'll get breaks you never could have planned for because you never knew they existed.

Let me make one more point. Different kinds of planning work for different people. There is another, more subtle kind of planning than the kind where you set a goal, and *this other kind of planning works just as well:* Every time you have to make a choice about anything, think "Does this go toward or away from what I want?" Always choose what goes toward what you want. If you're considering working on a farm this summer and you want to be an urban planner, skip the farm job. Get a job in the city. This is called "following your nose," and it's wiser than you think

—as long as your nose is always pointing toward what you want. Join everything. Talk to everyone. Don't worry, you'll tighten your focus as more data comes in. Whichever kind of planning you do, stay aware and adjust your path to your feelings as you go. Just use desire as your North Star and you'll be putting a powerful plan into action.

4. There's an Animal in All of Us—and It Has Great Instincts

Sometimes your wishes or your timing look a bit odd, but if they feel right, stick with them. You can trust your animal instincts. The animal inside us knows how fast to move and how much we can carry. And it tells us things that don't always make sense—at first. That's what happened to Jessie.

Jessie was about forty-five, very quiet and shy. She lived in Atlanta, Georgia, and ran an office for her husband, a well-known architect. He was a star in his community, involved with meetings and parties while Jessie did all the unglamorous paperwork.

Jessie had no idea what she wanted to do with her life. She joined a six-person Success Team (a self-help group of about six people who meet regularly to make each other's dreams come true). Jessie's team did everything they could to help her find something she'd love, but she couldn't come up with a thing.

"Why don't you look for a job you like better?" they asked.

"I don't know," she said. "I just don't feel like it."

Months went by.

Then one day, Jessie walked in to her group and announced: "I want to race sled dogs in the winter race at Bear Grease." (Bear Grease is a small town in Minnesota.)

Her team was flabbergasted. "Are you sure?"

"Yes," Jessie said. "That's what I want to do."

"Would you mind telling us why?" they asked.

"I don't know why," she said.

"Do you know anything about sled dog racing?"

"Nope."

That was the end of the team's questioning. They were so happy Jessie had found something she wanted that they set out immediately to help her find a training school, or a dog racer, or anything. They approached anyone walking any kind of dog and asked, "Do you know anything about sled dog racing?" Finally, somebody did know about a summer training camp for dog racers, and on a warm summer day, Jessie walked into that camp, went up to the trainer, and said, "I want to learn how to run sled dogs."

He looked at her, a tiny forty-five-year-old lady in a straight skirt and sensible shoes—and decided to discourage her. He hooked up a team of dogs to a training sled on wheels and gave her the reins.

"Here," he said. "Practice a little. See if you like it." Suddenly he shouted to the dogs and they took off running. Jessie could barely keep up with them. She tripped and slid and practically fell on her face, but she stayed with the dogs all the way around the track. When she finished and caught her breath, she smiled at the trainer and said, "I *love* this!" He laughed, and consented to train her.

When winter came and it was time to go to Bear Grease, Jessie realized she knew nobody. She asked her trainer if she could use his name for introductions and he said, "I can't do that, Jessie. You're still a beginner, and I have a reputation to maintain."

So Jessie's Success Team took her to the airport and saw her off with loud cheers and secret fears. When she arrived in Bear Grease she found a tiny town, mostly one main street, packed with snow and full of seasoned sledders sitting around in clumps with their dogs. She forced herself to walk up to one crew after another, asking if anyone needed a helper. Finally, someone who had lost an assistant to the flu took her on.

And Jessie ran with a team of sled dogs over a hundred-mile course.

Her Success Team went wild when she called after the race,

and when Jessie returned home, she was a satisfied woman. She told her team all the gripping details with a big smile on her face.

"Now, that's happiness," one of them said.

"It sure is," Jessie said.

"What now?" her team said. "More training?"

"No," she said. "I'm finished. I don't want to do that any-more."

There was a moment of stunned silence and then her team said, "Well, what *do* you want to do now?"

Jessie said, "Quit my job."

It had never occurred to anyone in Jessie's team that she would need to overcome a big challenge before she'd be ready to give up her thankless job and go out into the world. But the animal inside her knew.

You can trust desire.

Do some scanning until you find some desire, and be like Jessie: don't worry if it's practical or not. Start acting on it. There's a practicality in our longings that's beyond rational thought. Your desire will point you in the right direction better than any rules or well-meant advice.

Now you know four good reasons action will bring you the same kind of "good luck" you see happening to all those envi-able people who are doing exactly what they want to do.

Have I convinced you to get moving? Or are you feeling some resistance?

THREE

Resistance, or What's Stopping You, Anyway?

I'M CONVINCED that if you don't know what you want, something is stopping you from knowing it. Something—a hidden resistance—is making you hesitate to find your true desire and go after it. Positive thinking alone will never take you past this buried obstacle; pretending nothing is wrong won't get you anywhere either.

I would like you to find that resistance so you can figure out how to melt it.

I know one simple, surefire way to make your resistance come out into the open: *Start moving toward a goal you really want and the resistance will leap out of hiding and start trying to talk you out of moving.* Your resistance will show up and try to convince you that the obstacles to your goal are insurmountable. That's a promise.

All you need to do is find a temporary goal so attractive that your resistance will believe you really want it. Then you're going to take action and go after that goal—*right now.*

I've already given you four good reasons to swing into action as soon as possible: 1) it helps you think, 2) it puts a shine on your self-image, 3) it invites good luck in the form of information or opportunities, and 4) it sharpens your instincts.

Well, here's the fifth and most important reason: *If you can make yourself go after a goal when you're feeling stuck, you will activate—and expose—all the resistance that is causing you to be stuck.*

Your resistance will stay dormant as long as you're not threatening it. But it will wake up fast the second you start moving, and announce itself loudly: "What are you doing!?" "You're going to get in trouble." "This isn't for you." "This is a stupid idea." "You're going to fail."

How do I know a resistance is blocking your desire?

Because being stuck doesn't make any sense.

Logically, you know you could make a career choice, and if it wasn't perfect, you could change it. That's the way most people think. So what's the big deal? Why can't you get moving? Obviously there's *some* big deal, or you wouldn't have stayed in this uncomfortable spot for so long.

The only reasonable conclusion I can draw is that you sense some kind of danger in your path. Your resistance is trying to protect you from that danger. Take a look at an animal who won't move and you'll get an unmistakable message: There's trouble up ahead. *Animals don't necessarily have the best information or the most perfect judgment, but they always have a compelling reason for standing perfectly still.* The same is true for us.

When you swing into action toward your "dangerous" wish, every bit of resistance in your head will start proclaiming itself. It will try to block your path by making you feel guilty, or ashamed, or inadequate, or hopeless. "What about your poor mother?" your resistance will say. "If you're too good everyone will hate you." "You're supposed to be a lawyer!" "Your brother told you you're an idiot, and that's what you are!"

And that's exactly what we want.

We want those messages to blow their cover, because once you know precisely what you're up against, *you can design a strategy to beat it.*

So, let's start the big smoke out.

To begin, let me seem to change the subject and take you in a very different direction. I want to ask you some loaded questions.

WORTHY WORK

What is the real difference between "work" and "a job"? You labor at both of them. You could make money at both of them. But there's a real difference, and you know it. A job only pays the rent. After that, it might have no further meaning to you.

But your life's work feels worth doing. It's *all* meaning, whether it makes money or not.

"Meaning" is a very big word, a lot tougher to unpack than "job" or even "work." Let's take a little time to talk about it.

What do *you* think makes work *meaningful*? Do you want your work to be meaningful like Mother Teresa's work with lepers? Or Einstein's theory of relativity? Will you save the world from destruction or create an illuminating work of art? Or do you have to make millions of dollars? I'm not making fun of you; I'm absolutely serious. Inside most of us is the feeling that truly meaningful work has to be on a giant scale, or has to lead to a kind of worldly "greatness," like an Olympic medal. You need to find out what kinds of thoughts come into your mind about that phrase "meaningful work."

Exercise 1: "Meaningful Work"

Take out a piece of paper and write down as much as you can about what you think the world calls "meaningful work." If you wish, name some people whose lives seem especially significant and explain why you think so. To get to know you, we need to have these impressions.

What makes work really worthy? Don't worry if a Gallup poll, or anyone else for that matter, would agree with you. You can't make a mistake here, because we just need to find out what you *think.* So put down your thoughts as fast as they come to you, all the things that would make you say, "This is meaningful work."

Now read what you've written. Do your thoughts resemble this?

"Meaningful work has to do some good in this world. It has to help mankind in some way." Or this:

"To be meaningful your efforts have to make a splash. You have to be successful. No matter what the field." Or:

"I think people who have meaningful work are totally driven. They can't eat or sleep because they have discovered something, like Columbus, or Newton, or they have a huge vision, like Beethoven." Or:

"Well, I think the world finds it meaningful to do your best: have a family and a home and a good job. Be a pillar of the community."

If you're one of those people who thinks you have no problem with meaningful work, that you'd be thrilled if you could find *anything* to make yourself happy, don't be so sure. *Every time you worry that you could get trapped in some kind of work you don't care about, you're dealing with the problem of meaningfulness.* I guarantee that in the back of your mind is the thought that somehow you have to make a contribution to something, be acknowledged, *do something that matters*—or you're just fooling around.

But what happens to that theory when you hear someone say this: "When I walked into that bookstore backroom, stacked floor to ceiling with American 1890s periodicals, I felt as if someone were lifting a heavy coat off my back—like I was *home,* though *I'd never been in such a place before!* I knew most people might not care very much about that shop, but I feel I was meant to work there. Everything I'd been and done until then fell into place."

Dusty magazines might not mean much to you, or to the world at large. Not big, not a cure for cancer, not a great achievement—but I'll bet you wish *you* felt that way about *something. Well, you do.* You just have to forget whatever you were taught about "meaningful work" and start noticing whatever has meaning to *you.*

Real meaning, *your* kind of meaning, is as pure and unique as you were as a child. We do not know where it comes from. Like your identity, it just seems to be there. It doesn't have to be created, just discovered. Personal meaning connects your deepest gifts with the rest of the world. Whether you turn out to be a gardener or a builder, a filmmaker or a doctor—when you're doing the right work you will feel *connected,* both to your soul and to the world outside you. A gardener feels he's creating beauty and has reverence for nature. A builder or filmmaker feels she's using her best abilities to create something to delight the world. A doctor feels he's using his best skills and brains to heal people.

The very first step to finding work that fits *you* is to understand the connection between doing what you *love* and doing something worth doing, something that has *meaning.*

Because they are one and the same thing.

You'll never be happy just amusing yourself. I advise against choosing a long vacation as your life's goal. Even in retirement, even when you're only looking to get off the fast track and "smell the roses," you should be pushing past what you merely enjoy into what has real meaning to you. *When something really matters to you, you must bring it into your life.*

Without an activity that really matters to you, you're going to feel empty, even if you've set yourself up in Paradise and are living the life of the rich and famous. If you're not involved in something you truly care about, anyplace can seem like a prison.

And that's not all.

If you think it's selfish to put yourself first like this, think again, because when you're doing work you love *it's a gift to the world as well!* Picasso wasn't trying to help anybody. For that matter, Einstein wasn't either, not when he was working on the theory of relativity. They just wanted to do their work. That work seemed very important to them and they couldn't get their minds off it. Their efforts were personal, self-absorbed, even selfish—or at least, no one's welfare was in mind when they worked. Even the saviors of this world have some kind of personal vision they're fulfilling when they go out to help the sick or to heal the planet. They are listening to their own urgencies, not just trying to be good people. It's time to dismantle the myth that says you must choose between pleasing yourself and doing something meaningful.

To do one, you must do the other.

To do "great" work, you have to be in love. And with work-love, as with people-love, there's no accounting for chemistry. To live a life that is exciting and fulfilling, you can't do what's "right," you have to do what's right *for you.* In the long run, it's the most generous thing you can do. It can be heartwarming to think you owe it to the world to do what you're best at and what you love most. It gives you the right—by giving you the obligation —to *do* it.

Do you know how it feels to do work you love? I asked around and got these answers:

- "It fills you up, uses everything you've got."
- "I love my work because it's always a stretch and it's always new."
- "I know I love what I'm doing when I forget the clock."
- "It feels honest. Hard, honest work. Like a fireman or a farmer."
- "When I love my work, I'm the owner. I'm in business for myself. To really give my best, I have to feel that way, even if I'm actually being paid by someone else."

Nice work if you can get it, isn't it?

You *can* get it. The path we'll be taking in these pages may seem roundabout to you at first, but it leads, finally, to work you love. So free yourself up from any restrictions to your imagination, and get ready to do some freewheeling fantasizing. We're going to have a little fun.

GET A JOB

Exercise 2: The Job from Heaven (or Hell!)

Yes, I said "job." For this exercise, we won't need to do anything as ambitious as find meaningful work. This is a two-part exercise, and it doesn't matter which part you do first. If you can, start with Part A.

Part A: The Job from Heaven.

Let your imagination run free, and give yourself the gift of designing the world's most perfect job. Create your own hours, your own activities, your most desirable environment. Don't limit yourself with reality or practicality, because this is Fantasy Time. The only limitation is this: It must be a *job,* not a life. That is, it has to have tasks in it, hours to keep, and some kind of remuneration. After that, you can run wild. You can decide that you want to be a cowhand during the week, who gets picked up each weekend by helicopter and taken to a luxurious spa, and makes documentary films on winter vacation.

Remember to include those important categories: what, where, and with whom?

What would you be doing all day? Would you be shouting through a bullhorn on a movie set, biking or bargaining, designing or building or ice-skating or saving somebody? Would you be singing bass in *Boris Godunov,* or giving a speech to thousands of cheering people? Would you have a clipboard and be walking around your own factory, making sure your fabrics are being woven and printed to perfection?

Where would you be doing this job? Describe the environment: Would you prefer a cozy cottage with a roaring fireplace, Antarctica, midtown Manhattan, or a huge Kentucky farm where you're breeding Arabian horses?

You've had enough of jobs that didn't satisfy or please you. Now let yourself go. Go to that secret corner of your brain where you are a femme-fatale star-quarterback mom, or the rain-forest-saving gardener of the planet.

And don't forget to say who would be with you. Remember this is a job, so you need to imagine all the people you'd love to be *working* with—your boss, coworker, employee, business partner, or "right hand" helper—or competitor, for that matter. Would you like to have a team of assistants who carry out every wish perfectly and pick up after you without a complaint? Or a genius coach or mentor who wouldn't let you rest until you'd given your very best? Or the best, smartest, funniest, most cooperative teammates imaginable to work with you on a project?

This exercise usually causes an explosion of enthusiasm when I assign it in my workshops. So much of our time is spent at work, and so little of that time seems gratifying. Most groups I work with spill over with "Thank God It's Friday"–type relief when they get to do this exercise.

I always get a kick out of their responses and I think you will too.

Adrienne, forty-four, a lawyer for a corporation: "I want cameras and a first-rate crew and lots of money at my beck and call, and I'd document everything up and down the entire length of the Amazon River—and then move up to the highlands of Peru!"

Bernice, twenty-nine years old and a free-lance writer, said, "I just want to show up at some big downtown office every morning, with a desk and secretary, and a computer and modem and telephones and stamps and copy machines and faxes, and lots of people around all doing their work, and I want to do *only my own fiction writing* there. But I want to go to lunch with the gang, and have people to talk to at the water cooler, and set up dinner and movie dates and birthday parties all the time."

Philip, twenty-seven, a legal proofreader: "I want my own café on a Greek island. Then, after work I'd go eel fishing with my partner who is also my best friend, and we'd cook out on the beach and sing old songs, and talk about life and all the women who broke our hearts. In the off season, I'd sign up on the crew of a sailing ship and travel around the world."

Jeannie, thirty-eight years old, recently a manager in a Fortune 100 company, came up with this: "I'm the head of a unit in my company, and I have a crackerjack team working with me. Everyone, from the file clerk to my brain trust, is always awake, always in a good mood, and wants nothing more than to do a great job. Ha! If I had that, I wouldn't really care *what* I was doing!"

Louisa, thirty-nine, a receptionist in a law firm, said, "I want to deliver mail for the Post Office in a pretty suburb. I want to walk and be outdoors all day and I don't want to have to decide what to wear every morning. I love free health insurance, job security, and leaving work exactly at five P.M. every day. I'd love to deliver Christmas cards and Valentine's Day cards. And I like dogs. They'd never bite me."

What about *your* Job from Heaven? Was it fun to invent it? Or were you unable to do it at all?

"You've got the wrong guy," Bill, an ex-ballplayer, said. "I can't think of a great job. If I could, I'd *do* it!"

"You don't understand," Chris, a stagehand, told me. "I never get that enthusiastic about anything. That's my whole problem!"

Do Bill and Chris seem to speak for you?

Then I want you to do the other part of the exercise: "The Job from Hell." (I haven't met the person who couldn't do this one.)

Part B: Creating a Negative Picture: The Job from Hell.

Don't ask me why, but *everybody knows what they don't want, in detail.* If you had trouble doing the Job from Heaven, you probably will do just fine describing the Job from Hell. Put in everything you hate about every job you ever had or can imagine. If the devil himself took the time to design a job for you that was guaranteed to make you miserable, what kind of job would that be?

Remember to include *what* kind of activity you'd be doing, *where* you'd be doing it, and with *whom.* Incidentally, even if you did the Job from Heaven very easily, you might want to try this exercise for fun.

There's a horrible kind of glee that comes with doing this exercise. I've seen people make awful faces, squinting and grimacing, while they wrote about every conceivable dreadful aspect of their personal Job from Hell—but I couldn't get them to stop! They always wanted to write down just one more horrifying detail. I like to do this exercise in a group, where you spur each other on and get reminded of horrible details you may have left out. Here's what came up in a group I recently ran:

Louisa, whose Job from Heaven is to be a mail carrier, said: "I'm the baby-sitter for an incredibly rich, spoiled, angry movie star. I have no time to myself because she calls me at any time of the day or night. I have to live in the maid's room of her high-rise apartment in the middle of a big city. I have to do all the food and clothes shopping. (I *hate* clothes shopping.) The building staff is ice-cold and refuses to talk to me. I have to sit and watch soap operas all day, and game shows, and I'm never allowed to read. I have to wear a chartreuse uniform with hideous glass and gold buttons."

She stopped and Elliott, an MBA currently driving a taxi, was about to speak, when she started again. "Oh, and she only eats frozen dinners. And her microwave doesn't work so they're always cold in the middle. And I have to eat with her. Oh, and she could fire me at any time, with no notice."

Elliott said, "I work nine to five every day and get two weeks for vacation, one week at a time so I can't really go anywhere. I commute for four hours a day in traffic. I have to work with figures, do budgets. My boss is the owner's son and he's younger than I am and stupid and a real punk. I have to listen to him and smile! I'm on a big floor with a hundred desks and a hundred people typing or talking on the phone and we're not allowed to talk to each other. There are no windows. I can't stand this."

Juan, a banker, said, "I *have* my Job from Hell. I'd have to do exactly what I'm doing. Exactly. Every day forever and ever.

That's the Job from Hell. I'd have to give speeches with slides, about investment opportunities. And write reports. Lots of reports."

Martina, a single mother of two, said, "Well, the worst thing for me would be an office with a totally disorganized mess that couldn't get organized, and it's my job to get it organized, so I fail over and over and over. Every day. And I get chewed out for it every day. And I'm not allowed to stop trying. And I get called into the boss's office and lectured every Friday."

What's the purpose of all this silliness? It has a very important purpose.

For one thing, an attack of negativity is very good for you *any time* you're under pressure. It allows the side of you that is secretly, stubbornly refusing to cooperate with "pie in the sky" dreaming to have a small tantrum. Now you'll be able to relax and use your energies elsewhere. And I have somewhere specific I want you to use them.

Flipping the Negative.

If you were one of those people who couldn't imagine a Job from Heaven, this last exercise showed off your ability to be wildly, negatively creative. I really love negativity. It's funny and it's useful: being negative is often the best way to sneak around a stubborn strain of resistance that's blocking your imagination. Now you have invented a perfect nightmare of a job, which will show you exactly how to design a heavenly one! This nightmare job will be the map that guides you straight to your deepest wishes and needs, those wishes and needs you thought you couldn't remember. Let me show you how:

Take every detail of your Job from Hell—the hours, the activities, the environment, the attitudes of coworkers, even the weather, and especially the feelings you're having—*and reverse them exactly.* Find their exact opposites. If you said, like Louisa, that in your Job from Hell you're working for a spoiled celebrity, change her to a wise, considerate, obscure philosopher. If you said that you're commuting, change it to "I work out of my own home."

Get the idea? Then pick up your pencil.

Exercise 3: Job Rewrite, or One Negative Makes a Positive

Take your Job from Hell, and write down the exact reverse of it on a blank piece of paper. If you hate living in a high-rise apartment in the middle of a city, like Louisa, write: "I live in a wonderful cottage in the countryside," or whatever the opposite is to you. If you're like Elliott and to you Hell equals no time off, write: "I work only six months a year." If your Job from Hell has you isolated in a desert trailer court, put yourself in the middle of London or Paris and go dancing and eat great food. If you hate typing and filing, figure out what would be a wonderful contrast. Would it be designing clothes? Writing about Costa Rica? Producing plays? Helping people? Just figure out the reverse of everything you said—*and watch the outlines of a Job from Heaven emerge!*

You see, you've done much more than let off a little steam. You've exposed what is most important to you, by drawing up the negative and then printing it, like a photograph, to see its opposite! There it is; *you've created a picture that proves you know more about what you want than you ever realized.* Regardless of whether you started with a positive image or a negative one, you now have a picture of a dream job. Let's use that information in this next exercise, to create a wonderful job you could actually do.

Exercise 4: The Self-correcting Scenario

This exercise comes in two versions, one for people with a good buddy available to help, the other for people who prefer to do it alone.

Version No.1: Team Up and Write a Movie.

A scenario is nothing more than a brief description of a movie. When you want to "pitch" a movie to a studio you say something like: "This upper-class professor meets this flower girl outside of the London opera house, and he and a friend decide to fix her awful speech patterns and pass her off as an aristocrat at a royal ball. Then he falls in love with her." That's a scenario.

Well, I want your buddy to pitch a scenario of *your* brilliant career movie to you. How will your buddy do this? He'll work with those two descriptions: the Job from Heaven and the Job from Hell. Your buddy says, "Okay, you hate disorganization, so here's the scenario: You're working in a perfectly organized office, and everything is completely under your control. Every day you get praised for your wonderful performance."

Listen carefully to your buddy's scenario. When he is finished, help him improve the story. Decide if you're happy with the life he has described or if you'd like to correct it. "I like the perfectly organized office, but I don't think I want praise. I think I don't want any boss at all."

"Okay," your buddy might say, "let me start again. You're in a perfectly organized office and it's your own office. You're in business for yourself."

"Oooh. I like that."

Back and forth, over and over, I want your buddy to adjust the story, each time eliminating the things you didn't like, and putting in everything you want that got left out—and then try it out on you again:

"Okay, is it good enough yet?"

"Almost. What's my business?"

"You sell long underwear."

"No, I don't want to sell anything."

"Nothing?"

"No. I want to get something done in this world. I want to teach people how to make their lives better."

Oh.

Look who just figured out what she wants.

Little by little, by correcting that scenario over and over, you'll start to find what does really matter to you—"matter" as in "meaningful." The self-correcting scenario is a trick on your psyche. *We've used all the exercises in this chapter to sneak around your defenses, and finally we're producing some hard evidence!*

Version No. 2: Two Pens.

If you don't have a buddy around, this self-correcting exercise can be done just as effectively with a pad of paper, or a notebook, and two different colored pens—one to create the scenario, one to correct it. Just alternate roles: With one pen write your "buddy's" suggestions; with the other write yours.

Once you've created your perfect scenario, you will have a goal that feels—at least for the moment—worth going after. Remember way back at the beginning of this chapter I said that if you start moving toward a goal you will activate—and expose— all the resistance that is causing you to be stuck? Well, now you've got a goal. Let's see if I was right.

Exercise 5: The Temporary Permanent Commitment

Do you have your perfectly corrected scenario? No objections left? Okay.

Now I'm going to play a dirty trick on you. *I'm going to insist you promise to do it!* Yes, that's what I said. No more looking back, your decision-making is over. Your career destination is clear.

Before you panic or decide that I've lost my mind, let me finish my instructions: *I want you to do this for only an hour.*

For a little while, I'm going to take away your freedom, *because that freedom can be a killer.* The very words "You can do anything you want" create a private hell all their own. *Anything?* That's too many choices! Sometimes limitations can be an incredible relief, and right now you're going to get that relief. Listen, you know perfectly well that you hate the formlessness of being without a goal. You want more than anything to make a decision and get on with your life.

The only thing that's kept you in this free-fall of endless choices until now is the fear that you'll make the wrong choice and be trapped. Well, right or wrong, I want you to believe that you've made a choice and you are trapped.

You're going to make a total commitment to that scenario, the one that was so right you couldn't make it any better. All other choices are now closed to you, and you must roll up your sleeves and get started making your scenario come true.

For an hour.

Now, just a minute, you're probably thinking. You're not ready to make any commitment. Not even for an hour. For one thing, you didn't know that's what we were doing. If you'd *known,* you'd have been much more careful about the project, wouldn't you?

You bet you would have been more careful. *And you wouldn't have come up with a thing.*

"No, no, no," protested Georgia, a schoolteacher whose Job from Heaven was to be a famous poet living in Wales. "This isn't *really* what I want to do—I don't *know* what I want to do, remember? What if it's *wrong?* I mean, I'm sure it *is* wrong! You don't want me to make a commitment to something that's wrong, do you?"

I sure do.

But only for an hour. (Although this could be one of the longest—and most illuminating—hours you've spent in a long time.)

By commitment I mean I want you to stop the debate. Give up all your "what-if's." Your future is a done deal. I want you to say to yourself, "Okay, there's no point in thinking about it because there's no turning back. I will become a stand-up comic, or buy an island and become a telecommuter, or join a kibbutz. Now, what are the first steps I have to take to get there?"

Then I want you to actually look in your phone book, call a comedy club, check out the newspaper for island real estate, and phone a neighbor who lived on a kibbutz! *For the next hour I want you hot on the track of your goal.* Set the alarm clock for one full hour from now (take more time if you can stand it), and you can stop when the alarm rings.

*During the hour I want you to experience what it's like to be irreversibly committed to something—*and this scenario you have created will do as well as any other.

What was that like?

"It shouldn't have been such a big deal," one man said. "But it was! I tried to treat it like any other project—planning a dinner party, for example. The only difference is that this dinner party is my life!"

"I got a cold chill down my back!" Louisa the potential mail carrier said. "But I did it. I called a friend in Columbus, Ohio, and asked her how the mail was delivered. Sure enough, the mailmen are still walking up and down the sidewalks. I asked if the residential sections were still beautiful and she said yes. Then I called the Post Office and asked them to send me an application! I can't believe you're making me do this!"

Philip said, "I'm starting to feel burnout, and I haven't even begun yet! If this is just make-believe, why is it so damned scary?"

It's scary because you're pretending it's real, that's why, and it's waking up all that resistance that prevented you from taking action for so long.

If you skipped this commitment exercise and decided you'd rather watch old sitcoms, walk the dog, or even do your taxes than do the last exercise—and make a commitment—you may think you were bored, but you weren't. You simply ducked out before the voices showed up.

You ducked out because you were scared.

By the way, if your reaction to your one-hour commitment is not fright or ambivalence, if your reaction is unmitigated enthusiasm and joy, you're ready to go out and get that wonderful scenario you've created. Put this book down right now, and get going! Good luck to you!

But if treating your scenario like a real-life goal has unsettled you, great! Your resistance is about to declare itself. Get out some more paper—or a tape recorder if you prefer—and take down the voice of your resistance, which is on the tip of your tongue right now.

Exercise 6: Listening to the Voice

In a way, you've been hearing it for years. You may have called it the voice of negativity, but it's resistance and *it's there for a reason.* Your resistance says things like "I'll get killed if I try to be a big shot." "Nothing's any good once you get it," etc. Don't let these statements bother you. Just pay careful attention and think about your voice, because *this is what we've been waiting for.*

MEET YOUR RESISTANCE

Now your resistance is in plain sight. It's dug in its heels and is *daring* you to go after what you want.

Take a closer look. This little troublemaker thinks it is defending you by doing everything in its power to discourage you every time it senses danger—and it senses danger every time you reach for what you want. By whispering negative statements in your ear it is stubbornly setting itself against you and creating the conflict that paralyzes and confuses you.

But every word it says holds the secret to your freedom.

Now that you've brought your resistance out of hiding and you're listening carefully to its messages, you're in a wonderful position to understand how to move it out of your path.

That's what the rest of this book is about. Each chapter is dedicated to overcoming a different resistance and will give you tools and strategies to work with your particular resistance. Roll up your sleeves, and let's get going.

FOUR

The Sure Thing

You know someone personally who has a thrilling, exotic life. Some friend of yours—maybe your sister, or your spouse—teaches in Istanbul or writes in a cabin in the Rockies, or flies to Hamburg to make a deal with Mercedes-Benz. You daydream about how great it must be to live like that, but know it will never happen to you. You've stepped back from the exciting opportunities that came your way, because you wanted safety. Whatever courage is required to take risks, you're pretty sure you don't have it. *You're hugging the shore, but you can't take your eyes off the horizon.*

A lot of people hug the shore and are perfectly comfortable hugging it—but you are not comfortable. You are full of longing and regret. Deep down, *you want adventure.* You know perfectly well that you've stayed at your job too long. You know you've got more of the explorer inside you than you ever use. You know that a different kind of person would have sprung into action, seized the day, moved to new territories long ago, but somewhere you learned to hang on to what you have and not try for more.

* * *

Take a quiz: Are you a cautious person?

Let me ask you a few questions about yourself, just to make sure you're in the right chapter:

1. Are you always in rehearsal? By that I mean, do you take courses or learn a skill but never really put your learning to any use?
2. When it's time to take a trip or redesign your bedroom, do you find yourself making endless preparations, constantly hesitating, calling friends to check out their opinions on each action?
3. Do you find yourself fiercely resistant to being pushed or hurried one bit more than suits you? Do you ignore deadlines until they're dangerously near and become stubborn if someone tries to warn you? (Some people don't mind being hurried, you know. Others aren't crazy about it, but they don't go into gridlock. You do.)
4. Do you hang on to things too long—even bad things, like bad relationships or items of clothing, appliances, memberships that have outworn their usefulness?
5. Do you complain there's no time to do what you really want—but actually spend a considerable amount of your day watching television or puttering around the house?
6. Do you watch other people's lives as though they were a spectator sport? Sure Thing people are unusually interested in the lives of other people—famous or familiar. This interest may stem from the fact that they feel their own lives aren't full enough—or maybe they're watching for tips on how to escape!
7. Do you often think about changing your life—but never get past daydreaming about it?

If you ticked off three or more of those, you're a Sure Thing person for sure, and *you've got some thinking to do.*

Because you're playing with fire.

Safety is riskier than you realize.

You've cast your vote for security and you probably did it a long time ago. Most of us know by the age of eight whether we're going to play it cautiously, recklessly, or somewhere in between. Some kids leap before they look. Some look and then leap. You looked and didn't leap. There were reasons we made those choices; we've forgotten them now. The point is that when we grow up, we continue to play it the way the child designed it. We never stop to rethink the design. We never reexamine those rumbles of urgency inside us to see if they make any sense. Our habits take on a life of their own, and we just assume they're right.

The truth is, most of us don't really know why we're so cautious. If there ever was a reason, it's long gone. And we've overlooked something even more important: When you play it too safe, *you're taking the biggest risk of your life.*

From the front you look like you're putting your life together very nicely, piece by piece, but behind you, time is flying out the window like dollar bills. Time is the only real wealth we're given —but it's half gone before we understand that, because when it comes to time, children feel like millionaires. Old people know a lot about time and will tell you freely that their greatest regrets were the things they didn't do. You don't have to be very old to know what they're talking about. Look back at your adolescence and ask yourself, what do you regret most? Do you regret the things you did, or the ones you didn't have the courage to do? Do you regret the dances you went to, even when you were awkward and uncertain and felt like a fool? Or do you regret the ones you avoided so you wouldn't feel like a fool?

What's a person to do?

None of us wants to be reminded of what time spendthrifts we are, because what are we supposed to do about it? Most of our thoughts run like this: "Do you really think I'm going to sell all I own, buy a sailboat, and sail around the world? First of all, I don't think I could stand the life. Second of all, what happens after I get back from the trip and I'm out of a job and out of money? I am cursed with an awareness that truly adventurous people don't seem to have: I always remember there's going to be a morning after. When I get back from my great adventure I'm going to have to start all over. Thank you but no thank you."

I've got good news for you. *Your risk-versus-safety problem isn't real.* When you pretend that your choices are total risk versus total safety, that's what I call "a setup." Does all that talk about the morning after look pretty reasonable to you? Don't be fooled, it's nothing but safety thinking. That is, it calms you down, and stops you from thinking something that might make you uneasy. But maybe you'd better get a little uneasy, because you've been hiding from your life too long.

Reason One:
Nothing Is More Wasteful Than Ignoring What You Long For

You own a great treasure that you're not using, not sharing.

Inside you is a bona fide genius who's original, curious, and loaded with potential. That genius is dying for you to open the gates so it can jump into life with both feet. Until you act on that energy, the rest of your life goes on hold. When you have an unfulfilled wish waiting in the shadows, you don't fully invest in your work, or your family, or your vacations for that matter, you just fool around, halfheartedly.

You must go after your wish. As soon as you start to pursue a dream, your life wakes up and everything has meaning. It doesn't really matter what the outcome is. You've got to regain some meaningful direction if you want your life to be exciting.

So what's been stopping you?

This might be the answer:

Reason Two:
We've All Misunderstood What Adventure Is

Adventure is supposed to be thrilling and new and keep us excited—and it's supposed to be meaningful. If it doesn't have those elements, it's not adventure. And most of us think we have to risk our lives, or at least radically change our lifestyle, to get all that. We think we have to jump out of airplanes, take a raft across the Pacific, give up our families, homes, and jobs for sure.

Because we don't really know what adventure is. To assume that it is radical and requires the sacrifice of our entire lifestyle is to create a fiction that actually helps us stand still. Let me illustrate this point with a story about myself:

Once, many years ago, I performed in a little poetry reading of *Spoon River Anthology*—a group of poems that are spoken by people from a fictional area called Spoon River. The speakers are all people who have died. One by one, they come forward to tell the most important thing about their lives. I always found myself listening to the poem of a man talking about the carving on his tombstone. It showed a ship with the sails furled—because he had never left the shore.

To me it was the saddest poem in the set.

One night, on the subway ride home from rehearsal, I resolved that I would change my life and live it to the fullest. After all, I had started out as a very adventurous kid. I took off and did what I wanted, went to Berkeley, then lived in New York, traveled through the U.S. with friends—and when I got married, I persuaded my husband to forswear a conventional life and drive to Alaska with me. It was wonderful. And I was adventurous when my marriage went bad too. When it became clear it couldn't get straightened out, I took the kids by the hands and walked out. I had a lot of confidence.

That's when the game changed. With no money and big responsibilities, my confidence took a terrific beating. Safety took on a new attractiveness for me. So when I walked in the door this night thinking about really living an adventurous life again, I looked at my two sleeping children and I thought, "Just exactly how am I going to do this? Throw them on my back and head for Africa?" I was working two jobs, and clutching desperately to both of them. I didn't have the time or the money to go to a Tarzan movie!

So I dropped the whole idea of finding adventure and went back to my real concerns: paying the rent, getting the laundry done, and keeping the kids from falling out the window—and I decided never to make a move without looking again. Years earlier, a bartender in my dad's bar said to me, "Barbara, you've got more guts than brains." Well, in 1967, I got brains. And I lost my guts.

Who can blame me? If the way to have an adventurous life was to quit my job and carry my kids to exotic locales, I couldn't consider doing it. I think that was a pretty reasonable decision—*if going to an exotic locale was really the issue.*

But it never was.

I had one part right—a real adventure would have made my life feel exciting. And I was probably right about another thing— winding up in Africa with two small kids and no money wouldn't have been very nice. But I had the rest completely wrong, and I'll bet you do too.

Going on a safari isn't necessarily your big adventure. At least, that wasn't *mine.* Real adventure lifts your heart, opens your mind, and makes you catch your breath. And that's not the same for any two people. What I was doing was basing my notion of the "fully lived life" on my "escape" dreams.

Escape dreams are different from real dreams.

They're like escape hatches. They constitute a brief vacation from reality, and we seem to need them. We have escape dreams sometimes when we're on our way to work, or when we hear about the lives of the rich and famous. Then we sail off into being an astronaut or a rock star or a sailor on the high seas. I don't think we take these escape dreams very seriously, and in fact, they're not real passions, just momentary flights of the imagination. But let's take a good look at them because they hold some important information about your life.

Exercise 1: What Are Your Escape Dreams?

Do you imagine having millions of dollars, batting a home run in Yankee Stadium, being seduced by the most attractive human being alive? Let yourself go. Just make sure they're true fantasies, and not practical in any way.

Joe: I imagine being a fighter pilot in a great, hot jet plane, shooting down a really dangerous enemy.

Gert: I just watch lives of the rich and famous. It's not their goodies that impress me, it's their certainty, their carefree attitude. They have fun and they don't worry.

Moe: I imagine being a woodsman and a tracker. I don't know of what. I don't want to kill any animals. Maybe I track the habits of some animal, or something. And I live in a cabin and read a lot and then I go to a local roadside gas station and restaurant on the Alaska Highway and talk to everybody and drink coffee.

May: Making movies of Borneo, of cannibals!

Kelly: Just getting on a plane, first class, putting my feet up, and getting served champagne, flying far away.

Sue: Living in a mountaintop monastery where everything is clear and quiet. So quiet.

What about you? What did *you* say?

That escape dream holds a powerful clue to something you really need. It's like a photo film negative of your life. Whatever in your life is missing, wherever a blank spot exists, it shows up in this fantasy. Joe, the fighter pilot, needs some freedom and power. Gert envies the self-confidence and worry-free lives of the rich and famous. Moe needs a hideaway that's close to nature, and he needs time, and he needs friends who like to hang out and talk. (He doesn't really need to go to Alaska if he doesn't want to.)

We should all search our escape dreams because they send clues about what's wrong with our lives. And then we should do something about what's missing. *Because if you don't use that information to improve your life, you're using escape dreams to help you avoid life.* Use them as a pointer to the next step of your life, and you won't be needing them much after that.

Escape dreaming is so grand that in a million years you'd never seriously consider doing what you dream about. That makes it just another safe activity, and you're already too safe. That's not all. Escape dreaming keeps you from feeling confined and restless with your real life. Like a painkiller, it can keep you comfortable while you're stuck and stop you from changing.

We're going for the big stuff. We're going for your real dreams.

REAL DREAMS

Real dreams aren't escapist at all. The only reason I call them dreams is because they're in the future. When they arrive, they'll be very real indeed. Where escape dreams are shallow, real dreams are deep and utterly unique to each of us. You rarely see a movie made about real dreams, because deep down each of us wants personal pleasures that don't make a million hearts sing, only ours. We want to see our family's homeland, or go to school, or learn about astronomy. We want things we have a hard time explaining to people, no matter how sympathetic they may be. Because real dreams are like our fingerprints. They come from that inner genius I was talking about.

You can count on that. Anytime there's something you *really* want, something that rings a bell inside you and you don't even know why, it comes from a part of you that is unlike anyone else. That's the real you, the one with original vision, who sees the world in a way that is all your own.

Unlike escape dreams, you don't muse easily about real dreams. As a matter of fact you might have to go digging to find them, because they often hide themselves. Why? Because remembering them can be a very emotional experience.

They are the stuff that true adventure is made of. It's an interesting thing to note that grandiose escape dreams—like flying jet fighters, or wrestling alligators—are very easy to think about and very risky to actually do, while real dreams—like asking someone to marry you or deciding to go back to school at the age of fifty—scare the hell out of you when you think about them, *and usually involve no real risk at all.*

As I said, real dreams don't require you to abandon your family, quit your job, and move to Tahiti with your paintbrush. They just require that you search your soul for that deep dream you put aside—and go for it.

And watch your life light up.

You will find that the difference between your life when you're just marking time and your life when you're involved with a personal, beloved dream is astonishing.

There you are. All your excuses are gone.

So why are you still scared?

Because although you don't have to give up a life of security to lead a life of adventure, *you do have to take an emotional chance when you let yourself love something.* Daring to live your dream is very intense. It wakes you right out of that safety-sleep you're in. Being fully creative, or fully productive, even thinking that you have the right to live a wonderful life—this is no small matter. That's where the real fear is.

Of course, we try to pretend the practical obstacles are so great that it's much too risky to move. Let me give you a very common example.

Jerry says he *has* to change his whole lifestyle to follow his dream of writing screenplays. "Writing takes time! And I'm too tired at night because my job exhausts me. Anyway, my wife has a right to expect us to spend some time together."

His wife laughed. "Are you kidding? He's so unhappy that I spend the whole evening consoling him. I wish he'd do *anything* that would make him happy! I've got my own stuff to do!"

Jerry blushed, and said that was probably true. "I write and edit all day. They love me there, I'm good at what I do, I even have a future with this company. But I can't bear to think that I'm going to end up an editor. It makes me resent the hell out of this job, which is probably what exhausts me. Look, I wrote wonderful plays in college, I won prizes! I had a great future! I can't write with this damned job. And I can't quit it either. I'm not willing to starve and live in a garret.''

Mary Jane and Donna thought like Jerry.

Mary Jane: I *have* to leave my job. That way I'll be forced to take the big chance and sing professionally.

Donna: I have to leave this secretarial job or I'll be inferior like my sisters said I was.

But Jerry, Mary Jane, and Donna have it all wrong. They think they can't succeed *because* of their jobs. In fact, they can't succeed *without* them! I'll show what I mean:

Exercise 2: An Exercise for Job Haters

Take out a pencil and paper and write across the top of the page: *I don't want to like this job, because . . .*

Imagine yourself at work, right in the middle of doing whatever you like least. Imagine you have to keep this job for the rest of your life. Now write down what you're feeling. Hold nothing back.

Jerry: To like this job would be the worst thing in the world! It would mean I'm not a writer, I'm an editor. That would be the worst thing that could happen to me! All I want out of life is to be free—free to never have to write another word that I don't choose to write.

Mary Jane: I have to leave this job, because it's too comfortable and I'll never make myself go after singing jobs. I have to have nowhere to hide. I have to force myself. Otherwise I'll be an amateur forever, a teatime singer, you know, weddings and birthdays. Nothing real. No career.

Donna: If I liked this job it would prove I'm nothing but a dumb secretary. I'm a nobody.

Right now some of you may be standing and applauding—figuratively at least—Jerry's and Mary Jane's and Donna's cries for freedom. All of you writers, painters, and actors who, if it weren't for your draining office or restaurant jobs, would be racing ahead, bound for glory. Or would you?

We all think we need freedom to pursue our dream, but I've got a surprise for you. The opposite is probably true.

After three years of staying home, trying to be a painter, Nina gave up and went back to teaching. Now she paints more than ever!

"That was the worst three years of my life! It was too much free time. It was terrifying. Now I can't wait for Saturdays. I paint all day Saturday, and I'm starting to take a class on Wednesday nights. And I'm going to Maine this summer to take a two-week workshop with a great teacher!"

What happened? I'll tell you. *Human beings need structure.* We all need limits to things, even pleasurable things—and bottomless, creative things more than all the others! That job isn't keeping Jerry from writing. It's actually his friend. It can actually help him write. He's going to have to learn to love that job.

"Oh, no," Jerry moaned when I told him this. "You're putting a curse on my life."

For as long as he could remember, Jerry had dreamed of being a novelist. Not any garden variety novelist—it was James Joyce or bust. But while he'd given plenty of deep thought to his *Ulysses*, he had only a few pages of notes to show for it.

"How much do you write now?" I asked.

"Not much at all," Jerry said. "Well, notes. Every once in a while I make some notes."

Jerry needed:

Exercise 3: The Freedom Fantasy

Imagine that your wish suddenly comes true. You have nothing but free time to do what you want, and you will do nothing but pursue that dream full time. If you're a writer, you're alone in your study, sitting at a big mahogany desk with a blank sheet of paper in front of you. If you're a painter, you're in your studio, no phones or doorbells will interrupt you, you have your palette at the ready, and you face a large, blank canvas. An actor? You have nothing to do but scan for casting calls, get dressed and go out for appointments and auditions. A singer? You have the whole day to make phone calls to managers and opera companies to try to get heard. And so on.

Think about it for ten full minutes. Stay with it. Is it all you hoped it would be? Your wildest dreams come true? Sit in front of that blank sheet, that canvas, that copy of *Back Stage.* This is your life. How does it feel?

"Oh, it's terrifying!" Mary Jane said. "I'm not ready! Quitting my job wouldn't get me ready either."

"It's so incredibly lonesome," Jerry admitted. "I don't get it. This is terrible. Maybe I'm not a writer at all."

Sure he is. And Mary Jane is a singer. They simply have to start doing their writing and job-hunting immediately and quit fooling themselves into thinking their jobs are stopping them. After a few hours of writing or searching for an agent, both of them will be very relieved to warm their hands at their companionable jobs.

Now Jerry can relax and enjoy his job and quit worrying that he's nothing but an editor. He'll be writing every morning from six to eight. He'll know he's a writer. And Mary Jane doesn't have to quit her friendly job to force herself to get out into the world of professional singing. She just has to start going out on auditions *now.*

"Now" is the operative word. Everything you put in your way is just a method of putting off the hour when you could actually be doing your dream. You don't need endless time and perfect conditions. Do it now. Do it today. Do it for twenty minutes, and watch your heart start beating. You may not be able to stick with it that long! At the beginning you can only handle a little of that dream at a time. It's strong stuff. Much as we may long for it, following our dreams takes a lot of courage. *It's as adventurous as you ever need to get in your life.* Your feelings of safety will disappear at once, although you've kept job, family, and home.

And your feelings of boredom will disappear right along with them.

It's not actually the activity that creates the intensity, it's the love itself. Writing doesn't frighten everyone. Anthony Burgess says he had no trouble writing novels. He did it easily and for money, because it wasn't the thing he really loved best. What he really loved best was composing symphonies. And that was as intense for him as writing is for Jerry. He probably used his novel-writing to avoid writing symphonies! Jerry, Mary Jane, and Donna got instructed to start working on their dreams at once and to report back in a week. Here's what they said at the end of a week.

Jerry: My job is actually a relief, a place to run and hide! At work I can get a dose of feeling competent and sure of myself after hours of writing screenplays and being in outer space! It isn't that I don't like editing. I just didn't like thinking of myself as an editor. Now I'm a screenwriter, so I don't mind.

Mary Jane: The people are so nice, so supportive. My boss said he'd give me any time off I wanted for auditions, even for road tours if I got them. They love my voice! They'd love me to become successful! They're just wonderful. They were never the problem.

Donna: I just realized something shocking. Whose side am I on? I'm helping my sisters by despising my job! Is it really such a low-class job? After all, I'm not a hit man or a thief. I have nothing to be ashamed of. And since when am I the same thing as my job? I'm not my job.

A coworker gave Donna a plaque that she proudly put on her desk. It says "If a cat has kittens in an oven, does that make them biscuits?"

When you quit blaming your job you can get started right away taking real steps that will clear things up for you.

Donna has signed up for a landscape architecture class. Taking the time to learn a skill from the bottom up will help build her feeling of competence and stop her swings of grandiosity and worthlessness. Moving out of fantasy into the real work of learning a skill will give her both humility and self-confidence. Jerry writes for two hours in the morning before going to work and spends very nice evenings with his wife. Mary Jane sets up auditions and leaves work to go to them—with her boss's blessings—and then comes back for some TLC from her friends at work.

And every one of them is living a life full of adventure, right now—without sacrificing a thing. Are you getting the picture? Whenever you do what you really love, your heart lifts, your mind opens, and everything changes. You wake up.

That's what true adventure really is.

Don't let anyone tell you otherwise. And I don't care if that adventure takes up less than an hour a day or takes place with a pencil and paper in your living room! That's where Einstein's and Newton's and Kepler's greatest adventures took place. And Shakespeare's and Mozart's and Leonardo da Vinci's too.

So, security wasn't the problem at all.

And you're still afraid.

What's the real problem?

Creative people have a problem that looks unique, but the truth is that all of us feel exactly like them when it comes to living our dreams. *Because to make art is exactly like living any dream: every moment is brand new.*

We all fear what's new.

"I don't know why I don't do my pottery," a friend said to me recently. "I love it, but I don't do it. I find all the time in the world to organize things, to go bargain shopping, to sew things, and then I complain that I have no time to do my sculptures." What's dangerous about being creative? Well, for one thing, it's scary to change gears from low-anxiety, maintenance-type activities to the intensity of a level of consciousness where everything is new. Learning and creating are high-risk enterprises. Even thinking about doing them can drive us into all sorts of avoidance behavior. Perhaps when you create, you see too much. Perhaps you fear the size of your own gift. (Don't underestimate the scariness of a real gift.) Having a real gift is like having swallowed an atom bomb. It's terrifying. Artists have to strip away what is familiar so that they can see what is new. *And so do you,* whether you're an artist or not. What's new is risky, and evolution has worked for a long time to teach us to avoid risk. It's developed a powerful mechanism inside all of us that works to turn anything new into habit.

INNOVATION VERSUS HABIT

I work very hard to get used to things, to make them second nature—and so do you. I know I'll never be able to maneuver my way through this world if everything stays brand new. I've got to be able to do most things automatically or I'm going to have to think too hard before I can pick up a fork or cross the street.

What a powerful, exciting, terrifying experience it is to take our first steps, to go to a new city, to drive a car for the first time! Our love of excitement and intensity is always in a struggle with our need for what is familiar. We'd never survive without being able to absorb new experiences and make them habitual. So our habit machinery is our friend.

The problem is, it doesn't have an OFF button. It operates all the time! It doesn't like *any* excitement!

Well, don't get too worried about it, because learning how and when to sidestep our habit machinery is exactly what real adventure is all about. And again, that's not just true for creative artists—that's true for the rest of us too. When shy people take a bold step toward a new career or personal life, it's as fresh and frightening and beautiful to them as singing an aria to a packed house is going to be to Mary Jane! When "good mothers," people who spend their days taking care of everybody else, spend one afternoon doing what they really love—even if it's reading a book—the experience is fresh, and intense, and just as creative as making art!

The "good mother" is anyone who is always putting other

people before him or herself, such as Virginia, a gifted writer who is also a writing teacher, giving all to her students and leaving very little for herself, and Sue D., a supermom, who works, volunteers, and helps her husband with his projects and her children with their school, and carries the major burden for the running of the house. Their generosity is very gratifying to them. It's an expression of love, and makes the giver's life very rich. But past a certain point it clearly becomes a Sure Thing choice. When you give too much—when it costs you something essential from your own life—you too are choosing the sure thing over the adventurous life. How? You're choosing to be indispensable, a good person, to feel you have the power to make things come out right. Also, any guilt you ever felt in your life is being nicely worked off.

What to do?

I have a quick little exercise I want you to do.

Exercise 4: The Love Showdown

Choose one activity you are going to give up every day—and replace it with something you love to do. Here's the requirement: *You have to give up something you do for someone else.* It can't be something you do for yourself! Think for a moment, and make a decision. You can stop shopping, chauffering your kids to the pool, or taking your husband's clothes to the cleaners. It has to give you at least thirty minutes for yourself, and that thirty minutes has to be spent doing something that is only for you, only for pleasure.

That's it. That's the whole exercise.

I tried this on a women's time management workshop I ran in Eugene, Oregon, and the women were stunned. It took them a few minutes to understand that I really meant what I said, and then they started to stand up one by one and say what they were going to give up.

"I'm going to stop ironing shirts," one woman said.

"I'm going to give up typing everybody's school papers," another said.

And then it caught on! All night long, after the workshop and into the next day, you could find them in the hotel lounge, the elevators, and the restaurant, looking conspiratorial and saying, "What are you giving up?"

To protect them against the guilt they were sure to feel if their families complained, I had them write down a little speech that they were to say—a very tough but very true statement. Here it is, in case you want to use it:

"I shop and cook and make your beds and drive you places and earn money to share with you and I do it all with pleasure because I love you. I want your minds to be free to study and to do your personal work and to have a great life. What I want to know is, do you love me enough to let me have a half hour a day for the same thing, *or do you love dinner more?* If you love dinner more, I really ought to know that."

It's time to wake up the mamas *and their families too.* Put a sign on the refrigerator: "In this house, *everybody* gets what they need, even Mom."

And on the day that the kids come home from school and start cutting up vegetables for dinner because Mom's in the study reading poetry, *a whole family is going to find out what adventure is all about.*

Now, permit me to ask you a very big question.

What's your adventure going to be?

WHAT'S *YOUR* REAL WISH?

If you're a Sure Thing person, you're different from others who aren't doing what they love, because you often *know* what you really want. You cling to your Sure Thing job to keep you safe from that Unsure adventure that's enticing you. You almost always know exactly what that Unsure adventure is. Still, it takes a little courage to think about it, so let me make this as safe as possible. Let's imagine two things. First let's imagine that you are very bold, nothing stops you. You know how to fantasize that. Now let's imagine *you can't possibly fail at anything you try.* And now write or talk into a tape recorder and tell me exactly what it is you are doing.

Exercise 5: What Would You Do If You Were Bold? What Would You Do If You Knew for Sure You'd Succeed at It?

Sue D., forty-four, supermom, and community volunteer: I'd study the history of Greece, and get fluent in Greek, and spend my summers there, reading Plato.

Virginia, thirty-three, writing teacher: I'd write fiction from nine to twelve each morning, play with my kids all afternoon, write another two hours after dinner—every day.

Bob, fifty, scientist: I'd live in a different country every year.

Judy, thirty-three, computer programmer: I'd get a job working with people instead of machines.

Cindy, thirty-four, administrator in a community college: I'd move to California and start my own business.

But don't you think most people are being lazy and need to "Just do it?"

Not a chance. *It is one of my deepest beliefs that nobody is lazy.* Just take a look at how you run when you're trying to catch a bus, how painstakingly you dress when you really want to look sensational. If you were really lazy, you'd be lazy on those occasions too.

I bet you think you're pretty lazy when it comes to putting up the storm windows and washing the car, don't you? Surely that's laziness?

Nope. That's resistance. You just don't *want* to do those things. You'd refuse if you could get away with it. Since you can't, you're dragging your heels. It's silly, I suppose, but we all do it. (I invented the Hard Times Gripe Sessions to blow off the resistance, get you laughing, and get your energy back. It's in *Wishcraft.* Take a look at it when you have that problem.)

But when you really *want* to do something and you still don't do it, you're dealing with something much more loaded than resistance. You're in a wrestling match with yourself, and it's so exhausting it's got you all tired out.

You're dealing with *your inner conflict.*

Whenever you pull away from doing something you really want to do, there's an inner conflict. Conflict means two strong forces pushing against each other and causing immobility. One says "go." One says "stop." The result is a dynamic "stuckness," an uneasy immobility.

Our attempts to lecture the "go" force into overriding the "stop" force produce only small, temporary solutions. You can't talk yourself out of a problem any more than you can talk yourself out of a stone in your shoe. Slogans and clichés like "Just do it!" and "Ignore those negative thoughts. Life is what you make it. *Tell* yourself it's safe and it *will* be safe" are simply too superficial to help for long. The only way to deal with the "stop" force is to respect it, get to know it, find out where it's coming from and why it's stopping you.

Let me show you how Judy did it.

CAUTIOUS JUDY

Judy was overcautious about almost everything. Every decision required endless investigation, many conferences with people to get their opinions, and often a last-minute cancellation of very elaborate and extensively planned projects like vacations. She is a computer programmer and never really liked it, but was indecisive. Her dream might not seem huge to you but it looked as unreachable as heaven to her. She wanted to get a job working with people, not computers. But she couldn't take the first step toward it. With Judy there was no apparent reason for this hesitation. In real terms, it was hard to see any risk. But everything Judy did was like that. She just got stuck.

"I won't even look at the test dates that are posted on the bulletin boards and I don't know why." Like a magnet pointed the wrong way, her resistance pushes her away from action.

Judy is scared to death and she doesn't know it. She doesn't experience the fear, because she plays it safe. As long as she doesn't start reading those test dates, what's she got to be scared of? The danger begins when she takes her first steps, so she's not taking any steps.

What scared Judy?

THE SAFETY IN YOUR BONES

If you had stored up enough safety in your childhood bones, you would be very comfortable about pursuing adventure. After all, nature wants us to have both: safety so we live long enough to reproduce our species, adventure so we become hunters, explorers, and can find mates.

When you see someone who won't try to go after what they want, they don't have safety in their bones. They sense some kind of danger, and *when there's a sense of danger with no apparent present cause, it's a good idea to go looking into the past.*

In Judy's case, the cause of her feelings of danger was clearly her early home life. Judy's childhood family was a disaster. Her mother, a childlike woman, was abandoned by her husband and left with five children to raise. Nothing was organized or done right, and the family was always on the verge of disintegrating. By the time she was six, Judy had her eyes wide open for mishaps. One time her mother left her baby sister in a supermarket. When her mother got home she burst into tears and couldn't function. Six-year-old Judy ran out to find the baby. It took a long time to find her because Judy didn't know at which store she had been left, but finally she found her—sitting quietly in her stroller at the end of an aisle. Judy pushed the stroller out to the street, greatly relieved—but she had come so far from home she had a hard time finding her way back.

That was the biggest of such events, but smaller ones abounded. Judy's mother was out of control. So Judy spent all her energy trying to make sure nothing bad would happen since she believed that her life would fall apart if she took any risks.

Everything looks terrifically risky to Judy.

It's tough to overcome Judy's kind of cautious behavior. Judy knew about her background, of course, but she didn't know how powerfully it could still control her. Many of us don't even realize that events from our childhood are causing our cautious behavior.

But sometimes that's what it is.

That's why you'll never hear me saying it's your own fault that you don't have what you want. I hope you won't let *anyone*—not even *you*—talk you into the fact that you're not trying hard enough or you don't really want to change, because that's like telling a car with no gas that it isn't doing its best to run. Believe me, you're not cautious because you want to be that way.

And there is a way to change.

It's important to understand that this problem doesn't yield to a frontal attack, much as we wish it did. That's the attractiveness of all the power-plus self-improvement programs that tempt us into laying down lots of money for "Five Easy Steps to Personal Perfection."

EST called its audience "assholes." That's extreme, but every success program seems to have at its base some kind of scold. "Just stop being such a jerk!" they imply. "You're creating your own lousy reality." "All you have to do is change the way you see things!"

And we love it. It's so refreshing and invigorating. We march out with renewed resolve.

But after a little while, we slip back into our old ways. Why? *Because the underlying reason we were doing things in an imperfect way was a damned persuasive one, and it was never taken care of.* You can't brush your whole history under the rug and then be able to dance on top of it. You will trip for sure.

SOMETHING SCARED YOU

You're not scared because you chose to be a coward. *Something scared you!* The problem is just that you can't exactly locate it anymore. Believe me, underneath every cautious person's surface there's a mighty drama being acted out. And you've got to know what it is.

But first you've got to stop scolding yourself.

No one is as hard on themselves as people who chose the Sure Thing. They somehow picked up the message that if you were hard on yourself, that might cause good behavior.

"It's my own fault," each says. "If I had any guts I'd just pick myself up and do it. I'm doing this to myself."

But scolding yourself is a wasteful thing to do. When I was a kid, it was the fashion to assume that kids simply *loved* to do the wrong thing. Whoever originally figured that one out was doing some fancy intellectual footwork, because *nobody enjoys ruining their own life.* Check it out: Did you ever feel that it was a lot of fun to get F's, or to get fat, or to have your folks angry at you? Of course not. The same thing goes for playing life too safe: You *don't* want to.

Anyway, even if you were right about all your faults—which I insist you are not—scolding yourself wouldn't do the slightest bit of good, because scolding has no effect on the will. As a matter of fact, *being judgmental about your own behavior is actually another cop-out because it makes you feel as though you're doing something virtuous.*

Trust me, it's an illusion. Slapping your own wrist does nothing but fill up your agenda. When you stop scolding yourself, a nice big space will appear and you'll have plenty of use for it.

Don't let other people judge you either. Being judgmental is cheap. Any fool can do it.

To cause real change you must realize that there's a good reason for your problem—and find that reason.

Then you'll be in a position to fix it.

Why weren't we taught to seek the good reasons for our bad behavior? I think the real reason we're taught to be judgmental is because it's so much easier—in the short run—than being thoughtful.

So, let's *think* about your situation for a moment.

WHO'S THAT VOICE IN YOUR HEAD?

There are three kinds of voices:

1. That "no" voice inside you belongs to a grown-up who was training you to be scared—a parent, a teacher, an older sibling. You have taken their voice inside you and that's what's stopping you.

Alicia's parents reacted fearfully to every attempt she made to make friends or try new activities; they admonished her to be careful, do what was safe, as though there were danger at every turn. Both of her parents were youngest children in immigrant families whose lives in the new country had been tightly controlled by older siblings. As a result, Alicia's parents lacked initiative, the ability to make their own decisions, and the experience in the world that would have given them some confidence. Even when you know they're foolish, the messages get inside. That's how we learn. Our minds are set up to protect us from danger, and as a small child the best way is to take those voices inside to remind us, over and over again, that someone said the world is very dangerous.

Alicia never had much trouble telling her parents *they* were too fearful, but their voices got inside her head. Now every time she does something bold, she panics and tries to undo it. She walks out of new jobs, stands up dates, avoids social gatherings.

2. Your parents were so out of control that you created a parent-voice.

If you had a parent who was irresponsible, unreliable, or out of control, you had to parent yourself. How? You created a parent-voice to keep you safe by scolding you, reminding you to be orderly and not reckless. The more out of control your parent was, the stronger the parent voice you created.

CONTROL ISSUES AND MAGIC

We humans do a strange thing when we fear our world is out of control: we invent magic. We try to control the universe with little control games. Actually, there's very little we can do to make life completely safe—ill health, war, and weather can get us at any time. Somehow animals seem to live with this helplessness, but we can't stand it so we pretend we're doing something. Nadine is very strict with herself about her clothes. They have to be clean and in perfect order in her drawers. She's done that since she was a little girl. It's her form of magic. Like an Indian rain dance, it makes her feel like she's having some effect on an out-of-control universe. How does it show itself? With a scolding parental voice that says, "Now look at you! You've gotten your dress dirty. Your socks have holes in them. You're disgusting." Every year the stakes go up . . .

And now Nadine has a tyrant in her mind as fierce as any parent could have been, and it's controlling every step she takes. Until she understands that folding her clothes neatly will not change her mother into a normal mother, she's trapped into compulsive behavior.

3. The "no" voice was a silent command in your family—you never heard "no" but you felt it in the air.

Sometimes the voice in your head is well hidden, like Cindy's. Cindy had a wonderful childhood. She remembers it fondly. Her parents never seemed frightened because they had everything under control. "Nothing ever happened in our house. Everyone was nice, everything was done right. We were all kind of happy. No one got sick, and the soup never boiled over. My father was home at five thirty every work day of his life, and my mother had dinner ready. It was actually the most perfectly run home life I've ever seen. We never had a flat tire!"

Cindy went to a neighborhood community college, and on graduating took a job in their administration department. She liked the work. She developed an exciting system, cleaning up an incompetent, outmoded financial system with miraculous results. "I just have a natural feel for systems and numbers and organization. I love it." But she was consistently underpaid and underappreciated. She'd love to do the same kind of work somewhere else, maybe in California. I told her she could start a consulting service, cleaning up the administrative problems of community colleges all over the country. We brainstormed ways for Cindy to get herself written up in the right magazines, and the plan started to look quite feasible. But finally she admitted she was terrified to leave her present job. She was afraid of "things going out of control." Why would she be so afraid? Absolutely nothing in her childhood had been out of control.

I encouraged Cindy to ask her parents about *their* childhoods and an amazing secret came out. Her father had had a terrible childhood, and she never knew about it. His brother was a schizophrenic who had terrorized the family. Cindy's father did his best to protect his childhood family, but he finally walked away from it. He had seen the world out of control and he wanted no part of it, so he married a sweet woman who liked to play house and hated conflict, and between them they created the safe haven that was Cindy's home. *But everything he did was an affir-*

mation of safety and control and a memory of the danger he had lived through, and somehow the children picked it up.

Once you can hear the "no" voice, how do you respond to it?
You can't just ignore these voices, but you do not have to be restricted by them either. Sometimes just seeing that the problem is a voice from your past is enough. But sometimes insight isn't enough and you'll have to work on the problem before you can move on.

Here's how Judy and Cindy did it.

Judy took the tiniest steps so she wouldn't activate her alarm system. Her only goal was to desensitize herself to being in motion. Because she finds it frightening to act on impulse, she's given herself orders to go out and get an ice cream as soon as she even considers it. It may not look very dangerous, but it's the first step to breaking all Judy's rules of safety. Once she's comfortable with tiny steps, she'll be able to devise bolder steps—and take them.

Cindy started looking for a job in the career counseling department of a community college in the town she wants to move to; she also makes herself look at the local want ads. Because she'll have to stay in touch with all the corporate opportunities in the area in order to develop a program she can sell to the community colleges, one of these days she may find a job that's so right for her she'll keep it for herself.

Everyone who chose safety over adventure needs to practice taking tiny steps in an adventurous direction. So set a goal, no matter how tentative, and start the planning process. Decide to become an actor or learn karate or go camping. Don't worry too much about whether or not you actually achieve this goal. Taking steps in any new direction is adventurous. All you really want to do is start behaving in new ways at the lowest risk possible.

Write up a list of what you'll have to do to get to your goal. *Don't set a time limit on achieving any goals or subgoals, just put them in the right order.* (There are tips about how to do planning in Chapter 6: "I Want Too Many Things.")

Don't leave your Sure Thing just yet. First, begin to practice taking the small steps, doing the things you've avoided doing before, experiencing the "little" risks and the "little" adventures until your love of doing what you want and your experience at taking risks makes you confident enough to feel that living your biggest dream is only one more "little" risky step.

Some people have made big intellectual strides without ever leaving their Sure Thing jobs.

Wallace Stevens was one of the greatest American poets of the twentieth century. He played it safe too, by holding down a very safe job in an insurance company—and writing great poetry on his own time.

And my hero, Albert Einstein, was a patent clerk and liked it just fine.

There was a man named Cornelius Hirschberg who worked at a job he didn't care about in the garment center for forty-five years. Every day he spent an hour on the subway going to work and an hour coming home. He wasn't crazy about the work, or the people, or even the pay, although he managed to raise a family quite adequately. But Cornelius loved his job because it left him completely free to do what he loved most in the world.

He read on the subway to and from work each day for forty-five years, and he became a learned man. In his book *The Priceless Gift* (Simon & Schuster, NY, 1960), he wrote of his life, "I do my duty earning bread. Reading and thinking are my own. . . . So now I show you how you can delight yourself as I have delighted myself all my life long, in a noble world of song, color, form, ideas and truth. To think a thing out—what a joy! To see a new truth or a new beauty—you can have this so far as I have had it."

FIVE

Fear of Success: Leaving the Ones You Love Behind

You'VE got a problem a lot of people wish they had: you fear success. Most people don't have to fear success, because they don't think they're in any real danger of getting it. To them it looks like you have a luxurious fear, like the fear of enormous wealth.

They don't appreciate how painful it is for you to keep dropping the ball just when you were about to carry it across the line. They don't understand why someone with your abilities keeps messing up terrific opportunities. It's a mystery to you too.

You know you're gifted, because you get noticed. You've been offered a lot of chances, and the people who've offered them weren't wrong. They saw what you were capable of.

Yet whenever you get near what you want, something happens—you lose focus at a crucial moment and turn your energy to something unimportant, or your mood mysteriously drops and you get tired just when you need energy the most.

Sometimes, instead of sabotaging yourself directly, you simply lose sight of what you're doing. "This job is leading nowhere. I might as well quit," Lisa Q. said, oddly discouraged after enjoying three months at a fabulous job that would have led straight to her dream career. She started taking long weekends and began to miss important meetings. At first, Lisa had plenty of excuses, but one day she realized she really had no idea why she was acting so strangely.

Something was behind Lisa's incomprehensible behavior. Something's behind yours. And you've got to find out what that something is, because *what you don't know is hurting you.*

Take a careful look at your life and you'll probably see a history of missed opportunities that stretches all the way back to your childhood.

Your past won't determine your future if you can find out *why* you have such an odd relationship with success. And that's what I'd like you to begin doing right now.

Exercise 1: Backing Away from Success

At the top left margin of a piece of paper, write the earliest age you think might be relevant to your fear-of-success chronology. If you're not sure, write "5 Years Old." Continue down the page, putting a number for every five years up to the present. Alongside each age, write down anything you remember doing to avoid getting something you really wanted. If you don't remember a self-sabotaging incident, write down any highlights of that year as they occur to you. You may be in for some surprises.

Here's what Beverly, thirty-one, an office manager in a real estate firm, remembered:

5 years old: I did whatever I wanted. I learned to read! No problems.

10: My brother got to be very mean to me. He stopped being my friend. I played private games in my room. I tried to keep out of the spotlight.

At school, I talked too much to my friends in class and got in trouble with my teacher. I tried to be quiet in class, but I kept forgetting. I started feeling that people who didn't smile at me didn't like me. I tried to be funny, so everyone would laugh.

15: I was crazy about boys. They didn't want to date brainy girls so I tried acting stupid around them, but I always got interested in what they were talking about and forgot to keep my mouth shut. I felt I lacked whatever it was that made boys love you.

20: I went to college and finally became popular, but I wasn't happy about it. The boys didn't seem to really like me, they were just pressuring me for sex. I guess I wanted somebody to really fall in love with me.

For the first time I did badly in school and found myself losing interest in classwork. I just couldn't see the point in studying anymore.

Later, when I finally graduated, I was kind of depressed. I could have gone to graduate school, but didn't bother. I could never figure out what I wanted to study.

25: After a series of part-time jobs I took a job as an office manager. I've been doing that ever since.

Beverly stopped her chronology at twenty-five years old because by then she felt she'd locked her self-sabotage into place.

But when Marcia, forty-three, a voice coach, did this exercise, she didn't see any problems *until* she was twenty-five! She'd had a difficult childhood, with two alcoholic parents, yet she'd been determined to survive and make a life for herself. Carefully putting a career plan together, she trained to become a motivational speaker and lecturer, but on the night of her first big speech she lost her voice. Visits to doctors showed no physical cause for her voice problem, so she worked hard once more, but a few months later it happened again. She gave up public speaking and started gaining weight. Heartbroken, she studied voice for years, finally becoming a voice coach. She had learned enough about voice to do well whenever she started speaking again, but now weight became the obstacle to her success. She refused to lecture until she lost weight. And she didn't lose weight. She wouldn't let herself succeed at *that.*

What's your story?

Take a long look at what you wrote.

Can you see some places where you created a problem for yourself just when things might have gone really well? You're not sure? Ask yourself the following questions:

Did you speak up when there was something you wanted? Did you persist in going after what you wanted even when the going got tough? Did you introduce yourself to people you wanted to know or *needed* to know to get what you wanted? Did you enjoy doing well at sports or on exams or at parties? How did you feel when you brought home athletic prizes, good grades, wonderful dates?

Sometimes the only thing we do to avoid success is refuse to be energetic on our own behalf. I'm not talking about anything extreme, just normal, healthy eagerness, the kind every child starts out with. *You started out with that energy too.* Where did you lose it? Were you always this way? Or were you fearless and feisty until ten, or fifteen, or twenty-five before you began to show confusion about getting what you wanted?

Beverly was surprised at how clearly—and early—her chronology showed her conflict: "I learned *fast* that it was bad to be smart! I knew I couldn't get love if I had brains. My whole life was about having love versus having brains. Like they were opposed to each other. But I never realized I gave up before I was ten years old!"

Before you jump to any conclusions about this chronology you've just written, I'd like to give you three tips:

Tip No. 1: Backing up isn't always a sign of fear of success.

When you back away from something that looks like a great opportunity to other people, but not to you, *that is not an example of fear of success.*

Most of us remember a time when we decided against a scholarship, or a job that looked good, or an offer of marriage to some-one who looked like a great catch. People thought we were crazy, and we might have agreed with them. (You can get con-fused when an opportunity looks so good you think you *ought* to want it.) But we just couldn't bring ourselves to *want* that oppor-tunity. It wasn't right for us and we knew it in our bones.

Saul, forty-one, a university professor who was having a hard time finding a teaching job, got offered a position heading up program and curriculum planning at a wealthy community cen-ter. His friends were happy for him. He thought he should grab the job. But the idea of locking himself into curriculum planning, hiring other teachers to do the actual teaching, felt suffocating to him: "I'd rather keep looking for a teaching job. Teaching is what I love. Not planning programs."

Here's the key. If you've always wanted something and you push it away just when it's in your grasp, *that's* self-sabotage, that's fear of success. But Saul could have *always* told you he didn't want that job. Of course, it's always all right to take interim jobs that pay the rent even if they're not exactly right—paying your rent is essential to success—*but never forget what you really want.*

If you persuade yourself to love a career you really do *not* love —just because you think you should—you're looking for unhap-piness. Remember, *rejecting what you don't want is not a fear of success, it's a fear of getting pulled off course.*

Tip No. 2: You aren't the cause of every lost opportunity!

That's right. You don't control the cosmos.

If your industry has gone into a major wobble, or you're trying to get something that's almost impossible for most people to get (like an acting job on Broadway), you may start believing that you didn't try hard enough, imagining you were self-sabotaging when you weren't. But the truth is, you can't always make things work out the way you want *in the short run.* There's a real world out there. It doesn't consult us whenever it decides to make a move.

It's essential to distinguish between events that are really beyond your control and events you caused yourself.

Tip No. 3: Don't think the reason you haven't tried is because you fear failure.

As far as I'm concerned, people who think they fear failure have got it wrong. They really fear success. *If you truly feared failure, you'd be very successful.* People who truly fear *anything* stay as far away from it as possible. So, if you're operating below your potential, and you think the reason you don't try for what you really want is that you're scared of failure, forget it. In your eyes, you're a failure right now; so how afraid of failure can you be?

But what if you feel you're not afraid of failure itself, you're afraid of failing at something *specific*? "What if I try my hardest to be a writer, give it my best, and fail at that? Then my worst fears will be realized. I'll know I don't have what it takes," you might say.

You won't know any such thing. If you try to go to law school or be an artist or find a mate, and you fail, it doesn't prove a damn thing except that *it's hard to succeed.* That's not news. It's common sense to keep trying until you get it right. If you can't bring yourself to keep trying, I'd get a little suspicious. Maybe you don't want to succeed, maybe you just want it to go on record that *you tried.* You're looking for an alibi and now is the time to get curious: Why would you want to set up your life like that?

WHAT'S HURTING YOU?

Remember, there's always a good reason for everything.

"I feel like Ulysses's wife, Penelope, who wove all day and unraveled her work all night, because if she finished she'd have to choose a husband and she was waiting for Ulysses to come home," Lynn said. Lynn has a business putting together research information packages for scientists. She loves her work and does a great job. But at the last minute, at the moment she's handing in a report, she often loses a crucial page, or forgets to check her material for mistakes.

"I *know* I should recheck the material. I know it. But somehow I talk myself out of it, saying oh forget it, it's okay. Later, I'm always sorry."

If you're like Lynn—and most people who fear success *are* like her—you can see the deliberateness of your self-sabotage but feel unable to stop it. That's because your sabotage is only half-conscious. We blow our chances just as we do when we're trying to diet and we reach for a piece of cake. It's almost as if somebody else is taking over! And in a way, someone is.

Who's running this show anyway?

Look again at Beverly's chronology. Beginning with the resentment from her brother and her teachers, all her experience made her see that whenever she was too smart people became cold. After a few years, she connected being smart with being unlovable. But she never made a *conscious* decision to hold herself back. Beverly worked hard to make her life come out right, but after a while she "mysteriously" developed trouble concentrating. Her grades tumbled and she finally decided she wasn't very smart after all. Without actually knowing what she was doing, Beverly submerged her talents.

When a reaction is unconscious, it's on automatic pilot and resting comfortably. It's done its job of controlling you so well that it doesn't have to keep an eye on you anymore. The best method for waking up that hidden resistance is to *give it something to worry about.*

For five minutes, I want you to push away the controls. Imagine that nothing has stopped you and you've gotten your biggest dream.

Exercise 2: Let Your Success-Loving Voice Sing Out

One side of you actually enjoys success—and that side has a voice. It's clear as a bell, strong and beautiful, and it says, "I love getting what I want!" It's dying for exercise, so I'd like you to give it something to crow about.

Imagine you have gotten everything you ever wanted. Pick a life that feels closest to your dream of success. That is, pick *whatever you'd have today if you'd never dropped the ball.*

Close your eyes and imagine: What does it look and feel like to have everything you want? Walk through every part of it, as if you were really there. Stay with this exercise for as long as you can—for up to five minutes—without stopping.

You're doing exactly what you always longed for. You're at your desk signing big checks, looking out over a beautiful skyline in your favorite metropolis. Or you're on stage singing like an angel in front of thousands of adoring fans. Or you're in the best research lab in the world, discovering the cure for AIDS. Or you're on the dais at the Olympic Games, the gold medal around your neck, your national anthem playing.

Don't forget to furnish your successful life with all the honors, accolades, and respect you'd have if you were completely successful at what you love.

How does that feel?

Now I want you to talk about it. *Out loud!* Stand up, look out the window or into a mirror, and let your success-loving voice have its turn to speak. Tell the world why your life is wonderful.

Andrea, forty-two, a bookkeeper who had always wanted to be a professional dancer, visualized her triumph as a Broadway musical and music-video star: "Oh, I love it. I'm wonderful at something I love. This is pure heaven."

Saul, the out-of-work professor, saw himself at one of the world's great universities, winning all the student votes for best teacher, being honored at a black-tie dinner: "I feel so wise and so generous and everyone around me is so appreciative. Every moment is interesting—even lavish, lavish food and wine, lavish hearts and minds!"

Beverly, the office manager, described herself reading on the back porch of her own beautiful country cottage, just reading a long book on a summer's day: "I'm being restored, relaxed. The air's so fresh. I'm free of responsibilities."

Are you having trouble being wildly enthusiastic? *Well, just keep trying, because we have a special reason for this exercise.* Force yourself to cheer your fantasy life for at least five minutes!

After five minutes, how are you feeling?

Andrea, the bookkeeper-dancer, said, "Something's wrong. I feel uncomfortable. I've felt this before."

Did that happen to you?

After a few minutes at this exercise, the self-sabotager usually suffers a mood change. All this happy racket has awakened your resistance—and that's *exactly what we wanted to happen.*

Saul, the professor, found himself furiously angry. Beverly just got anxious: "I got the jitters, like something bad was about to happen. I thought if I got up and started to mow the lawn, I'd feel better. My country house is going to have very short grass!"

Why on earth would it not feel entirely wonderful to taste sweet success?

Because success holds danger for you. By avoiding success you are avoiding danger. What could possibly be dangerous about success? *Built into the spirit of every one of us who fears success is some expectation of emotional pain—and instinctively, involuntarily, like an animal, we pull away from pain.*

Because you forced yourself to consciously enjoy your dream long enough, your unconscious voice—your antisuccess force—has swung into action to save you from the danger of emotional pain; you can already hear its words. This is nothing new, but this time you're going to say them out loud just as you did with your success-loving voice—and we're going to listen to those words very carefully.

Exercise 3: Let Your Antisuccess Voice Speak Out

You *know* why it's a terrible idea for you to be successful, and I want you to announce it loud and clear. Say anything negative that comes into your head.

Andrea: Dancing's stupid. It's just showing off.

Saul: If I get honored as the best teacher, my father's going to take full credit for it. He's going to think *he's* done something great. I can't stand to let him have that satisfaction.

Beverly: I suddenly feel completely isolated, as if I'm on the moon. I feel like I deserve to be all alone.

Now, here's the important question: *Where did you get the idea that success was bad?*

Maybe, like Saul, you'll know right away why you're avoiding success—there's someone who wants to co-opt your achievements.

What if you don't immediately recognize where the danger's coming from? Here are two ways to find out.

1. Pick up that sheet of paper with your chronology on it and take another look. Focus on each point where you backed away from something you wanted and see if you've got any fresh insights about what made you do it. Was someone in your family unhappy or unsatisfied or a failure? Did they need you to succeed for them and forget that you needed your own success? Did someone get angry at your achievements and belittle you?

2. Ask yourself *Who does my negative voice remind me of?* Ask *Who says that?*

The first answer people give me when I ask "Who says that?" is "It's *my* voice. I'm saying those things because I believe them." Well, those things may *feel* like your lines, because you've memorized and practiced them for years, to stop yourself before someone else said them. The important question is: Who else would have said them?

Andrea, who thought dancing stars were deeply unhappy, neurotic people, asked the same question: "Who taught me that?'' and realized right away that her negative voice was her mother's voice. Her mother had always put down famous people or people who were successful by saying that they did it because they were selfish.

Our parents speak their minds and we never really ask ourselves what's behind their messages. We take them as givens—and design our lives around them.

It's not easy to learn that the world is not like your family. Some part of you wants to hang on to your childhood style—even when you know better.

YOUR CHILDHOOD

We like to think that since our childhood's long over, we're not affected by it anymore.

But we really shouldn't get too cocky about our maturity. When we're under stress, our most primitive—that is, childish—defenses swing into action. For someone who fears success this means that when success looms, sabotage is not far behind.

Exercise 2 will help you see that your underlying conflicts are alive and well. It's no fun to acknowledge our problems, but if they stay hidden they can stage an ambush just when you think you're finally moving ahead.

So don't be hesitant to take a hard look at your difficulties. You're in a good place when you can see the real shape and source of a problem. Then all you have to do is roll up your sleeves and get to work fixing what's wrong. As the great American novelist James Baldwin said, ''Know from whence you came. If you know from whence you came, there is no limit to where you can go.''

Your fear of success can come from more than one source. See if you're afraid of committing any of the following ''sins'':

1. Passing up someone you love.

Fathers and sons: You'd be amazed how many men won't pass up their fathers.

Males are cruelly tested in our culture by other males. They learn in the schoolyard how to back out or fight or tell a joke to avoid getting beaten down. Boys pressure boys to be tough and independent before they're ready. They start faking independence too early, when they're still children. There's a lot of leftover fear and vulnerability that men have to deny, so they're on a special kind of tightrope, fighting down any sign of weakness in themselves.

When men become fathers, they try to help their sons by encouraging them to be tough, helping them to stop those "dangerous" impulses toward neediness or vulnerability. But when a boy starts to be too strong, his father starts feeling his own uncertainty and switches into a competitive mode. Much as he may love his children, he can't help feeling threatened by the strength of another male.

Whenever you pass up your father, he's thrown into a confusing conflict of feelings. One side of him wants to tell his friends you're extraordinary; the other side of him wonders "What does this make me, second-rate?"

Now that high-achieving women are having high-achieving daughters, this problem is beginning to jump the gender line and some mothers feel conflicted at their daughters' successes.

Even children who become successful in professions very different from their parents' can feel that becoming a winner takes away the parents' "hero" status.

In family businesses, the power struggle often becomes very open. Children—boys *or* girls—work hard to make a real contribution, but often find themselves getting put in their place if they ask for any real control of the business. Sometimes the only way to become a success is to leave and work for a competitor—but very few children can bring themselves to make such a hard choice, so they become stuck.

Regarding unhappy mothers and their daughters: Many

daughters still feel the tragedy of their mothers' unfulfilled lives and find it very hard to allow themselves to become happy—as if through happiness they abandon the very person who made their success possible. You can't overestimate the drag this situation puts on a child's heart.

2. You come from a family with a history of failure.

When failure has eroded your parents' confidence, the history of that failure affects you. It can make you determined to become wildly successful—to break free of your parents' fate—or it can make you feel protective of your parents. This protectiveness conflicts with your attempts to create your own success, as though success would say to your family, "You didn't have what it takes," or "Your world isn't good enough for me. I've chosen a better one."

3. You were a trophy.

When you get the message that your success doesn't belong to you, something odd happens to your momentum. It's tough for parents to strike a balance between loving a child and realizing that the child's future doesn't belong to them. But few parents realize that pride in a child's accomplishments can be a tricky issue: it implies ownership. You wouldn't walk up to a famous athlete and say, "I'm proud of you." You *know* he or she isn't yours to be proud of.

As a parent, I have to confess it's tough to get it right. Are you *proud* of your kids when they do well, or are you *happy* for them? It's very hard at times to remember that your children don't belong to you, they belong to themselves.

When you're a child who gets a lot of approval, you may feel like a family trophy and be in danger of losing your autonomy. If your parents' pride in you is too great, you may feel that you represent your clan, instead of yourself. If you ignore their wishes you create disappointment and lose your usefulness. It's a painful choice.

This trophy conflict gets even more lively when your parent

wasn't the greatest parent to you when you were growing up. Then the idea of his taking credit for your achievements can feel unbearable.

Saul: I saw my Dad's shining face at my graduation and I remembered how rotten he was to me when I was a little kid, and how I became a top student to try to win his approval. I'd been planning to take graduate entrance exams at Stanford Business School. I knew that if I got in, my dad would throw his arm around my shoulder and call up all his cronies and pass out cigars. And I deliberately *blew* that exam.

Consciously or unconsciously, you can end up in a grudge match with your parents: refusing to succeed as a way of saying "I belong to myself—not to you."

4. You're waiting to be rescued.

Sometimes we let ourselves get into trouble over and over again because, unconsciously, we're waiting for someone to rescue us. Either our parents rescued us too much, or they let us down so consistently that we spend our adult lives in trouble so they can have another chance to come through for us.

When you're waiting to be rescued, you don't enjoy the power of being able to take care of your own problems like most people do. Instead, every time you make your own life work, it's an agonizing reminder that no one else wants to take care of you.

5. You've encountered envious people and other enemies.

Could we please stop being Pollyannas and start admitting that the world has lots of difficult people in it? It's not true that everyone means well and we just have misunderstandings. Sometimes there's *no* misunderstanding—*sometimes people* want *to hurt you.*

As far back as your birth you could easily have been the victim of jealousy or envy. You may have displaced an older sibling or even a parent as the center of attention. As normal as such things are, they have a powerful effect on a little child.

Mel, a carpenter: Boy, I know what jealousy is. That's my

older brother. I did everything to make him like me, but the only way to keep him from being mad at me was to stop existing.

If you were around an angry, jealous person as a child, you remember it when you grow up; you expect to provoke resentment whenever you get positive attention. And if you confront someone who really is resentful of you, you lose balance. I've seen people get physically sick because they had to work in an office with someone who was envious of them.

If you find yourself obsessively preoccupied with a person who resents you, even to the extent of trying to win their approval, you should realize that, like Mel's older brother, *jealous people don't want to approve of you.* The nicer you become, the angrier they become, because by being nice you're making yourself look good—and that's exactly what they resent.

If someone was envious of you while you were growing up and now you're afraid of success, *you have hooked your fate to someone else's drama.* Jealous people think if anybody gets more, they get less, and you've bought into that idea: you think if you get more, someone else gets less.

If this awareness shocks or frightens you, take a deep breath. You don't have to be their victim. This is just another problem and it can be solved.

6. *You're a woman (women aren't supposed to succeed).*

This cultural problem may be diminishing but it isn't gone; cultures don't change that fast. As a young girl, you get approval if you're considerate and helpful and disapproval if you're too interested in your own success. From kindergarten on, teachers (by their own admission) enjoy boys who are aggressive about getting attention but dislike girls who are.

We turn toward approval as plants turn toward sunlight, and shrink from disapproval just as strongly. It's still easy to convince women with careers that they're shamefully neglecting their family duties; men still feel their careers *fulfill* their family obligations.

7. Your parents were disturbed or unkind.

If your parents were disturbed, or if they were substance abus-ers—or child abusers—you took in a feeling of both guilt and unworthiness. If you feel you don't deserve success or love, you find yourself avoiding them because you feel that you've done nothing that deserves reward. Inevitably you have a feeling of emptiness. Striving for—but never actually achieving—success at work or in love feels "right." After all, your mind tells you, you must be guilty of *something*, or you would have been loved. Try-ing hard and never getting anywhere produces the unconscious satisfaction of doing penance.

Have you found yourself in these pages?

Did any of these stories remind you of your own life?

If they did, you can expect to be having a whole range of feelings—especially if the recognition of your own situation shocked you.

Before we start discussing all those feelings and the steps you can take to break these self-defeating patterns, let me explain something:

YOUR PRESENT SITUATION

The good news: Understanding the source of your fear of suc-cess means you've already taken a big step toward surmounting that fear. Understanding alone won't entirely solve your problem, but it's a major breakthrough to see what's behind your habit of "snatching defeat from the jaws of victory."

If your car won't run, and you don't know why, you're in major trouble. If you find out you're out of gas, you're automati-cally in a different position—*even if you can't immediately get your hands on any gas.* You stop wasting time trying to start the car or fix the carburetor. You start walking to the nearest gas station. The problem is half solved.

The bad news: Your parents, your family, can't free you even if they want to. You're going to have to (and you're going to be able to) free yourself from being tied to someone else's fate. And you're going to have to do it alone—although someone else in your past may have caused the entanglement.

If your parents realize and admit the harm they've done, it could add a wonderful new dimension to your relationship, but it won't have much effect on your conflicts from the past. The time is gone when a change in your parents' behavior could change your deepest feelings. Even if a jealous sibling is no longer jealous, and feels bad about the unhappiness they caused you, that sibling's remorse won't solve your fear of success: *you're* going to have to fix what's broken.

And you'll be able to do a better job of it than you expect. While it's easy to get stuck on the injustice of someone harming you and getting away with it, a way exists to lighten the weight of this misfortune.

It's not easy, but you can do it.

The hard news: You've got to process your past by expressing your old feelings now.

It isn't enough to know what's wrong, you have to resolve your feelings.

You have unfinished business to attend to. Now that you're an adult who does understand the world you grew up in, you're finally strong enough to take on those childhood feelings.

Someone once said "The greatest sorrow isn't the sorrow of childhood—the greatest sorrow is childhood remembered." The child you once were deserves your compassion. No one but you will ever understand the hurt you lived through when you were younger, so have the courage to let yourself cry if you can. Cry for the child, or cry as the child. If you can't actually bring up tears, just sit still for a moment and feel the hurt. That pain isn't endless and once it's released you'll notice surprising changes. Not only will you sense a great burden lift, you'll feel your conflict melting. Releasing those old feelings will begin to free you from old dramas and let you move on.

What if you're not aware of any old feelings? You might be willing to believe that the emotional events of your childhood are affecting you as an adult, but not find any feelings to process. Well then, you have to track them down. There are a number of ways to tap into buried sorrow, release it and be rid of it. You can join support groups where people speak about their feelings, or you can talk to a therapist. Getting to childhood feelings is one of the things therapists do best.

You might try this exercise to help you get started.

Exercise 4: Life Rewrite

Rewrite your past. Search your memory for some significant place you got pulled off course, some moment when you let yourself down and blew a big chance—or didn't even try. Look over the events of your past until you find a time you wanted to push harder but decided to back away. Now imagine that everything happened differently. Imagine you had stayed on course, had taken your big shot and hit it.

Where would you be now?

Remember Andrea, who wanted to be a theatrical dancing star? In Andrea's real life, she had been offered a part in a touring company of a Broadway show and had passed it up to accept a proposal of marriage. Now she's forty-two and furious with herself. She sat down and rewrote her life as it *should* have happened: "I was offered the job and I snapped it up. I told Alex to wait until I got back from the tour, and I think he'd have done that. I had a heavenly time, and I was sensational . . . and Alex waited for me."

When Andrea rewrote the past, she got tears in her eyes.

"Why did you pass up a chance at a Broadway cast tour?" I asked.

"Because of that voice, the antisuccess voice that told me I was a show-off, a neurotic."

"Where did you get that idea?"

"It's my mother's idea. She said it all the time."

"Do you have any idea where she got that opinion?"

"Well, she was really neglected by her own mother who cared about nothing but parties and high society." Andrea stopped talking for a moment. "Good God," she said then. "She was talking to her mother, not to me!"

What about you? What did you discover when you rewrote your past? Did the pain of what-should-have-been seem almost too intense to bear? Or after releasing some feelings, did you find yourself thinking "I was such a jerk! It's all my own fault." If you're blaming yourself, try to stop at once. It's unproductive, but that's not the real problem. The real problem is that *self-blame is based on an illusion you designed to make you feel more powerful than you really were.*

IT'S ARROGANT TO BE TOO HARD ON YOURSELF!

If you ever think "I had the power to do differently and I didn't. Everything is all my fault," you're on a power trip. It can actually make you feel stronger to be angry at yourself, as though you were the master of your fate. But you did *not* have the power to do differently.

Andrea left bookkeeping and got back into musical theater as a character dancer, but she still had days when she'd see somebody in *People* magazine and say "That could have been me." She would have to remember that when she was a twenty-year-old kid, she didn't have the strength to do differently. She had to remember that her particular childhood with her particular mother had *programmed* her to pass up success.

Why do we choose to blame ourselves rather than admit we were innocent? Because we can't bear to remember our tragic helplessness.

The illusion of power is a leftover from childhood, when we

desperately needed to think we had more options than we actually had. In fact, we never had the power to make our mothers' lives come out right, or to make a jealous sibling love us, or to make an angry father behave differently. That's very hard news. And if you blame yourself now for not grabbing the success that was within your reach in the past, you're continuing the habit of pretending you had power. Let me tell you something. *When people have the strength to do what's right for them, they do it!* When they're burdened by too many inner conflicts, they can't.

IT'S BLAME TIME! (TEMPORARILY)

Something did go wrong in your childhood. And if you don't put the blame somewhere outside yourself, you're going to blame yourself.

To get your self-esteem back, you have to take a few steps that may not seem very realistic. For one thing, you have to accept that *you were entitled to be born into a perfectly nurturing world.* You had the right to be respected, protected, encouraged, loved. Very few of us were actually born into such a perfect world, but we can survive the shortfall and actually thrive, if we let ourselves know that the imperfections in our environment were not our fault. Your parents may not have been able to deliver perfection, and eventually you have to admit that. *But if you forgive them too soon, you will blame yourself and get off to the wrong start.*

"No one had it perfect, let's just forget the past and get on with it," you might say. I understand the impulse to say such a thing. It's based on wishfully thinking that you *could* simply forget the past. But it won't work. *We all try to prove our parents right.* My friend Alma, who's about fifty pounds too heavy, does it with weight. Alma's mother implies she'd be happy with her daughter if she weren't fat, so Alma stays fat so she doesn't have to admit that her mother could never be happy with her—fat or thin. As long as Alma is fat, she can blame her weight, not her mother's inability to love her.

Nobody wants to face that kind of feeling. If your parents were unhappy because of you, all you'd have to do is improve yourself. But if your parents are unhappy for their own reasons, there's nothing you can do.

That's the self-sabotager's childhood situation. There was nothing you could do. Some temporary blaming—with some good old-fashioned angry outbursts (in the privacy of your journal) will unlock the gates of self-blame and allow you to walk out.

ANGER!

You know it's destructive to become too angry for too long. (It's also suspicious—anybody who hangs on to anger too long is usually avoiding some other feeling, often a deep hurt that he refuses to feel.) But anger is a necessary, temporary stage if you've been injured in the past. You can't sidestep it.

And you can't excuse your parents' behavior at the expense of your own innocence. You've got to get mad until you feel better—and then you can forgive. To clear out a tangle of leftover feelings, you've got to understand that your earliest feelings of fear and outrage and betrayal are based on *the child's rightful need for perfect parents.*

There are no perfect parents, of course. But you still must express the agonies of the child who *needed* perfect parents. I know it seems complicated, but it works.

Pick up your pencil and start writing out those feelings of hurt in a letter you're never going to send. After you've let the anger out, you'll feel very different: free of self-blame and ready to *truly* understand that your parents were just kids with their own problems, *and you won't blame them anymore.*

Exercise 5: A Letter to the Person Who Didn't Love Me Right

When Saul (the professor) got outraged with his father for treating him more like a trophy than a person, he wrote a letter saying "You should have been a better father. You made me take care of *you! That was selfish.*"

As I've already mentioned, your parents or siblings can't do much now to change your past. It's up to you. So, unless you have extremely understanding parents, don't send your letter. (Saul burned his.)

But do write it.

Remember, *the reason for getting to your anger is to complete an uncompleted process and finally leave the past behind you.*

If you find that expressing your anger doesn't leave you feeling completed and calm, you have simply opened up another wave of hurt feelings—and that's all right. You're entitled to grieve for past wrongs until you're finished. Don't worry that the grieving will never end. You may alternate between hurt and anger a number of times before you feel calmer, because there may be a lot of feelings to process. After all, you were a great kid and—intentionally or not—someone hurt you. Until you grieve for what that kid went through, the wound cannot heal.

Exercise 6: Life Rewrite No. 2

Write a play in which you tell your grievances to your parent or sibling; in your play your parent or sibling *wants to listen to you*—they're concerned about any hurt they've caused you, and sincerely sorry.

Your real parent probably couldn't say these lines, so write a play with a parent you didn't really have. This parent says, "I'm sorry I hurt you."

Here's what Lynn wrote:

LYNN: Mom, you really hurt me when I was little.
MOM: Tell me what you mean, I want to hear.
LYNN: You hated being a mother and showed us that every day. You made us feel like we were ruining your life.
MOM: I had no idea what you were feeling. I'm so sorry you had to go through that.

Your real mother might say, "Don't talk like that," or "I *loved* you! I gave you everything a mother should give a child!" or "Why don't you just forget the past?" But you don't need to hear that right now. You need a fictional *rewrite of your life.*

What do you get out of this imaginary talk? Well, if it goes well, you can actually melt the iceberg of a double injustice that has been hidden inside you for years: having been hurt in the first place, and having your hurt denied all your life.

Acknowledgment and compassion help us heal old wrongs, but our real parents might not understand what was needed and fall into the old trap of defending themselves or dismissing the whole issue as something too far in the past to matter anymore. Or they might feel so guilty you'll wish you hadn't said a word.

If you ever *do* try talking to a parent, ex-husband, or big brother who hurt you, help them out a little by saying, "I guess what I want from you is just to listen. I don't want you to shoot yourself or say you're the worst person who ever lived."

If they're strong enough to hear you out, you'll be able to say, "Look, it wasn't your fault. You couldn't have done any better."

You have to understand, as Andrea came to understand, that the reason she gave up her own happiness was not because she was a fool, or because her mother was a monster, but because she had enormous sympathy for her mother. She sensed that if she became fulfilled, her mother's life would present a painful contrast.

When you give up your illusions of power and accept your inability to fix your family, you can expect to feel the full tragedy —their tragedy and yours. One of the hardest things you'll ever have to do is take the full impact of that painful knowledge: *The parents you were born loving may never have gotten their chance at happiness.* Times may have been too hard, or their circumstances too difficult. But to avoid facing this tragedy is to forever misunderstand your parents, and worse, to turn your back on your own happiness for no good reason.

There isn't anything I ask you to do in this entire book that's more difficult than accepting and processing these feelings, but if you can do it, I have excellent news for you.

GOOD TIMES

The hard part is over.

All those painful feelings you've just processed will leave you free to walk unencumbered into your future. You see, in your campaign to end your fear of success you've discovered something you may not have noticed:

You thought you were afraid of your future, but you were really afraid of your past. Your feelings of uneasiness about future success were really uneasiness about awakening past hurt and anger. When the good times come, your mind will play another trick on you—you'll become terrified of losing what you've finally got. I've heard people say things like "What if something terrible happens and I lose everything! I couldn't bear that."

Once again, you'll think you're afraid of a future loss, but your loss has already happened. We never fully realize how bad things have been until life gets better. The full extent of past hurts only hits us when we feel the unmistakable contrast between our painful past and our happy present.

That's how human minds work. So, when you're finally home safe, take some time to let any sorrow hit you. Tears will heal you and let you live the good life without being afraid you'll lose it.

FASTEN YOUR SEAT BELT . . .

It's going to be a bumpy—but thrilling—ride!

Expressing all those leftover feelings has crumbled the foundations of your self-sabotaging behavior. You're ready for success now, but you can expect plenty of aftershocks.

Even after you've come through the insight, the anger, the sorrow, and the beginnings of healing, you're going to have slips —days when you still want to sabotage yourself out of habit or because more of the pain or anger is coming up. Your family may continue to see you as a trophy, or be jealous or make you feel guilty, and you may get the impulse to act as if you'd never read these pages.

Don't let that worry you. Change takes time. After all, you are beginning to do the very activities you've been avoiding for years. If you were avoiding being a successful salesperson, you're starting to make more and better calls. If you were stopping yourself from being thin, you're now on a diet that lasts.

This is a new life, full of new feelings, and all the familiarity is gone. More than any other time, you should get help and support for yourself. *This is a time when a buddy system becomes essential.* You need a friend to keep prodding you into exercising or to help you study. You'll often be tempted to slip back to the comfort of self-sabotage whenever your new behavior makes you feel uneasy, and a buddy will calm you down and replace the comfort you've given up.

You'll also need to have a few strategies on hand for daily maintenance. Here are some ways to trick those feelings that persist in making you feel you're doing something wrong.

Buy off your guilt with good deeds.

Elaine: First thing in the morning, I do the forbidden thing: I practice my singing and do the very best I can. After two hours, when I start getting nervous, I stop and clean the house. Then I don't feel selfish anymore. It's that simple.

Use a decoy.

Although we're usually advised to imagine a good outcome whenever we're about to do something risky—like go for a job interview—if you're afraid of success, imagining a good outcome will only create more tension. If that's the case, take a technique from those people in school who always said, "I know I'm going to flunk," and then went on to get the highest grades in class. *Indulge your fears that you're going to fail, and work for success at full speed.* Complain and fuss all you like—but do your best at the same time. This technique is perfect, incidentally, for slipping past the anger of jealous people you're carrying in the back of your mind. Suffer at top volume, and then sneak out and have a great time.

As time passes, you'll find you've dropped a lot of freight that's been holding you back, and your path to the life you've always wanted gets easier every day.

Every time you move toward success, those feelings are going to come back, just as they always did, but they'll be quieter, and this time you'll be ready. You'll know how to release some of that leftover hurt or anger or guilt, in controlled, constructive ways that don't mess up your relationships.

You'll find yourself doing things you weren't able to do before and you won't even know quite when you changed. You'll find yourself tossing the ball right into the basket without much thought.

And one day you'll find that the only time you get anxious about success is when things get so good they take your breath away. Now that you know what to do, that's not really so bad, is it?

Go ahead. Make a plan. Set your goal, and start taking small first steps toward your goal today!

That's what Marcia did: She joined a Toastmaster's club to give herself a safe way to begin giving speeches while she was still overweight. After getting wonderful responses to her short presentations, she developed confidence and began to do motivational speaking for her church group. After that, she realized that weight was no impediment to her dream, and now she tours the country giving inspirational lectures in all the major cities. She even started dropping weight. "I guess the weight wasn't serving its purpose," she said. "It wasn't stopping me. I'm giving my speeches anyway. Maybe I'll get thin now, and maybe I won't, but it doesn't affect my work anymore."

Beverly went back to school and got a Ph.D. in medieval history. She's now writing a book—at her country home in the Catskills.

Saul held out for a teaching job, and got one. "Am I happy I didn't go into curriculum planning," he said. "It was hard to resist the pressure I was getting. But what *looks* like success doesn't count. What *feels* like success, that's what I had to remember."

Lynn went through all the feelings she had to face and now doesn't need to mess up the details of her research packages for scientists. "I stopped having those blind spots, and it got to be a point of pride to do a complete job. But that's because I faced my own mother's tough life. It hurt, but I think that's what made it easier to concentrate."

Andrea just stole the show in *South Pacific,* a musical put on by the community center where she teaches. "It's a small step, but the important thing is that I felt fine about the applause. I loved it. I wasn't guilty. I think I'm going to start auditioning again for Broadway shows."

Remember: "Doing your own thing" is a generous act. *Being gifted creates obligations,* which means that you owe the world your best effort at the work you love. You too are a natural resource.

It's heartbreaking and unnecessary when a hidden obstacle keeps anyone from bringing her gifts to full flower. *Every single one of us can do things that no one else can do—can love things no one else can love.* Your particular loves are your treasure. They are nature's gift to you. If you keep yourself free from hidden handicaps, you not only create happiness for yourself, you also do the right thing.

We are like violins. We can be used for doorstops, or we can make music.

You know what to do.

SIX

I Want Too Many Things; I'm All Over the Map

"J ACK of all trades, master of none, that's what they call me. *But I like so many things!* I can't make up my mind," Eric said. He was twenty-seven years old, a sometime SAT-prep teacher with interests in sculpture, investment banking, and mountain climbing.

Robin, a thirty-five year old with master's degrees in botany and comparative literature and a blossoming interest in Japanese studies, said, "I don't know why I don't stick with anything, I just get bored with it after the beginning."

Gayle, a twenty-five-year-old waitress and word processor, said, "I can't decide whether to go to med school or become a high school teacher or take a junior management position in a big corporation. If I choose one thing, I'll miss out on the others."

Do any of these people sound like you?

If you, too, want to do many things and can't make up your mind, I know something about you—because I had the same problem and I know how it feels.

It's uncomfortable to sense that time is speeding by while you're not getting anywhere. You're not becoming a better dog trainer or real estate broker, you're not becoming an authority on anything. Just at the moment you could become expert in one thing, you get very interested in something else. You see people your age with no more talent or ability than you have, getting way ahead in their lives, while you're still at the starting gate.

To make matters worse, *you don't get no respect.* Our culture respects specialists. People aren't called "Renaissance men" anymore; they're called "dilettantes" or "jack of all trade," like Eric. If you do a lot of different things, your parents apologize by saying "She hasn't found herself yet."

And you're probably spending too much time in a job that doesn't mean anything to you. A person who can't make a choice often works far below her capabilities to avoid making a commitment and to send out the message that her present job is only temporary.

"No one would ever think I'm a career waitress or career typist," Gayle, the waitress and word processor, told me. "But if I took a real job, a job that goes somewhere, everyone will think I couldn't be a doctor."

Of course, it *is* sensible to get a temporary job while you're figuring out your life's direction. But Gayle's waitress job is a decoy, *not* a way station. *She's in terrible danger of job drift.* Years might easily slip by before she lifts her head and realizes she's been at her "temporary" job too long. Then she'll say, "I could have owned this restaurant by now. I could have gotten through medical school."

What's going on here?

If you're like Eric, Robin, and Gayle—interested in many things, unable to make up your mind, panicked by time's swift passage, demoralized by a lack of respect, in danger of job drift— *there is a way out of your dilemma.*

The first step is to understand who you really are—that is, *why* you want so many things. Once you know that, I'll show you some further steps you can take to get yourself a life that suits you.

There are two big reasons you might be wanting too many things and feeling all over the map about it.

Reason No. 1: You're a born scanner—you're a person who delights in the astonishing, unending variety around us—*but you don't realize that being a scanner is a very respectable profession.* You don't yet know that scanning is a talent, the key to a very good life.

Reason No. 2: You're a born diver—you're like a deep-sea diver; your curiosity makes you want to go deeper and deeper into your subject until you dedicate your entire life to it—*but you appear to be a scanner at this moment because something's blocking you from diving.* In spite of how your life looks now, you are not really a scanner. You are the kind of person who loves to delve deeply into a subject. You need to figure out what's stopping you from diving.

SCANNERS

Scanners want to taste everything. They love to learn about the structure of a flower, and they love to learn about the theory of music. And the adventures of travel. And the tangle of politics. To scanners, the universe is a treasure house full of a million works of art, and life is hardly long enough to see them all.

Robert Frost defined divers and scanners very neatly when he said "A scholar is someone who sticks to something. A poet is someone who uses whatever sticks to him."

Because our culture values the diver's specialization and determination, we too often think of scanners as people who simply won't get down to work.

This is a foolish cultural oversight.

If you're a scanner, *you have extraordinarily special and valuable skills.* You love what is new, and you don't suffer from fear and indecisiveness. You're highly adaptable to new cultures; you're so flexible you can turn on a dime. You're a lightning-fast learner, curious about anything you don't already understand; you like and respect all kinds of thinking. Although you may be unwilling to dedicate yourself to one path, you don't lack discipline or have a low IQ. On the contrary, you're dedicated to learning all that you can, and you're intelligent enough to delight in all that you learn.

Having It All: At Once

In many cases the only problem for scanners is finding the kind of work that will allow them to use their talent for scanning.

Career aptitude tests tend to miss scanners.

Take Jack, for instance.

Jack went to the most respected career testing service he could find. His tests showed he was equally skilled in music, nature, mathematics, science, and literature. As a matter of fact, there was *no* subject for which he showed no aptitude!

The career counselors who tested him told Jack there was no way around it, he'd have to make a choice. "You can be a musician, a science teacher, a mathematician, or an editor in a publishing house. Which one do you want?"

Jack knew he wouldn't be happy at any of them: "I've never gotten past Anything 101. In college, when I would take second and third courses in some discipline, like pre-med, or French literature, I'd feel like I was on a detour, off my path. What I really loved was the *overview,* the sense of where philosophy belongs in a person's life, or history belongs, or physics, for that matter. Once I'd get something located, I wanted to look at something else.

"My advisors didn't know what to do with me. They called me a perennial student. But I couldn't make a choice. I racked up so many credits they *had* to graduate me after a while. And there I was, no wiser than before about what I was supposed to be when I grew up."

Jack wandered for a few years, until he accidentally stumbled into a writing assignment for a newsletter to be handed out at a convention for inventors. He really enjoyed interviewing all the different inventors for this article, so he went looking for other writing assignments.

That was twenty years ago. Today Jack is a successful free-lance writer, and he loves his life. He just got back from touring the Far East with an American opera company, and this fall he'll be on Mont Blanc in France with a group of French mountain climbers to write about their climb.

Jack is—and you might be—a popularizer. He can learn about biology, but what he likes to do with his knowledge of biology is translate it to the world—he's a communicator. He's a teacher.

It can take time and ingenuity to find a scanner's niche, work that accommodates all of a scanner's many interests. But the results are worth it.

Scanners *are* poets—and librarians, documentary filmmakers, explorers, brilliant salespeople, good managers, naturally gifted teachers.

We're trained to believe that we only get one choice in our lives. But to scanners, one choice sounds like someone's saying, "You can have a coloring book *or* you can have crayons, but you can't have both," and they're onto something. Scanners know that life is not stingy. If anything, life is too generous. The choices are dizzying. But there's a way to manage the riches.

Having It All: Sequentially

One of the things that drive scanners to distraction is that they're in a terrific hurry. But, although you should not waste any more time by being stuck, you should never hurry, because 1) there's more time than you think, 2) hurry is inefficient, and 3) part of your problem is caused by what I call time sickness. Time sickness is a form of hysteria that makes you believe you must fill every waking hour going after what you want, that everything must be done at once because time is about to end. You have no sense of the future, the leisurely course that time actually takes in most of our lives. Writing lists only makes your problem worse, and calendars have to be used with great care or they'll become packed with enough projects for a dozen people.

But the truth is, if you want to do a lot of things, you *can* do them all. Leonardo da Vinci, Thomas Jefferson, Ben Franklin, and Ted Turner knew that.

You just have to be shown that there is more time than you ever imagined.

Exercise 1: Time Management for the Person Who Loves to Do Too Many Things

1. Ten lives.

If you were ten people, what would each of you do with your life? Take a pencil and a blank sheet of paper and write down each life. (Do you want more than ten lives? Go right ahead. Write down as many lives as you like!) When you're finished, take a look at your list.

You might say, I want to be:

> a poet
> a musician
> a successful businessperson
> a scholar of Chinese culture
> a gourmet cook
> a world traveler
> a gardener
> a husband and father
> a journalist
> a talk-show host

With this list of everything you ever want to do, take a look at the available pieces of time in your future. *You're about to find a way to live every one of your lives.*

2. Available time.

Quickly answer each of the following questions with one of your ten (or more) lives. Don't think too much. Put down the first answer that pops into your head as you read each question. (It's okay to use the same life several times.)

- Which life can you devote yourself to this coming year?
- Which life can you do when the first one is completed?
- Which activities can you do for twenty minutes or less each day?
- Which ones can you do on a weekend?
- Which ones can you do once in a while?

Answering these questions should give you a more realistic look at how people actually do things—when they're "Renaissance men" like you are. Maybe you'll stop thinking in either/or terms, as Ralph did when he said, "How can I go off and write poetry, and learn Chinese, and take violin, and still run my business and travel? Oh yes, and be a gourmet cook and garden?"

Here's how: Don't *go off* and write poetry. Just write poetry. Write a line at night before you go to sleep, and you'll find yourself getting up very early to write some more.

If you get excited by your poem, push everything else aside. On your coffee breaks, pull out that poem and work on it. *And a few days later, you'll be finished.* Then you may not want to write another poem for a month.

When will you study violin? How about next summer? The point is, you can do it all, if you schedule it right.

If you want to start a business but you also want to see the world, you can combine them or you can do them one at a time: business now, travel later.

3. Make a quick three-year plan.

Year 1:

Year 2:

Year 3:

It's funny how we forget the sequential possibilities of time. It's as if we think if we don't do everything *right now,* we won't get to do *any* of it.

You've got more time than you think. Our days and years aren't as neat and tidy as we think. People like us, who are torn between doing many things, want to break time up in an unrealistically rigid way, and we may feel a little slapdash when we don't have ourselves on a tight schedule, but life *is* slapdash. I'll show you what I mean.

4. Map your life.

Look into your past. Did you try mountain climbing once? Do you go to movies a lot in one year and then stop going for two years? Well, that might be exactly the right way to live. You must learn to respect the wisdom of your natural instincts, because they are probably superb when it comes to weaving everything you need into your life.

The truth is that too rigid a schedule might *prevent* you from doing all the things you want. "I never get to draw anymore," a busy home visiting nurse said to me recently. "I haven't for years. I wish I had more time."

"How much time does it take?" I asked. She looked surprised, as if she hadn't thought of it that way. I asked her to take out a pencil and paper and do some drawing for three minutes. She did, and when she lifted her head she had a big smile on her face. "That was great!"

Maybe for the next few months she can only draw for a few minutes at a time, but this summer she might be able to take two weeks and go to an art workshop in the woods somewhere. If drawing makes her happy, there's not a thing in the world to stop her from starting today.

Don't forget to plan for another of those lives you wrote down. You can do it three or four years down the road. By then you're going to be interested in new things. You might want to make a twenty- or thirty-year plan so you can fit in *everything* you ever dreamed of doing.

If you're a scanner, don't do a thing to change yourself. Instead of designing yourself to fit the world, you can design a life to fit your abundant gifts.

But what if you're really a frustrated diver? There's a very special group of people: they look like scanners and they act like scanners, but they aren't. *They're actually divers who are afraid of diving.*

DIVERS

Musicians, mathematicians, scientists, artists, professional athletes often fall into this category. They delight in the depths. When something interests a diver, they become transfixed. If scanners have wide-angle vision, divers have telescopic vision.

Divers aren't satisfied with beginnings or quick insights: they like to hang on for the whole ride. They need to see how things come together in the end. If they find there is no end, no bottom to what they study, it's because they've opened up a new depth, revealing new secrets and new puzzles, and then a diver is in heaven.

For example, to a diver, a flower is a pretty thing on the surface, but he wants to go deeper and learn about its amazing structure, and even deeper until he sees the flower as a tiny world with an old and honorable history. A diver knows that if he delves deeper into knowledge of a flower, it will transform itself into biology, chemistry, into molecules, into atoms. And this makes a flower open up to become the universe itself.

Such are the rich rewards of diving.

But if something's blocking a diver's desire, he often lives like a scanner—and is very unhappy with the scanner's life. For a diver, to refuse to land anywhere, to hover and always keep all his options open, *is to do nothing.*

A happy scanner moves from one subject to another, sipping nectar like a bee, and says things like "That was great. What's next?"

An unhappy diver says things like:

- "I can never stick to anything. I hate to keep dropping my projects, but for some reason I just can't stay with them."
- "I've lost touch with whatever it is I'm supposed to be about. I'm just fooling around."
- "I've never done what I wanted because I was afraid of committing and then finding out it was the wrong thing."

If you sound like these unhappy divers, what we're looking at in your case is not a bunch of abilities in search of a job title, *we're looking at a problem.* You know perfectly well that you get restless and bored as long as you stay on the surface of things, but every time you start going into deeper waters, you mysteriously lose focus or get anxious. You don't know *why* you can't change *because you don't know what's causing the problem.*

First, *find out if your inability to focus has a physical cause.* You may be one of the many people with Attention Deficit Disorder (A.D.D.), a physical condition caused by poor regulation of the neurotransmitters in the brain that help people focus. If your mind wanders while you read and if it's sometimes an hour before you notice that your mind has wandered, if your friends and colleagues think you're hyperactive, or if you've simply always been frustrated because you've never been able to focus and follow through on projects you like, you may have A.D.D. A psychiatrist can diagnose you. A psychopharmacologist can prescribe caffeine or Ritalin to help you. And it's even *more* important for you than for the rest of us to break down every big goal into small, specific, achievable steps *and* to get a person to hold you accountable for completing each of the small steps.

The Unfulfilled Diver

If you find no physical cause for your inability to focus, then you're a diver who's behaving like a scanner. Changing your mind all the time isn't an exercise of free choice, *it's a defense mechanism.*

Consider the story of Lydia:

Lydia worked as a street vendor and made good money, but she couldn't see street vending as her lifetime career. "I just happened into it, and I started making good money. But I can't figure out what to do next."

We did some questioning for a little while and then she said, "I almost signed up for a business course that teaches you to make a good salary working at home on your computer. But what if it isn't what I want?"

"Do you like working on your computer?"

"I love it," she said. "I love spreadsheets. I love doing the number crunching everyone else hates. But I can't sit home and do spreadsheets for myself. And I don't want to do temp work. It's corporate and it doesn't make enough money."

"Why couldn't you run a business doing free-lance work for corporations, rush jobs they're understaffed for?"

Lydia started to look interested, so I continued.

"You could start a spreadsheet business and still keep your vending job. Just try it out. Sounds like a no-risk way to try to be a computer entrepreneur."

Lydia was interested. She immediately thought up a sales slogan for her business: "Why tie up your executives for days crunching numbers, when I can do it for you overnight!"

"I could contact hotels and provide a spreadsheet service for traveling executives. I even know of one or two large corporate clients who would give me more than enough work," she said.

And if she got too much work, she realized she could find other people with computers to help *her.*

"Hey, this is exciting!" she said.

"Okay, very good," I said. "Let's make a list of your first steps."

Suddenly, Lydia's enthusiasm faded.

"What about animals?" she said.

"What about them?"

"I love them and I think a lot about being a veterinarian."

Fear of commitment had reared its ugly head.

I could tell, from long years of experience, that we had just run into commitment phobia. But I didn't want to mention it right away. There was the outside chance that Lydia *should* be looking into a career as a vet instead of starting the home business, and it would do no harm to take her at her word.

"Have you ever looked into being a vet?"

"Well, yes. And decided against it for a lot of reasons."

"For instance?"

"I don't know," she said. "I really don't like medicine much."

I said, "You're going to have to find a touchstone for your love of animals. Find out what you love most about being with them. You can design a goal that will allow you to do that. Would you like to investigate your touchstone right now?"

Lydia fidgeted on the couch. "Not really. Boy, I feel very strange. Very blank, suddenly."

"Like you've gotten off the point?"

"Like there is no point. Like I'm back where I started."

She *was* back where she started! On the verge of making a move, she suddenly (and unconsciously) stopped herself.

Why?

If you're like Lydia and have a dread of anything that looks remotely like a commitment, I'd like to give you a friendly little lecture, because I don't think you're clear about what a commitment really *is.*

A commitment may feel to you like some kind of trap, but it isn't a trap. You can put your whole heart into it and give it your best—and if it doesn't work out, *it ends.*

You should know that most people enjoy making commitments. They find it satisfying to dedicate themselves to learning piano or creating a garden. They like to see the results.

People who fear commitment don't get results. Although this makes them very unhappy, they're afraid that once they sign on, they'll never be able to leave. So they are forever locked outside any arena that could give them satisfaction.

They are unhappy divers.

* * *

In my experience, there are three kinds of unhappy divers.

1. Divers who don't know how to learn.

Sometimes people who are unusually bright can't get past the enthusiastic, creative period where they shine and into a period where they have to slow down and learn the material. They *want* to follow through but they never learned how to learn. So they become frustrated with the difficulties. Sooner or later they drop out and go looking for the high of beginning a new project. They hope *this* time they'll be able to follow through, but then they crash again.

They don't understand what slower children learned very well —*if you stick with learning there's a big payoff at the end.* People who don't stick with exercising or a sport are the same way. They don't see the point in staying with anything that doesn't pay off immediately. They never did it, and they're not used to it, and they don't believe it works.

Sometimes these people were bewildered by too much unwarranted praise when they were children. The overpraised child never learns how to work hard at something until he has accomplished his goal. He's never tested his stamina or developed self-discipline, and therefore he lacks self-confidence.

Carol was a great beginner in college, but when the going got the least bit tough, she gave up. "I secretly thought I was stupid, and I'd get found out. So I'd come in, dazzle everybody, then disappear before they could find me out," she said.

Carol's parents had tried to give her everything and cushion every step, but when she went to college, nobody acted like her parents. In college, you passed your exams or you were history. This depressed Carol; it seemed cold and judgmental. She eventually dropped out and came home, her self-confidence shattered. She had no tolerance for even a small amount of frustration.

But think about the uses of frustration.

Frustration is supposed to create action, not make you give up. We all need to learn how to handle frustrations so we can stick with things until we have some capability; that's how to develop self-confidence.

2. Divers who are addicted to novelty.

"My therapist told me that I escape into action. Instead of facing a bad feeling, I'll go do something," a woman in one of my workshops said. In other words, whenever she was depressed, she could get a high from starting something new. That high—like highs from drugs or auto racing—is short-lived. The second a new activity becomes "old," the high evaporates for you and your old feeling seeps into the new activity. When you need a "high" you're probably avoiding a "low." Check yourself out to see if you're fighting chronic heavyheartedness (read Chapter 12: "Nothing Ever Interests Me").

In the short term you may be avoiding unhappiness by constantly going after what's new and exciting, but in the long term you're avoiding happiness.

There is a way to break out of this demoralizing cycle. It has two steps. First, go inside yourself and try to find your reason for giving up after each new beginning. *Second, and most important, you've got to force yourself to stick to your work.* Nine times out of ten, completing a project will make you feel much better— even when it feels meaningless. But it's sure to kick up some of the worst discomfort you've ever felt. More than most people, you need to experience pushing right through your discomfort and coming out the other side. It can be a revelation.

The first time you succeed at fighting your way through those unpleasant feelings, take a piece of paper and write down the process you experienced. Then tape the piece of paper to your wall, so you can read it the next time you get anxious or uncomfortable and want to run from what you're doing.

3. Divers who experience a jolt of alarm when they let themselves dive.

Where the first two kinds of unhappy divers feel uncomfortable after the initial phase of any project, this diver experiences real fear. Whenever he stands somewhere too long, the ground under his feet starts to burn, and he has to jump somewhere else.

Lena, forty-four, a homemaker and political campaign volunteer, said, "It makes me feel bad to say this, but I gave up everything I liked, one by one: writing, drawing, singing, school. I didn't want to give any of them up, but I did because whenever I start to do something I love I get so nervous I just can't do it."

What's going on here?

Lena's life—and maybe yours too—is a tragedy of unfulfillment for reasons that seem hard to fathom. Why would anyone become alarmed when they're doing nothing more than becoming happily absorbed in something that fascinates them?

There are a number of possible answers to that question, and all of them point to childhood. You may be the child of controlling or manipulative parents or siblings, and your survival depended on learning how to avoid entrapment. Or you may have experienced some kind of abuse or abandonment in your early years, and you've promised yourself to stay alert and watchful so it doesn't happen again. Then, every time you allow yourself to become immersed in something, you wake with a start, as though you had dozed off on guard duty. Whatever your particular problem, you're afraid something bad will happen if you delve deeply into what you really love.

If you find yourself saying "I start to feel guilty when I get into something I love and I feel I should start doing something for someone else," you think diving is *selfish.*

Sometimes, when we've had unhappy families, we won't allow ourselves the pleasure of becoming immersed in our favorite activities. It's not only that we feel ashamed of enjoying ourselves when our mother or father always felt bad, *we actually feel we're helping* lessen their burden of unhappiness by depriving ourselves.

One day it finally dawns on us that depriving ourselves didn't help anyone, that it wouldn't have made the slightest bit of difference if we had allowed ourselves to be happy. While this knowledge sets us free, it also leaves us with no defense against the agony of witnessing the unhappiness of someone we loved.

But a parent's sorrow is not in our power to fix, and as hard as that realization may be, it allows us to finally give our parents the sympathy they really deserve, instead of offering them our unhappiness as a consolation prize.

First Aid for Unhappy Divers

What should you do when you're delving into a marvelous book on naval aeronautics and you suddenly realize you want to study opera? There are three cures for this problem, depending on its source.

1. *If you're someone who gets jolts of alarm* when you start becoming absorbed in a subject, if you feel you've forgotten someone you love, you need to learn that it's okay to be happy now, but it takes some tears to really let the news sink in. Take a few moments to feel your feelings, *then go back to work.*

2. *If you don't know how to learn,* your worst enemy is frustration. The first time you outstrip your abilities, you'll feel that familiar, hopeless feeling that you don't understand anything. *But this is your chance to finally break through that pattern. This time you're going to learn how to learn.*

   Patience is the key here. Learners know that learning can be slow, but they understand that there is always a payoff. You've never experienced that payoff because you were always faster than anyone at the start of any project— and gave up the minute you got lost. To break out of that pattern you must learn to cherish something you have always dreaded: the ignorance that a newcomer inevitably feels. Zen calls it "Beginner's Mind," and honors its nobility.

3. *If you're addicted to novelty* then you're afraid that com-

mitment to one thing will deprive you of all the other wonderful things you want to do. You need a lost and found for your dreams.

A Lost and Found for Dreams

Take a small box, a shoe box will do, and place it on the floor beside your work desk. Call it "Lost and Found for Dreams." Now, every time you want to jump prematurely into a new project, write on separate slips of paper all the pursuits you fear you'll never get around to if you make a commitment to one goal. See if you can come up with lots of projects, small and big, that you want to do someday.

Lydia did this. Some of her slips said:

—work with animals
—start a home computer business
—travel to Thailand and Hawaii

Keep that box near you whenever you're working on a project. Anytime you make a commitment, and your little army of "yes, buts" comes out and reminds you of all the other goals you could be pursuing, write each wonderful idea on a slip of paper and put it in the lost and found.

The day may come that you'll actually be free and looking for some of those dreams, and can't remember them. But if you've saved them in the box, they'll be waiting for you.

And every time you've finished writing down that dream and putting it into your Lost and Found for Dreams, *get back to work.*

You must always get back to work because the real cure for an unhappy diver is working at something until he gets very, very good at it.

Only sustained effort will develop the mastery that an unhappy diver really craves. Always feeling like amateurs, but sensing their considerable talent, these people are caught in a nightmare of self-evaluation: Am I a genius or am I a fool? That seesaw thinking is a painful mistake people make when they haven't worked enough. An inexperienced actor might say, "I am probably the greatest actor who ever lived. I can just feel the talent in me." And the next moment he thinks, "I'm the biggest loser who ever lived; I can't act at all."

Well, *he's neither.* He's certainly not the greatest actor who ever lived no matter what he feels inside himself *because he hasn't developed his craft.* And he certainly isn't useless because even bad actors are just on their way to becoming good ones. *Only skill will pull you away from those extremes.*

A person who has taken the time to learn his craft doesn't bother himself wondering whether he's a great master or just a minor talent. He no longer knows or cares about what such words mean. He's concerned with improving a technique or expressing an idea and has no time for self-evaluation.

A commitment to challenging work takes your attention off yourself at the same time as it quietly adds to your self-esteem.

Mastery gives life meaning.

Learning to master a skill—any skill—is like having a keel on your boat. Mastery will steady you and calm your fears.

And you can start to become a master right now.

I'd like you to try a low-risk experiment. Make a very small commitment and stick to it for thirty days.

Exercise 2: Your Thirty-Day Very Small Commitment

The instructions are simple: Spend one half hour each day doing *something* until you get good at it. It's not important what you do: make an omelet, or do sit-ups until your tummy is flat, or learn to juggle. *But do it every day and try to get it right.* Keep doing the same thing over and over until you begin to notice results.

You need to let this information seep into you: *When you stick*

with something you learn things you can't learn any other way.
You learn that beginnings do not represent complete experiences.
The beginnings of juggling, for example, are ineptitude and frustration. You keep dropping the balls and can't believe you're ever going to get the hang of it.

But ineptitude and frustration will pass, and then you'll start to feel pleasure with acquiring a new skill. Now when you see a master juggler you'll really appreciate what she's doing. You'll begin to admire craft no matter where you see it, in all arts, in all professions.

Sticking with a simple little project for thirty days can make you realize something that could change your life: *Commitment and mastery do not close doors; they open them.* For the first time you will begin to know what high achievers always knew. Making a choice doesn't lock you into limits, it sets you free to fully develop your gifts.

Have I convinced you that it's a good idea to make a commitment to something?

Okay, you might say, now I understand, but that doesn't always change my feelings. How do I actually do this thing? I'm the one who runs from commitment, who has trouble learning, who is overcome with heavyheartedness or worry whenever I try to stick to something. What am I supposed to do when the going gets tough?

Here's what you're supposed to do: *Put one foot in front of the other.*

As soon as you start getting jumpy or distracted, or you start asking yourself "Why am I doing this?" always remember the answer: You're doing it because you decided to. That's all, and that's enough. You don't need a better reason. This is no time to reevaluate your efforts. Just put one foot in front of another, and do not stop.

That's how you stick to a commitment.

You'll be surprised to find your interest reviving again, popping out like the sun, after you've braved that blizzard of feelings.

But the feelings will probably come back many times; they are not easily bought off.

Don't worry. You won't have to fight them alone. In your push for mastery, you have gained a powerful ally.

Nature.

A Last Bit of Wisdom for Unhappy Divers: Trust Nature

When you see how many inner conflicts unhappy divers are engaged in, you realize that they feel very alone. If you're an unhappy diver, I'd like you to know something I learned over the years that has made an enormous difference to me.

Nature will come halfway and help you.

What do I mean by nature? I mean the materials you work with. Your materials might be numbers or sounds or words or wood—or gravity or weather or physics. If you're working with people, your material is human nature. Whenever you give your focused attention to your work, your materials will guide you.

What does this mean in actual terms? A very fine cook said to me, "My secret is that I let the food tell me what to do. I don't plan ahead, I just go to the market to see what's fresh. I come home and lay everything on the kitchen table and I look at it and try to imagine what it can be. The spices, the timing, the pots and pans are, to a certain extent, beyond my choosing. I have to do what's needed."

A sculptor working with stone knows that the stone has its own rules and the sculptor must obey them, learning, bit by bit, what the stone requires. But without the sculptor the stone will stay forever a block of stone. The two are engaged in a delicate partnership to create a statue.

All good work is a partnership between you and nature, and that partnership will end your feeling of isolation. Nature will help you every step of the way. As any deep-sea diver will tell you, when you are in the sea, you are never alone.

SEVEN

On the Wrong Track, and Moving Fast

I F YOU'RE in the middle of a dazzling fast-track success but you don't know what you *really* want, you've got some special problems: the jet-setting pace of your life, your material rewards, and the admiration you get from society excite and confuse you. They make you afraid to stop moving. So you zoom on. And you start to feel like you're speeding in the wrong direction on a superhighway and can't seem to spot a turnaround. You may not be sure what your real life's work is, but you're beginning to suspect it's slipping away from you.

Moving fast and getting more and more lost is the only thing I can think of that's worse than being stuck.

And the unexpected and tragic truth is that in this wonderful land of opportunity it's remarkably easy to get trapped on the career fast track and not be able to get off. If you're speeding along, succeeding at what looks like a great job (even if you're *miserable*), we both know what everybody thinks: "You've got it made. You're one of the lucky ones."

And you *are*.

You've got the success everybody wants. You're working for a top company, making good money, and getting respect. It's true that your hours might be long, and maybe you're under a lot of stress, but after all, that's why they pay you that big salary and those terrific bonuses. You've got so much glamour that you actually looked forward to your high-school reunion; compared to you, everybody else felt second-rate. You look damn good and you know it. And you enjoy that.

The problem is, you don't really enjoy anything about your job *except* the glamour: you like how it makes you *look.* However, behind how you "look," either the work you do is dreadful, or the work is okay but takes so much time and energy, is so hair-raising and absorbing that there's nothing left over for the rest of your life.

You never cook a leisurely meal and enjoy it with your lover because you haven't had the time to find a lover—or to buy food, for that matter. You never play the guitar the way you always meant to play it, because your brain goes into a stupor as soon as you get home—at 10:00 P.M. Your personal life is nothing but a pit stop in this race you call your career. You use all your time off to rest up and get ready for the next lap.

The fact that your life isn't really so hot does not occur to anyone, and you're not in any hurry to enlighten them.

So what I'm about to say may surprise you: I feel sorrier for you than for almost anyone else I talk to. Other people may be unhappy in their jobs, but they're allowed to complain about their rotten situations. "Lucky" fast trackers like you think they've got the brass ring so they don't have any right to complain. But they're looking around bewildered—trying to figure out what went wrong. They don't suspect they've been duped, or misused, by the culture. Yet this happens more often than anyone realizes. Every culture promotes its own ideas of winner and loser, and no culture checks things out with the kids.

Think about what our culture tells us. Do you remember anyone at the dinner table, in your senior year at high school, or in your college, telling stories of happy, fulfilled dropouts? Which alumni were invited to speak to your class, the ones who live in a cabin in Alaska, or the ones who are making $150,000 a year at a management consulting firm?

You got very specific marching orders: become a most-valuable player. Make a lot of money, or get a lot of prestige. Whatever the markers are, every insider knows them very well. And, whether or not the people in your family made it into the winner's circle, the advice they gave *you* was clear: You know what you have to do, kid. Be a winner or you'll be a loser.

Now, if you follow *my* definition, a winner is anyone who is doing what he or she loves. Whatever that may be! And a loser is someone who is losing time doing something they don't like. My losers list includes anybody in a Rolls-Royce who isn't happy. *Because they haven't yet invented the shiny thing that makes up for the loss of a fulfilled life.*

If you don't get to live your life, you've lost an incalculable treasure. Fate gives every single one of us the most astonishing uniqueness. Each person is a complex mesh of finely woven styles, viewpoints, abilities, tastes, and gifts. *There's no one in the world who can do what you can do, who can think and see the way you do, who can create what you can create.*

Listen to me carefully: If you're unhappy, something *important* is going on. When your body hurts, it needs attention. When your heart hurts, it needs just as much attention. Your mind knows what you've been taught, but *your heart knows who you really are.*

And it's trying to tell you something!

Pay attention or your spirit will get worn out. It's possible that you're going to need a complete overhaul of your definition of success. I'm extremely cautious about burning bridges, but this is one case where you might have to change everything around. You've got to make sure that this success is really *yours,* not somebody else's, and that it really suits who you are.

If you're a winner for the world and a loser for yourself, you've struck the worst bargain of your life.

So. What do you do? Walk away from a great job and live in the woods with the sprites and fairies, eating moonbeams? Of course not. *I just want you to stop thinking that your story has already been written.* The stakes may seem high to you, because you've got something to lose, but your life is too precious and rare to give away to a culture that doesn't know who you really are. Your past does not have to control your future. As a matter of fact, your past—along with your present—is going to help you create a new life if you want one.

First, before we do any problem solving, you need immediate relief from all that stress you're under.

I want to remind you of a safety valve that you used to know very well when you were little.

Your feelings.

HOW TO LOWER YOUR STRESS LEVEL

Feelings Management

Do me a favor: Don't put on a happy face. When you feel rotten, admit it, don't try to brainwash yourself out of it. You might want to cover up in front of your boss or your clients, but *never hide your real feelings from yourself.* A whole generation has been raised on the virtues of seeing life through "rose-colored glasses," trying to talk themselves out of what they feel, thinking they can change their situation by trying to see it differently. "I can create my own reality," they often say.

Every time I hear that I want to cry, "Please don't create your own reality. There already is one!" Don't change the word "problem" into "challenge." A problem is a perfectly decent thing to confront, and we're problem-solving animals. We like problems. They make us creative! Don't call a disaster an "opportunity." Who needs such opportunities? You don't have to plunge into despair when things go wrong, but for God's sake, *call them by their real names.* When there's trouble, you need a clear head!

Why force yourself to reshape all your natural responses when you don't have to? Nature has provided you with superb equipment to handle *anything that happens to you* with strength and precision, and it's called *Your Real Feelings.* You pay a high price when you talk yourself out of your real feelings. All your energy goes into pretending you don't feel bad, but buzzing in the background is the truth: you feel very bad indeed. After a while you get very nervous, and to calm yourself down you might take something that's probably not good for you: like Valium or candy bars or alcohol.

If there's any one thing I'd love to teach you, it's this: *Your feelings won't kill you; repressing them might do just that.*

So, what should you do, walk around feeling lousy all the time?

Not at all.

The best and most natural way to manage feelings is to release them on a regular basis.

Remember the movie *Broadcast News?* Holly Hunter played a network news producer who kept sitting down by herself and suddenly starting to bawl. No comment was made in the film about her odd behavior, and I liked that. It implied that this was a perfectly good way to release tension in a high-tension job. If you aren't ready to leave your high-tension job, let's buy you some time and use some "Holly Hunter" techniques: releasing feelings —or at least, facing them.

Why You Should Regularly Visit Your Feelings:

Your feelings are there—that's not a matter of choice—and they'll cause trouble if you don't check in on them on a regular basis. Whenever I find myself rushing too fast, piling on task after task, being critical of how slowly everyone around me is working, I get suspicious of myself. It's taken a long time for me to understand that I'm not relating to reality at all, that the external world is exactly the way it was when I felt fine the day before. Therefore, the problem is me. So, with very little immediate understanding of what's going on with me, I know enough to sit down, take a deep breath, and say "Hello feelings. What's going on in there?"

I can tell you what happens with me. (Each person is different.) The minute I slow down and visit my feelings, I usually feel some kind of sadness rush up. I heave a sigh, or sometimes find tears coming to my eyes. Sometimes I even fall apart—I do a "Holly Hunter."

Then, like a small miracle, my feelings of desperate rushing melt away. Why? Because I sensed something bad was about to happen, so I was rushing around to fix the world. But the thing I was afraid of wasn't the world, it was some inner hurt. The minute I went inside and connected with my feelings, the hurt came right up. And then there was nothing to be afraid of. The world suddenly looked calmer, more reasonable, more manageable.

What was I sad about? Who knows? Maybe a friend had just moved out of town and I knew I'd miss her. Or maybe I really was overwhelmed and felt like a little kid who wanted a grown-up to rescue her. In any case, whatever it was, I handled my day's work —and my own needs—much more sensibly when I stopped being frantic.

You should visit your feelings on a regular basis. And you should try to figure out what *your* pattern is. My "rushing around trying to organize and fix and accomplish against all odds" pattern is usually a cover for hurt feelings. Some people have a pattern of getting exhausted to cover up resentment—or one of grouchiness to cover up fear. Check out what you're feeling. You may find you can't concentrate. Go inside yourself and visit your feelings. You may find yourself running for the nearest alcoholic drink or chocolate candy bar. Wait before you take a drug that will hide the feelings too well to find them. Wait, and go inside for a visit. Just sit down, close your eyes for a moment, and run the four feelings through your mind: Is it anger? Fear? Joy? Hurt? One will reverberate—sometimes more than one. And when you sense what it is, express it. Sigh, or cry, punch a pillow. That's nature's way of helping us handle the insults and outrages that life visits upon us. Whenever we take in an insult, nature says we must release feelings. That's a truth, much like a law of physics: energy in, energy out. Even if someone tells you a joke and you take in a jolt of humor, you have to release it in laughter. Feelings are the tools to keep your body and soul humming like a happy engine. Don't be afraid of them.

Mapping Feelings

There are roughly only those four feelings: anger, hurt, fear, and joy. You could probably name others: guilt, humiliation, uneasiness, and many more. But if you follow any feeling to its bottom you'll almost always find that it falls into one of those four categories. Guilt usually reduces down to shame (hurt) or resentment (anger); humiliation is made up of hurt and anger; uneasiness is a version of fear. Once you get to the bottom of a feeling, it's a much more direct matter to express it. Feelings like guilt, humiliation, uneasiness tend to get clogged within us and don't release easily.

If you're not used to paying attention to your feelings, you're going to need a little practice. I'm going to show you an exercise that will help you understand that inner country better and begin to map out its terrain.

But I'm going to ask you to do the opposite of what you may have been told before—don't focus on "joy." I don't want you to write about joy. If you're feeling it, you don't need to work on your feelings, just enjoy them. My point is: *If you're feeling miserable, I don't want you to think happy thoughts.*

That's like pretending you're clean before you've taken a shower. If you're feeling rotten, I want you to do something about it, not just paint a falsely rosy picture.

Exercise 1: Your Feelings Speak

Get yourself a notebook for this exercise. At the top of page one write "Anger." Skip about ten pages, and head a page with "Hurt," and ten pages later, write "Fear" at the top of the page. Pick whichever subject feels easiest to write about, and start writing. If you've chosen "Anger," write down anything you can think of that makes you angry, and don't stop unless 1) you run out of things to say, or 2) the feeling changes. If the feeling changes to hurt, move to the "Hurt" page and write down everything that makes you want to cry. (If you actually cry while you're writing, that's great.)

If you start to get scared, there's a bit of good news. What you're afraid of is probably just another feeling—usually hurt or anger. What's so good about that? Well, all you have to do then is write it out. Or say "I'm damned angry," and give a King Kong roar—or say "I *hurt*," and have a good cry. *Express the feeling and the fear will go away.*

No one says you have to punch anyone in the nose. As a matter of fact, violence usually comes from people who are holding down their feelings and feel pushed past their endurance to control themselves. If they felt able to just shout or cry, they wouldn't have to break anything.

Remember, feelings are allowed. Any feelings—even hatred or meanness—as long as they're only feelings, and as long as you're the only one who knows about them. Confronting other people requires that you try to be reasonable and fair. Feelings are irrational and might be unfair, but you can't help having them! *So you simply deal with them before you go public.* When you've calmed down, you might decide it's unwise to mention them to anyone—or you might decide it's the wisest thing in the world. Once the emotional storm has passed, reason will make an appearance to help you choose.

Okay, that's step one. Feelings management. Now you've got an outlet for your feelings so you can process them the way nature meant you to. Every time it gets to be too much, you won't crack up, drink up, or drop out—you'll just run into a private place and visit your feelings.

Now, the other stress reliever.

You Need to Start Socking Away Money

One of the benefits of this fabulous job of yours is the big paycheck, so let me ask you a question: How much have you saved? You and I both know the answer: You're a couple of paychecks away from bankruptcy. How did that happen? More than likely, much of your money went for consolation prizes. When you're giving your life away to success you need a lot of toys to make up for it.

Julie, thirty-four, a management consultant with one of the top firms in the country, had so little time left over from the job to enjoy herself and so much money in her paycheck that she started doing some major spending. "First it was clothes, beautiful, expensive clothes. I loved them and really needed to look good at work, so that seemed okay. Then I needed a condo, for tax reasons, and then a BMW because I just needed to lift my spirits. Furniture, rugs, gifts, I bought everything but vacations, because I never had time for those. I think I'd like to leave this job, but I'd be totally broke! I couldn't afford to pay my mortgage, and I can't sell my condo because nobody's buying these days. I'm really trapped! And I keep on spending to cheer myself up for being trapped."

Julie is in a never-ending cycle of deprivation and reward. Spending money isn't going to satisfy her. There's something she needs to know, and you need to know it too: *You can never get enough of what you don't really want.* When you want ice cream, twenty candy bars won't satisfy you. But one ice cream cone will! The soul, like the taste buds, does not accept substitutes. You give your soul what it wants or it will give you no rest.

What does Julie really want? She wants a job that feels worthwhile, that does something valuable for the world. She wants time to read, to walk her dogs, to fall in love. What has she got? A fancy car with no time to drive it, an expensive apartment with no time to entertain in it, beautiful clothes with no place but work to wear them.

Okay, I've convinced you to start saving. But how on earth are you going to save money when you're up to your eyeballs in obligations? I don't know your exact situation, but I do know you can stop buying expensive clothes, drive the old car, let your house paint peel, stop eating out, stop taking cabs, refinance your mortgage, sell your second home and forget about renting a summer place.

Agony? Most of those lovely things are nothing but consolation prizes for an unhappy life. *By any measure—time, money, energy, focus—those toys cost too much!*

What if you have a family to support?

It's a lot harder to save money when you have people who depend on you, who are used to a standard of living that makes it impossible for you to budget. They need to cut back too. But don't start trying to reform your family until you've reformed yourself.

If you're anything like me, you need to feel like The Good Provider. You'd rather have that power than share the burden, even if your family is willing. What should you do about it? I think it's time to take a look at the high price of being a hero. Don't abandon your family, or drop your obligations. Just look at the emotional structure of this position you've chosen. You might make some surprising discoveries.

Melanie, thirty-three, a banker whose husband is in school: "I'd feel so useless. Like Mike would have no reason to be with me."

Ron, forty-five, a small-business owner with a family of four: "I'd feel like a loser, not as good as my older brother. I'd feel like a stupid kid. This way I may be working myself to death, but I feel like I have some real value."

Here's my message: There's nothing wrong with taking care of your loved ones. It's an expression of affection and commitment that's good for all of us. But *if you're overdoing it because you want to make up for feelings of worthlessness, you're sure to get stuck—and to mess up your family's values to boot.* A buried agenda makes it almost impossible to change the surface of your life. Once you're ready to let go of a little power, *then* you can start asking your family to help you economize. Then, if they need some time to fret and adjust to the new regime, you won't start feeling so terrible that you cave in and sabotage the process.

Let me stop for a minute and explain something: I have nothing against conspicuous consumption, or if I do, that's my business and I don't intend to influence you. If there's nothing else you want but money and toys, I think you should go for it. You'll be perfectly happy getting and spending, and your happiness is what this book is all about.

But if you were *trained* to want toys, and made to *forget* what you really wanted, you're the victim of a cruel joke—you've been robbed of your own world, and put on a wheel like a hamster— and you're running after nothing. And maybe the cage is made up of expenses you simply can't see how to cut back. *Maybe you're just pretending that somehow you'll leave someday, when actually your living style is making that option impossible.*

How much money would you really need to live your dream life?

If you don't know what your dream life is, hang on. We'll get to that in a moment. For now, just for practice, take a wild guess about what that dream life is, and think about the price of living it.

If your dream life is to own your own yacht, you'd better hang on to this job and take another one too. If your dream life is to work in the same career, but in a better work environment, all you need is some money to tide you over until you've relocated. Sometimes that means you're going to actually take some time off. If possible you should stay at your present job until you find a better one. Even then, however, you may have to take a cut in pay for a while. If you have a nice chunk of money in the bank, you have that choice. But if you have to make what you're making now, your choices narrow considerably.

If your dream life is to live in the country, run your own home business, and raise Irish setters, you need enough money to start that business. Once it looks viable, you'll be able to get the house and the dogs one way or another. (I know people who've done both for very little money. I'm one of them!)

Gwen, twenty-six, a lawyer: All I want to do is live abroad, in a different country every year. I know how to live on $15,000 a year if I'm careful. So I'm going to save enough for three years of travel, and I'm going to find some kind of temporary job in the states for six months a year, so I can stretch the savings for a few more years. If my languages get good enough, I might be able to get a job traveling. (In fact, she found a stateside job working for the tourist departments of a number of other countries, selling their attractions to travel agents, and she travels for free!)

Roger, forty-seven, recording engineer: I'm going back to school, and my target date is a year from today. I'll have to turn down jobs and take a cut in salary, so I'm cutting expenses while I'm still working full-time, to build up a nest egg. Then I'm going to work part-time forever.

By saving money and cutting expenses, Gwen and Roger are buying the most precious thing in the world: time. *You need time more than anything else;* time to start working fewer hours so you can try out your love of study, or train for a different career, or even go fishing.

Now we've got a mechanism for you to let off steam (visit your feelings), and hopefully I've convinced you that you need re-sources for a life change (putting away money). The immediate danger of walking out on your job is past and the future danger of being without choices is being taken care of.

Okay, let's talk.

Let me state your problem again. You're on the fast track, doing well, looking good, and making money, but you're not happy. You think you'd like to change your life, but you're so conflicted about leaving that you're walking around mumbling to yourself in public places.

Don't get worried; it's not such a big deal.

You may not have to leave the fast track at all—you may be able just to change some of the details, or some of the ways you react to your work. And if you do need to leave your job, the good news is that *there is no dilemma without a solution.* I guarantee that this steel-hard dilemma of yours has loopholes big enough for a genius like you to climb through easily.

Let's look at how you got here in the first place.

WHAT'S A NICE KID LIKE YOU DOING IN A JOINT LIKE THIS?

Successful people become successful for different reasons, and they become unhappy with their success for different reasons too.

I'm going to list five different scenarios. See if you can find yourself in one or more of them:

Scenario 1: You Never Exactly Decided (to Be a Stockbroker, Lawyer, Management Consultant, etc.)

You were good at school, and never thought much about what you really wanted to do. Maybe you went on to graduate school because that was the logical next step, and you had the grades. When the time came to get a job, you chose the most prestigious firm that wanted you. It never occurred to you that you could do anything else. But you never really liked the job very much. Now you've got a good car, a good apartment, and a great sound system. Everyone in your personal life is impressed with you or envies you. But this success thing isn't all it's cracked up to be.

Is that you? Let me give you some real-life examples you can compare yourself to:

Randy, twenty-eight, liked school. He was a good student, and sort of slid into a career. It took six years and two big promotions for Randy to admit he's drifting. He says he doesn't know what he wants.

"I never made a decision," he says. "I just took care of each step, and found myself here. I'm very capable. I can get good grades, do a good interview, fulfill my job. The only thing I apparently lack is remembering to pick a goal!"

Kathleen K., twenty-six, just ran for district leader—and made a very good showing. Everybody thinks she has what it takes and she's gotten some interest from powerful backers. But politics really isn't fun for Kathleen. She isn't even sure how she got into it. "I was only playing the game, and when I looked around, I was signed to the team!"

Secretly she's always wanted to work with children. She's patient and happy with children and always wanted to be a grade school teacher—or a nanny, for that matter. But the district leader post is her chance to make it big. Her family thinks you shouldn't waste brains on children. (As if we had a more valuable resource!) Everyone expects her to have a glittering career in politics—to carry the banner to the top of the hill for her family.

Scenario 2: Your Work Eats Up the Rest of Your Life

You fought hard to get where you are, and you never minded the work. It was part of the fight to get to the top. You may have gotten pleasure out of winning the competition and being really good at what you do, and you feel very lucky to be on top. It wasn't until a few years went by that you looked up and noticed what all this success was costing you: a normal life, a happy family, and perhaps some dream you really love but no longer have time for.

Marguerite, a thirty-five-year-old futures trader on Wall Street, had studied American literature in college and loved it. After graduation she didn't have enough money for graduate school, so she took a job as a junior stockbroker. The job lacked interest for her so she nosed around and eventually wandered into the futures trading department, which looked like much more fun. She asked what the gang there was doing, and watched, and before long she was good enough to transfer into their department. After eight years she was making more money than she had ever imagined possible. But she didn't have a minute to herself.

When I met her, she was tense and unhappy. She said, "I work fourteen hours a day! At first, I loved it. And then eight years passed. I'm about to get another big promotion, but I haven't had time to devote to my relationship in years. I'm thirty-five years old! I haven't been out of the city for anything but business for eight years. I have a degree in Comparative Literature, but I haven't read a novel in eight years. Every time my birthday rolls around, I hear a background voice saying 'Something's wrong—and time is passing.' "

Scenario 3: The Work Is Fine, but You Can't Stand the People

Our environment is what makes us strong and open and happy—or it makes us sick. A toxic environment doesn't just have cigarette smoke in it, it has difficult people in it, and they can make you as sick as any toxic chemical.

Sometimes it isn't just one or two people, it's the whole place. It's so riddled with politics you can't do your work. You may have walked into a sick corporate family. You picked the right work, but the wrong place to do it.

Billie's job used to be wonderful, then somebody came along and spoiled it for her. A new boss changed the entire temperament of the company, firing Billie's beloved supervisor and replacing her with a man who was both unkind and unfair. Now Billie's job is simply hell.

This is no minor issue. In 1990, a study found that one third of all unhappy workers attributed their job stress to *other people on the job.* You can become sick if the community you work with is toxic.

How do they make you sick? You have terrible feelings and begin to think there's something wrong with you. You find yourself not wanting to work at your very top level because you're angry and demoralized, so your work suffers and you lose the pride you had in doing a great job. But most of all, the injustice makes you sick.

Scenario 4: The Work Isn't What You Expected. It's a Terrible Disappointment

You became exactly what you wanted to be—and then found out your work wasn't what you thought it was going to be. It's heartbreaking but true: most of us are sold a bill of goods when it comes to choosing a career. Law students spending summers at a firm, encouraged by happy parents, proud professors, seductive employers, do not find out until much later that the real job isn't like the summer job.

Most of us trick ourselves. We hold some kind of vision of our fast-track career that we got from fantasies or films. We see ourselves in front of a jury, fighting for the life of an honorable client, but instead find ourselves pushing mounds of paper for a utility company. We imagine ourselves draping gorgeous fabric as only we can and then watching our models dance out on the runway to TV cameras and applause, only to find ourselves fighting our factories and our creditors to get hundreds of ladies' sweat suits delivered on time to enraged department store buyers. This isn't what they told us, but there's no way to leave now. And the money is good.

Marlene loved medicine and medical school, but she got a job at a health group that wouldn't let her practice good medicine. She doesn't know where to go, and may leave the field entirely. "They won't let me do good medicine where I work; they make me see eighty people a day and won't let me spend more than five minutes with each one!"

I know television sitcom writers who have a hard time living with the outright idea-theft that sometimes comes with their territory, and I know idealists who joined organizations so they could fight for good causes—only to find the organizations riddled with politics or corruption.

What are they supposed to do? All these people made a big investment to get where they are, and if you're one of them you know what a tough decision lies ahead: either you stay and sign up for unhappiness, or you leave and resign yourself to having wasted all those years.

Well, don't throw anything away just yet. There's a good chance you'll be able to salvage everything of real value to you.

Scenario 5: The Trophy Leaves You Feeling Empty

All you ever wanted was to be the best, better than anyone else. You were competitive and you were good, and nothing could stop you. Others fell by the wayside, but you never stopped and now you've got the trophy. Your drive was unstoppable, your focus never wavered, and now here you are, the winner, in any-body's book. The game's been won, and *you don't feel a thing.*

We all read about big stars—musicians, athletes, self-made millionaires—who fought their way to the top and wound up on drugs and alcohol. Sometimes they come to see me, and they always say the same thing: "I had to get to the top. Nothing else mattered. It always seemed so urgent. And then, when I finally made it, something was missing that I thought would be there, and I don't know what it is!"

I want you to ask yourself the same questions I ask them—and this could be a little painful. If you have the courage to answer, you'll take your first step toward real happiness, the kind you can count on.

Question 1: Was there someone in your past, a disappointed parent perhaps, who needed a trophy? Sometimes there was a parent or older sibling who never got what they wanted—and you took on the job of making them feel better.

Question 2: Was there someone in your past who didn't see your value? Did you win that trophy to make somebody love you?

If the answer to either of those questions is yes, you've got a very special problem on your hands: you worked at something you were gifted at, something you loved doing, to be a winner—for reasons you didn't exactly admit to yourself. You had a dream in the back of your mind that was so pervasive or so disguised you forgot it was there. You knew you simply had to win and you wouldn't stop trying. Absorbed in your own determination, you never got the bad news until you won the big trophy and then it hit you like a ton of bricks. The sad person is still sad, the person who didn't love you still doesn't love you.

Little kids can't bear to think that a parent's dissatisfactions are unsolvable. It's too terrible for a child to accept that his or her family will never be happy, either with their own lives or with the child. It's touching but tragic that when we're children we decide to tie our fates to theirs. If I make it to the top, Dad will stop being sad, my big sister will start to like me.

Sooner or later we all have to face the hard truth—children don't have the power to rescue adults. Maybe nobody has the power to rescue anybody—without a lot of cooperation, anyway. People have to rescue themselves—if they want to. And if they don't, well, we have to learn to respect their choices and get on with our lives.

You can't make anyone love you either. You see, you were perfectly lovable from day one, and if someone didn't love you—or seemed not to—*it's because they didn't want to.* You may never know why, because it probably had very little to do with you, but the key here is this: no amount of success can change their opinion of you, because *they don't intend to be forced.* The better you become, the less they like it!

One more point: Those disappointed or unloving people I've been talking about have the same influence on you even if they've completely changed now that they've grown older. Even if they're no longer alive, the influence is there. I think that's why it's sometimes so hard to identify what's going on. When you've made it to the top and everyone is applauding, you can feel as though it's not enough. You feel that somebody is missing, and you have to think for a moment to realize it's someone who's no longer alive, or someone who stopped being hard on you and loves you very much today.

Why do you still feel the applause is not enough? Because the child inside you is running this show, and nobody told him it's really over. You're going to have to do that yourself.

Those are the five major categories of discontent that I've found. And there's a logical solution attached to each of them.

But first I think it's important to discuss another possibility. Maybe if you weren't so burned out, you'd want to keep your job and your career!

BURNOUT AND BOREDOM—THE CURE

You may sense that quitting is really not the right thing for you to do. Just because changing jobs is the right thing for some people doesn't mean it's the right thing for you. Sometimes leaving a job is exactly the wrong thing, and your resistance is based on good sense more than fear.

You may have just what you always wanted: all the excitement you can handle, firing-line intensity on the job, hair-raising missions as part of your daily work. The stock exchange floor, a television news program, or the emergency ward of a busy hospital are all very exciting, but they take their toll. The pace is intoxicating and you're caught up in it, but one day on your way to work, you realize that what's ahead of you is really no different from what you did yesterday, and you feel exhausted in advance. Intensity can be its own kind of drug and it can lead to its own kind of burnout.

The cure for your situation is not a vacation, believe it or not, although a couple of weeks off will give you a good start. But you know as well as I do that going back to work will erase your gains within hours. And don't take a year off with no plans, or you could be in for a nightmare. Some friends of mine took a year to travel the world and found themselves in a bar in Bali looking around and thinking, "What the hell are we doing here?"

I'd like to spare you that. Experimenting taught me a better way.

The cure for sorrow is to learn something.

Merlin, the wizard, says that in *Camelot.* Merlin has not only cured sorrow, he has also come up with the cure for burnout. If you're burned out, learning something new or doing something creative is the cure. Plain and simple. It not only begins the healing process immediately by refreshing your mind, it wakes up the imagination you forgot to use. It rests the part of your brain you used too much by waking up the part you hardly used at all.

Don't let anyone talk you into basket weaving, for heaven's sake, unless you're secretly a wildly talented basket weaver. Nothing is creative or interesting *unless it's creative or interesting to you!* Search your memory. I promise you there's something you always wanted to know something about, but never had the time to learn. Find something sweet, because nothing else will refresh you. It can be anything from the history of toolmaking to higher mathematics or a new language or filmmaking.

And don't start taking classes in your present field.

Some people think that if you take a class, it should be to enhance job skills. *Forget your job skills.* You've got too many already, that's why you're in this pickle. As a matter of fact, to get the most radical refreshment, you should take a class that is as distant from what you do as possible: if your job uses language, take a painting class, or the history of architecture. If you work in a small, contained atmosphere, go mountain climbing or hang gliding. When you start using senses that you've neglected, your reward is to see the world with completely fresh eyes.

That's first aid for burnout—and it works every time.

Burnout makes you sick, but if you don't take care of it, you're in for meltdown. Meltdown will make you do things on impulse that you won't be able to straighten out later, so don't mess with it.

Later, if you like, you can start learning things in your field. After all, you must be pretty good at it or you wouldn't have done so well. But your gifts have been misused so they have to be left alone for a while, like a field that's been overplanted.

Now let's solve each of those five scenarios.

THE SCENARIO SOLUTIONS

Scenario 1: You Never Decided to Be What You've Become

If you're like Randy, who backed onto the fast track without ever actually deciding to, *you need to find out what you really love,* and forget for a while what you're capable of. You're obviously capable of achieving a lot, but *ability can never take the place of desire.* Don't be tempted to do something just because you *can.* That's what got you off course in the first place.

I know very well that it's not easy to recover that fierce and loving core inside you, that private language that I call your "genius." It's been covered up by a well-meaning cultural program designed to teach you the language of your society. Still, there are pointers everywhere, indications of your true gifts, and they're not hard to find as long as you aren't misled into thinking that your genius is the same as your skills and abilities. That's just your surface. Your skills and abilities are valuable, no question about it. They'll keep you alive. But skill alone won't make you happy. This is a source of great confusion to fast trackers, so I want you to pay a lot of attention to what I'm about to say. *The indicators of your personal genius are not necessarily what you're good at.* When I say "genius," I don't mean "high aptitude."

Look around at what you love, what you'd do with your time if all the necessities were taken care of. Look at what lifts your heart, and you'll hear your genius talking. Follow that voice, and you'll find your *gifts*—not just your abilities.

I don't think we were put on this planet so we could be slapped into service by the prevailing ideology. Life is too precious to get caught on a route that someone else chose for you without your even knowing it. But before you change direction, you've got to have a dream.

Is there a dream you left behind? I hope so, because it's going to save your life. True desire is like a crowbar to a jail door. It can bust it right open and set you free.

If you can't remember a dream, there are lots of ways you can awaken your original self—the one that did the dreaming; that creative, hopeful person I know you were before you ever heard of a grade point average or investment banking.

The time has come to find yourself.

a. Read autobiographies.

You don't need action stories right now. Donate them to the local hospital and go pick up some autobiographies of people in very different fields from yours.

Lots of people have told their lives in ways that can teach you how to live. Who should you read? Just ask the bookstore owner to recommend the best autobiography she knows of, and read that one. Great people are great talkers, and at bottom they only talk about one thing: how to live.

You need the contrast to your own life too. On the fast track you tend to be isolated. All the people you know are doing the same thing you are, and what you need more than anything is a look at some alternatives.

When you read a quality autobiography, you'll have some quality companionship. You've needed that for much longer than you realize.

b. Write your autobiography.

Keep away from the last ten years. Write short vignettes, at random, about moments out of your early childhood. Anything before you graduated from high school—the earlier, the better—should refresh you enormously and remind you of who you were. I know someone who set himself the task of writing one hundred stories about his childhood. I thought that was such a great idea, I started to do it too. I got up to about seventeen little one- or two-page vignettes before I ran out of steam, but I loved every minute of it.

I'm delighted I started it and maybe someday I'll finish. And maybe I won't. I think there's a special saint who protects unfinished projects. Unfinished projects are just as valuable to us as the projects we finish. So it's very possible I'll never write a hundred stories about anything, but I'm very glad that I reminded myself of these seventeen richly colored moments from my past. I've enjoyed showing them to my friends and my kids. I wish my grandparents had done the same thing, and left the stories for me to read.

Maybe we all owe it to the people who come after us to tell them about our lives. If you're willing to believe in the value of your story, telling it will come easily. The person who will benefit most, of course, will be you.

c. Enlarge your experience.

Take a two-week summer photography workshop in Maine. (Look in the photo magazines in February or March for ads.) Take a writing workshop in Montana and go fishing when it's over. Especially if you think you can't write—or fish.

What you're doing now is gathering together raw materials for your personal life sculpture, and that's why I want you gathering marble from brand-new quarries. You never know what's been passed over in the narrow path you had to choose. Focused people often do well, but they pay a price for it, and often cannot regroup when the time comes because their experience isn't wide enough.

I know a man who took a photography workshop and came away realizing he wanted to work with the forest service. He wasn't a photographer in his heart, but he was a lover of trees and hadn't really thought about it before. Now he has contacted a sympathetic writer, and they're putting together a pamphlet, maybe an article, about the nature of trees.

He didn't take up photography—and he didn't quit his job either. And he isn't burned out anymore.

d. Enlarge your imagined experience.

Try a little pretending for refreshment. Here's a game I use in my workshops:

Exercise 2: I Am a Stunt Pilot

Sit down and put a clock in front of you. Now, for thirty seconds, be a stunt pilot and make it sound so wonderful that anyone in the world would want to be you. "I am a stunt pilot. It's great to just play in the sky. The part I like best is soaring around and over mountains, following a river right through the mountains. I love the noise, and I love the power."

Got it? Do it for yourself, and start with stunt pilot, just for fun. Then do this exercise over and over again, using a different profession each time! Be a prima ballerina in the Bolshoi Ballet, be the richest woman who ever lived, be a tide-pool researcher who studies the complete little worlds that exist in tiny tide pools. Come up with anything, and then make yourself its biggest promoter. If possible, get some friends together and do this in a group. I promise you'll love it.

Dee, twenty-nine, from an executive search firm: I'm with my husband in a very glamorous international business where I travel all over Asia, interviewing the most important people in each country. We get so excited about their issues that we stay up all night talking and making phone calls all over the world! Their chauffeurs take us back to our hotels at dawn.

Cora, thirty-three, a secretary at a community college: I design *huge* sets for big presentations and international festivals. I walk around with a clipboard in my hand and a megaphone, shouting to my staff to move one backdrop over here, and another over there. I make a huge amount of noise and raise a lot of dust! I can tell them to bring elephants on stage if I want! I make things happen!

The second time around:

Dee: I work in the arts and I meet all the most brilliant playwrights and dancers around. Maybe I'm a publicist, but I don't sell anything. I come up with great ideas on how to publicize these artists. What's best about it is that everybody is interesting. Ideas are always floating around. It never gets dull.

Cora: Let's see. This time I'm a meeting planner. I love bossing everybody around. I plan huge rock and roll concerts and meetings with business people from all over the world. I make sure that the translating machinery is in place, and that the food is served at the right time.

Fast trackers are more likely than the rest of us to get drafted into living other people's dreams—they're not given much time to think. They chose from whatever was available without ever getting the chance to develop the genius that's inside of them.

You need to do some exploring, and the way your most creative side explores best is by playing games. Hang on to your job for a while (at least) while you play with different experiences, and check out your interests, and try on different lives in your mind. Pay careful attention to anything that excites you—even a little. Interest is a powerful clue, and any stirrings will unfold into a bigger picture if you are patient with those messages you're getting from your original self.

Now, if you suddenly realize what you want—and it's radically different from anything you've ever considered—poke around among the chapters in this book. You may need solutions that are in other chapters. (One good bet is Chapter 8, "I Want Something I Shouldn't Want—It's Trivial or Unworthy.")

Randy, the hotshot business consultant who never really decided, enlarged his experience by volunteering at a retirement home. He remembered that he was always interested in helping people. He toyed with the idea of studying psychology, but continued to try out new experiences. That's when he realized he was interested in photography. His interest lasted only a few weeks, but in that time he got some important evidence. He found he wanted to take pictures of little businesses—very little ones, like grocery stores or shoemakers. His grandfather had run such a business on New York City's Lower East Side when Randy was a little kid. So he walked into small stores to take pictures, and got into conversations with the owners. He took some pictures, but gave advice too and enjoyed that, more than being a psychologist. Soon he was spending Fridays and Mondays helping out small retail businesses. One day he was put in touch with an eastern European family, and now he runs classes on accounting techniques for small businesses in eastern Europe. His firm lets him go to Moscow, Prague, and Sophia three times a year—with their blessing. It makes them look good, and he does some business for the firm over there. He says there are lots of financial organizations helping out in eastern Europe these days, and he's met great people, both European and American. Randy doesn't mind his job anymore.

Kathleen K., who has such a great future in politics, has gone into children's advocacy. She's the "child's representative." Who votes for her? Apparently everybody. One reason is that she has a radio show every Saturday morning on which she reads stories to children. And she's in the park some Sundays, doing the same thing. Her opponents think it's a clever gimmick and wish they'd thought of it, but it's no gimmick at all. "If I couldn't have found a way to work with children, I'd have left politics. I don't like politics. I like children."

Scenario 2: Your Work Eats Up the Rest of Your Life

If you're like Julie and Marguerite and Roger, intoxicated with being able to handle a high-paced job and pull down an astonishing amount of money, but sacrificing a personal life, you've got some tough decisions to make. You might have to say, "That's enough," and walk away. I prefer compromise but sometimes no compromise is possible. In many fast-track jobs you must give everything to the job, or you can't stay in at all.

It's an odd dilemma. You wonder who sets up a company that way. Does the boss go home to his family and let everyone else do the hard work? Or has he lost his family? It's very clear that people who are willing to be that kind of "winner" cannot have complete family lives. Some people manage to live without family lives, although at what cost, I don't like to speculate. But most of us can't bear to face the fact that the cost of success is so high. We try to find ways to wiggle around and avoid making a decision.

Marguerite had a very hard time letting go of her prize job. "I know this job is killing me and ruining my life. But I can't stand to let it go. It's so much fun sometimes."

So why consider leaving at all?

Because Marguerite is involved with a wonderful man, and they want to get married and have a child. Her husband-to-be says she can call it any way she wants. He'd be happy to have a baby, but he can live without one. He's a teacher and would be very willing to take care of a baby if they have one. The situation looks workable, but Marguerite says it isn't.

"No woman here has a family," she says. "Because nothing can come before this job. Joe is great, and if I didn't want a baby, maybe things would be all right. But I know the reality."

The truth is, Marguerite is facing another weaning. Many times in our lives we have to give up something we love in order to get on with the next phase of our lives. If we never let go of our mother, we can't become free—and neither can she. If we refuse to leave our familiar home to go to school, we miss out on whole worlds! There seems to be no end to the weanings, as you know when you've given up familiar relationships that were bad for you. Or even given up moping about somebody who walked out on you!

I believe you can have whatever you really want in this life, in one form or another, sooner or later. All you have to do is take care of your health and be lucky enough to live for a while.

But you can't have it all at once and you can't have it forever. No life has the room for everything in it, not on the same day. Think back on any period in your life that was sweet—say, when your children were babies, or when you got your first old car and fixed it up. Or think of any country you visited that you fell in love with. There's a wistful sweetness in those memories. You wish you could visit those times just a few times more. But you wouldn't want to be stuck with little babies all your life, nor with junky old cars, no matter how wonderful. And if you only visit London every time you travel, you'll never see Paris.

You can keep moving, or you can stand still. You can hang on to what you've got, or you can move to the next stage. So Marguerite has some tough decisions to make. She can keep working, but she will have to let go of the constant rush from her high pressure setup if she wants a richer home life.

Scenario 3: The Work Is Fine; You Can't Stand the People

Do you identify with Billie J.? She loved her job at a major cosmetics company before she started being knocked around by political games. Now she wants to quit. It's all been spoiled for her.

Billie needs to learn to do two things before she takes any steps. She has to learn how to survive in the company of difficult people, also known as "jerks," and then she has to decide if she really wants to.

Is a jerk at work ruining your love for your job? This is a case where you never really had a complaint with the fast track, and you never felt you were moving in the wrong direction—until now. Now you're getting sick with stress and you feel you can't handle a high-powered job.

Don't blame yourself. You were great at handling a high-powered job before someone sapped your energy by their behavior. You're just overwhelmed and you need to do something about it. Difficult work relationships are a major problem in the work force, and labor experts say they are *the* major cause of low morale on the job. But there are steps you can take to solve this problem.

Step 1: Ventilate.

Let yourself—*in the privacy of your own home, not in the public arena or to anyone's face*—blow your stack. Figure out how King Kong would handle it. And when some of the heat has subsided, have some fun with diabolical revenge fantasies that you're never really going to do. That will get you laughing and release the rest of the heat. And then your head will clear up a bit and you'll get some perspective.

Aren't you supposed to forgive your enemies?

Not exactly. Not yet.

Forgiveness may be necessary in the long run, but done too soon it only muddies the waters. If you try to forgive somebody because you're *supposed to,* you're biting off more than you can chew. You cannot forgive somebody you're mad at until you're ready. *And you can't pretend to be ready.*

On the other hand, if you can't find some way to get past your anger, this person will control your life. You've got to find some way to get free. And there's a way to do that, a distancing technique. *You have to role-play the jerk.* If you can put yourself in this jerk's position and begin to try on his behavior, you can get a rare insight into how he looks at the world.

Step 2: Role-Play a Jerk.

It's hard to pretend to be somebody else. Just remember that to imagine you're somebody else you do not have to act like him. You just have to sit in his chair and look at the world from his perspective. Try it out for a moment, and see if you get a glimpse at what's motivating him. Here are some guidelines to help you get into the role. Imagine that you're at the jerk's desk, wearing his clothes, and have his responsibilities. See the office staff from his viewpoint, *and start talking:*

Mandy, twenty-nine, product developer for a photo company: Okay, I'm the manager and I don't want to help any of these people on the staff because I'm afraid of getting into trouble. I'm up for retirement in a few years. Hey! No wonder he tries to sabotage our ideas.

Amelia, thirty, a surveyor: My assistant acts so nice, I didn't know why I wanted to choke him, and why I was feeling so unsure of myself! Now I can see it. He really is competitive!

Can you see how that kind of hard clarity changes the whole situation? Now you can figure out what to do. And for some reason your frustration sinks to very low levels. Because you understand that it's not possible to expect reasonable behavior from the jerk, you no longer expect it.

What then? Well, now that the problem is clear to you, you have some options. You can figure out how to sidestep the conflict, or work around it—or you fire somebody, or you quit. And your head will be very clear about which one of those actions is the right one.

But sometimes, no matter how you try, your mind will not clear up. When that happens, you're caught in a web because this person has reactivated something from your past.

Step 3: Back to the Future.

We're all very aware of how much our childhood experiences influence our personal relationships. We usually forget that those same experiences can mess up our relationships at work. We might get especially upset by an angry boss because we had an angry father. Or we may feel too guilty to leave a bad work situation because it reminds us of our unhappy family.

Sam B., twenty-five, had just started an investment bank training program. He'd been excited about starting the program, but by the end of his first week he was almost ready to quit. Why? Because a coworker was making him so uncomfortable that he couldn't concentrate.

"I think this one guy hates me and I don't know why. Every time I turn my head, he's staring at me. The boss really liked one of my comments today, and I think this guy hates me." Sam wasn't delusional. The man *was* jealous. But Sam was overreacting. It took just a few minutes to realize that the reason Sam was overreacting was because this coworker reminded him of his jealous older brother.

When we confuse people at work with people from our families, normal situations turn into excruciating ones.

What to do?

Exercise 3: Take the Feeling Back Home

Ask yourself the key question: Is this a familiar feeling? Have you ever felt it before? If so, you might have a case of mistaken identity.

The cure: Find the original scene where it all got started. *You have to "take the feelings home," that is, back to the place they originated—and have those feelings about the right people.* If you're upset by an angry boss, and you remember feeling exactly that way about your angry father, go back into the past and have those feelings about your father. Remember all those things you want to say to your boss? Well, say them to your father of the past. "Don't you dare yell at me! You have no right to make me feel this bad! You big bully!"

I know, and you know, that you couldn't have said those things to a parent when you were little. *But you wanted to.* They're waiting inside for a new situation to come along, and here it is with your boss!

Well, don't confront your boss until you've gone back into your past and let that long-gone angry daddy have it. When you're finished you may be very surprised to find that your boss's snarls don't bother you nearly as much.

Scenario 4: The Work Isn't What You Expected

Are you like Marlene, whose love of medicine forms the essential core of her life, but who is disappointed by the realities of a medical career? Marlene works in such a big institution and has to see so many patients each day that she doesn't get to practice medicine the way she wants to. "I don't want to do patch-ups. I want to do some real good in this world," she said.

When she was convinced that there was no way to do that, she had some hard thinking to do. Would she have to give up medicine completely? After a bad moment, the answer became clear. She called her favorite teacher from medical school and said, "I want to do research and I want to teach. Can you help me?"

You may have to find a way to let go of your career while hanging on to your passion—that is, by isolating the essence of what it is you love and building a different career around it. Look around you and see if you can become inventive. After all, when fate slams a door, they say it opens a window.

Is there some way, some place, where you'll be able to do what Marlene did and rescue your love of your profession from the aspects that are ruining it? You might have to strike out on your own, start your own business, and do it your way. Or keep your passion for your private hours, and make your living doing something else. Not all passions have to make money. Only you know what you really need.

But never give up on that part of you that loves your work. It must be rescued, one way or another.

Exercise 4: Do It Your Way: Imagine Your Own Business

Imagine you're in charge of redesigning your profession to suit only people who are exactly like you.

Go into detail. What duties would you add; which would you drop? How would you change the time you spend with each patient or client? Would you spend more time as a figurehead, or more time researching, or more time in the field with colleagues or others? Would you have more or fewer assistants? Would you work without any hierarchy? What would be essential; what could you eliminate?

Georgie N. quit her $85,000-a-year corporate job because, although she liked the tasks, she didn't like having a boss at all and she felt it was meaningless for her to stay in corporate life since she would always have a boss. "I decided I want to go on with the *best* of my life, rather than just the rest of my life" is what Georgie told me.

So she hung out a shingle and pursued a career as a self-employed consultant, controlling her own hours, her own earnings and investments, and often being hired—at more money *and* more respect—by her previous employer! The important thing for Georgie was to have more personal control and by being in business for herself, she got it.

Even if you change careers, you can take what you like about your job and leave the rest behind you for something far more satisfying. If you've been through undergraduate and professional school, you've got transferable skills. If the work isn't what you expected, don't despair. Go looking for something you love, and take your skills along with you.

Scenario 5: The Trophy Leaves You Feeling Empty

Did you fight your way to the top thinking you'd be happy when you finally made it, only to find it empty? Then you've got to do some thinking to find out if you used your talents to win someone's approval—and didn't get the approval you hoped for. The question is, can you love yourself enough to value what you won just for yourself? Now that the old reason you pursued success is lost, can the success have new meaning for you?

Devon, a world-class athlete, won prize after prize until she became a national champion, and the Olympics were the next step. But one day, in a minor running meet she came in third.

When she looked up, she saw her father gazing at her with open dislike.

Everything crashed. Devon dropped out of sports and left her hometown. She took a few jobs but they never felt right.

You'll find some solutions to this scenario in Chapter 5, "Fear of Success." Devon's solution—after letting herself face the sorrow of having an unloving father—was to remember how much she loved running and get started again. Today she's a running coach. She trains girls to run and to win for themselves.

So those are the five groups of discontented fast-track people I've found, and those are the five solutions.

If you found yourself in this chapter it means you've used your outer life—your accomplishments, your possessions—to stand for who you are. That's a guarantee of dissatisfaction sooner or later, because there's more to you than any job. It doesn't matter how much your accomplishments and your future successes mean to you and to your family. And don't fool yourself by making lists in your head of all the great things in your life. *Happy people don't have to make lists.*

You're going to have to take charge of your fast track lifestyle before it eats up any more of your very precious time. You've got to find some way to make your job work for *you,* or you've got to leave it and start something better.

The work you give yourself to can enrich your life or seduce it away from you. Ask your heart what it really wants—and listen when it tells you the answer.

EIGHT

I Want Something I Shouldn't Want—It's Trivial or Unworthy

MAYBE the nurses in the maternity ward made a mistake, maybe the stork got his delivery orders crossed. Whatever reason, cosmic or clerical, Marnie was born into the wrong tribe. It happens all the time.

Marnie's parents own a bar in New England. They are, in fact, members of the large and proud tribe of bar owners: self-reliant, self-employed individuals who look down on people who work for others.

Marnie wanted to be a college professor.

Without studying particularly hard or well, Marnie's natural intelligence and curiosity landed her in college. Within a week she knew that this was where she belonged. The sudden lush oasis of ideas made her feel that her life until then had been an intellectual desert. Brimming with excitement, she phoned home.

"Dad, I know what I want to do with my life! I'm going to be a college professor."

Her father's reaction was not at all what she hoped for. "A professor? I had professors mopping floors for me during the Depression. If you're smart you'll get married."

Marnie was determined not to let her father's words affect her, but it was no use. She started to wobble in her resolve. She became uncertain about her ability and her first semester was a disaster. She was overwhelmed by assignments and could not get organized. She bought so many books that she had no money left for food, and often they were the wrong books. She studied all night and slept through exams. Finally, she became so frightened that the words in her textbooks stopped making sense; her mind became a sieve, incapable of retaining the simplest facts.

Marnie had strayed from the beliefs of her tribe and was now paying the price. Her father's words worked on her like a spell, planting seeds of self-doubt that led inevitably to her self-sabotaging behavior. Although she refused to drop out of college and went on to struggle through four years of classes and exams, the joy of ideas that had briefly illuminated her life was gone. Despite her intelligence, talent, and passion, Marnie did not become a professor.

Marnie's problem was that she did not share the values of her tribe. Jane Fonda was lucky, she liked acting. The Wallenda children, members of the famous trapeze act The Flying Wallendas, liked to fly. But many of us are not so lucky.

Rejecting the values of your family—your tribe—is one of the most difficult things a person can do. These values have been instilled in us since infancy and seem secured with the unbreakable bonds of love. But sooner or later every one of us has to find our own values, to cover our ears and stop listening to family instructions and start listening only to ourselves. In no other way can we discover the life that's really right for us. Pulitzer-Prize–winning poet Mary Oliver should know; few tribes encourage and teach children to be poets. In her poem "Journey" she wrote:

> *One day you finally knew*
> *what you had to do, and began,*
> *though the voices around you*
> *kept shouting*
> *their bad advice*
> *. . . little by little,*
> *as you left their voices behind,*

the stars began to burn
through the sheets of clouds,
and there was a new voice
which you slowly
recognized as your own,
that kept you company
as you strode deeper and deeper
into the world . . .

THE UGLY DUCKLING SYNDROME

Hans Christian Andersen knew all about this problem, and he wrote about it in his famous story about the ugly duckling, which, you will remember, was neither a duckling nor ugly. He was a swan raised by ducks, just as Marnie was a professor who was raised by bar owners. And as in the fairy tale, this little swan's family thought she was a very peculiar kind of duck. But heredity is just as strong as environment in determining who you are. Every human being is carrying genes from unknown ancestors, like a chest of buried treasures. That's why a family of singers can have a child who loves farming; a family of judges and lawyers can have a child who is a gifted actor. "Being born in a duck yard does not matter," Andersen concludes, "if only you are hatched from a swan's egg."

So what kind of egg were you hatched from? What kind of animal are you? In the course of working with Marnie and other "ugly ducklings," I developed a set of five exercises to help people claim with pride their valuable differences from their tribe. The first of these exercises is to stage a debate.

Exercise 1: The Great Debate

Whenever you leave your tribe, or even consider leaving your tribe, you set off a debate in your mind between two skilled and ruthless teams of debaters, each of which claims to represent you. When Marnie decided to become a college professor, the debate team that represented her family, what I call the "tribal voice," immediately began shouting her down. When she tried to give up academia, the team on her side, the "personal voice," told her she would be wasting her life to walk away from her beloved school. The debate in her head was unending. If you're like Marnie, I want you to make those debaters in your head go on record. Their arguments contain important information for you and you need to get it onto paper where you can take a good look at it.

Here's how to do it.

Divide a sheet of paper into two columns. In one column I want you to record assertions of the personal voice, so label this column "Personal." The other column is for the voices of conformity, the tribal voice, and should be labeled "Tribal." You can decorate the columns with appropriate signs, like smiling and frowning faces. Marnie wrote "The Battle for My Dream" on top of her paper.

Now all you have to do is start the debate. This should not be hard. One surefire way to start an argument in your head is to make a strong positive statement about yourself and your heart's desire. Write it down in the personal column and wait a moment. If you're in a tribal conflict, your tribal voice cannot remain silent when provoked by a strong personal statement.

Belinda, a woman in one of my workshops, triggered her debate by writing in her personal column: "It's a very good idea for me to be an arctic explorer because I want to do it, and I know I'll be good at it. When I went to Alaska with Earthwatch, everyone was impressed with my work."

Belinda didn't have long to wait for a negative, tribal response. It came to her immediately, loud and clear: "Big deal. We're not impressed. That doesn't prove anything!"

She started to record this statement in the tribal column, and before she had even finished writing, her personal voice answered: "You're not impressed? That doesn't prove anything? You're wrong! The Earthwatch scientists are world famous. *They're* impressed."

Got the picture? Remember, this is a debate, so keep those rebuttals coming—tribal and personal alternating until both columns are full.

Here's how Kate, another of my clients, did this exercise:

Kate wanted to be a fashion designer, but everybody else in her family, living and dead, was a social worker, public defender, or philanthropist. Kate's family had little respect for fashion. They thought the only worthy pursuit was to help others. By the time she came to see me, Kate's unhappiness about a career had gone on for so long that her family would have supported any career choice she made, just as long as it made her happy. The family in her *head,* however, was not as sympathetic. Kate had internalized her family's values and was ashamed of what she wanted. She had to debate her inner voices and win. She had to convince her own faultfinding inner voice that fashion design was a worthwhile pursuit.

She started with a positive personal statement: "I will become a great fashion designer because I love designing clothes." Her negative tribal voice shot back, "Fashion design? When people are starving on the street? What a waste of time!"

In the personal column, Kate countered with an argument that took her by surprise: "Dressing well enhances everybody's self-esteem: Park Avenue matrons, high school kids, and people who are living on the street. Social work is not the only way to help people."

Kate's tribal column filled up as quickly as the personal. As she wrote she created a powerful position paper about what it meant to her to be a fashion designer. By arguing with her tribal voices, Kate became proud to claim her right to design.

In a case where the conflict between self and the family is so strong, affirmations are not enough. Merely walking around thinking "I'm entitled to be a designer" could not combat Kate's inner anxiety. She had to get down inside herself and challenge the particular negatives being hurled at her by her internalized tribal voice. You too will need to stand up to the negative voices in your mind, so stage your debate on paper like Belinda and Kate did.

After you've completed this first exercise and you've given those inner tribal voices a good battle, they will never again have the same power over you. *Even if you didn't win the debate, you've made one enormous change: You have sorted out your voice from the tribal voice.* This awareness means you have already taken a big step toward defining, and defending, who you really are.

Your tribal voice will not disappear, of course. It will keep disapproving; that is its nature. But from now on you will stop confusing it with your own.

Keep the written debate handy. If your negative voice comes up with new arguments, write them down and formulate rebuttals. You're going to get very good at debating, and after each debate you'll find yourself more determined, less intimidated. Now that you know this tribal voice can be challenged, you'll see that the decision of how to run your life is far too important to leave to anyone but *you.*

Exercise 2: Design Your Perfect Family

You have now convinced yourself that you are not an ugly duckling after all; you are a swan who grew up in a duck pond. The problem is, you still do not know much about being a swan. Had Marnie grown up in a family of scholars she would have begun leading the life of the mind while still in her crib. Books would have been stacked everywhere. Her family would have discussed St. Augustine over breakfast and debated issues of epistemology at bedtime. With such a childhood, Marnie would have found it easy to live like a true member of her tribe.

You can't change the past, but I'm going to ask you to imagine what your life could have been like if you'd had tribal support from the start. The next exercise is designed to help you invent a new personal history for yourself, in your imagination. What's the purpose of creating such a fantasy? Certainly not to make you bitter about what you didn't have. And I don't believe for a moment that you can or should replace your real history with a fantasy. I have a much more important purpose.

I want you to experience the best support situation you're capable of imagining. I want you to walk through it and see how it makes you feel. *Because once you allow yourself a glimpse of what your family life could have been, you'll change the way you feel about yourself.* And once you've imagined a different past for yourself, you'll be ready for a different kind of present—and future. So get another piece of paper and pencil ready.

I want you to design another family, the family who would have welcomed and understood you from your birth. In fact, I'm going to ask you to design two versions of this ideal family, one after another. There's an important reason for doing both versions of this exercise, and I'll explain it when you're finished.

Version 1: The famous family. Create a family full of people— real or imaginary, historical or fictitious—who are completely knowledgeable in the area of your dream. If you love physics, get Stephen Hawking in there. You like acting? Why not choose Sarah Bernhardt and Robert De Niro as your parents, Macaulay Culkin for your little brother? You might pick filmmakers, financiers or farmers, painters or paleontologists. Whoever you choose, make sure they have the deepest respect for your goal, and for you. Imagine you're all sitting outside on a summer's day. Write out what your family says about your wishes. Here's what Marnie's ideal family said:

MARCEL PROUST:	*Why, she loves to study! Let her be! It's for people like her that I'm writing!*
MADAME CURIE:	*A natural curiosity is the mark of a wonderful mind. We must send her off to a fine college.*
JO (FROM *Little Women*):	*Hang the disbelievers, Marnie! You just hole up with those books of yours and let them stew. I did!*

When you've written out what each member of your imaginary family would say, take a look at their words. Surprised? Marnie was completely taken aback. "I see myself so differently in that imaginary family. Like I'm wonderful, not weird. It's a strange feeling."

This is no small change. A few minutes later, Marnie started feeling very emotional. "There was nothing wrong with me. I don't have to explain myself to anybody."

Take a few minutes to let the impact of this exercise settle in for you. Then we're going to do a different kind of ideal family.

Version 2: The psychological makeover.   In this version of the ideal family, you start with your real family and totally reverse their negative attitudes. If they were angry, imagine them as patient and kind; if they were sad, make them happy; if they were fearful, make them brave—and if they were critical, make them supportive.

All right, begin the fantasy.

You're at dinner. You present your family with your current goal and get the most delightful response possible. Take some time to imagine each member of your family energetically encouraging you.

Here's how two people imagined such a scene:

Joe, twenty-three, a student in graduate business school: We're at dinner, I'm just out of college and I've just announced that I want to visit the Himalayas instead of looking for a job. My dad, instead of exploding, is interested in everything I say. He listens intently and even says he might like to go to the Himalayas sometime himself. He even tries to help me figure out how to make my dream practical.

Bill, twenty-nine, a high-school teacher: My mother isn't at all worried. She says, "Okay, acting it is. Maybe we could think up some kind of work that would help you pay your rent without cutting into your acting."

Version two is a very different experience from version one. Unlike version one, these faces are familiar ones. Only their difficult characteristics have changed.

This is an important vision you have just had. Imagining your own family without their fears or their resistance presents you with faces you have always loved giving you the respect you always longed for. Like the exercise about the other ideal family, this can be an emotional experience, but it has different results. Instead of giving back your self, this exercise will start to heal some of the hurt your family has caused you. Not only that, but seeing your family as they probably wish they could be will soften your feelings toward them, and this is essential to you. You need to feel affection for your family or you'll be handicapped when you strike out on your own. I'll talk more about that later.

But for now, you've imagined two ideal families. You've stretched your experience to include what your family should have been. You now have a sense of how ideal families can allow themselves to enjoy and encourage the personal visions of each of their members.

Of course, you did not have an ideal family, and neither did your parents for that matter. No act of the imagination can change that. But with a clearer idea of who your ideal family could be, you can go out and look for them. It's time to find the people who will have no trouble accepting your dream—real, available people who can help you do what you are here to do; people who understand the part of you that baffled your family. Here's how to do it.

Exercise 3: Stepping Out

I know a man who always wanted to work with animals. His family thought he was out of his mind. "We're not farmers, we're financiers. The closest we ever came to working with animals was the time we sold hog belly futures short." So he subscribed to *The Wall Street Journal* and forgot about animals. One day a friend took him to a dog show. Despite all the books he had read about animals, he had never been to an animal show of any kind. On this day he was a little afraid of being reminded of what he could not have: He was like a dieter who averts his eyes every time the dessert cart rolls by. What he had not anticipated was that the room would be filled not only with dogs, but with hundreds of people who raised dogs for a living, people who thought working with animals was the greatest thing in the world. They were happy to talk and glad to share what they knew. For the first time in his life he didn't have to justify his love for animals. Everyone in the hall thought that loving animals was perfectly normal. He had found his people.

The moral of this story? You must begin a search. You won't find your people by sitting at home watching television. You've got to look for them in their natural habitats. Here are some tips on how to find people who are like you:

1. *Think like a hunter.*

    Do you want to be a journalist? Find out where they go after work. Give it a little thought and you'll know where your people hang out. Go find them. Be outspoken: tell the people you meet about your interests. Even if they aren't the right people after all, they might point you in the right direction.

2. *Send up a flare.*

    Personal ads are too good to be used only for the romance market. Place an ad saying "Is anyone interested in talking over coffee about trekking across Antarctica? Call me."

3. Read journals left by someone who knew the territory.

You're different from your family, but someone out there who was just like you has written a book. Find it, and paste up quotes all over your house so you never forget who you are.

4. Do anything.

Avoid tunnel vision. Look for offbeat things to do. Accompany your friends when they go places you might not otherwise go. As many people find their tribe through serendipity as through design.

THE SHAKES

You're doing great. You've debated your negative voices and won, you've imagined an ideal family and have begun meeting your people. You're on your way to breaking away, breaking all the tribal rules. *Now you can expect trouble.* This is the moment that the child's fear of being punished for breaking tribal rules could begin to affect you.

You might start missing appointments, or be overcome with fear that you don't have the talent to reach your goal. You might hate yourself when you mess up, and you hate yourself more when you do well because you feel like a show-off. As happy as you were with your new friends, you may suddenly feel like a fraud on the verge of being exposed and find yourself asking "What am I doing here?"

Why is this happening? Because you've given up the safety and support of your family to pursue your adventure, and not only are you a bit afraid, you're finding that sometimes the joy is submerged under the weight of loneliness.

When you're gripped by this kind of anxiety it is important for you to remember that what you are going through is normal. Take heart. You're having growing pains, and the course you've set for yourself is still a good one. If you need reminding, go back to the minutes of your debate with your tribal voice.

Just remember, when you go after your true identity, some part of you feels like you're breaking the rules. It comes with the territory. It just means you're human, and one day it will pass.

THE OUTSIDER

In your newly chosen field you will be something of an outsider for a while, but that can be an advantage. Being the outsider affords you a unique perspective. The novelist Joseph Conrad is a spectacular example of an outsider who made good. Conrad's native tongue was Polish, yet he is widely considered to be one of the supreme masters of the English language. What was the secret of his achievement? Conrad maintained that precisely because he wrote in a language unfamiliar to him, little slipped his notice. As an outsider Conrad was able to notice aspects of his adopted language that escaped the attention of a native speaker.

Like Conrad, you too will bring a unique point of view and set of experiences to your newly chosen field. These final exercises will help you discover how your background can give you an advantage in the world you have chosen.

Exercise 4: The Perfect Fit

This is an easy exercise. No writing. Simply ask yourself: Why is someone with my talents, from my background, an exceptionally strong candidate for my dream job?

Kate, the would-be fashion designer from a family of philanthropists, answered: "My background has taught me to care about people, not just haute couture and not just making money. That's going to give me an original perspective about comfort, cost, and pride in appearance."

Marnie, the would-be professor from a family of bar owners,

noted: "Many academics forget to ask the obvious questions. They live in a very small world and know nothing about the realities of life I picked up around my father's bar. I can see when the emperor isn't wearing any clothes."

You should take pride in the fresh view that you can bring to a subject; it comes from your roots and it is your birthright.

Exercise 5: Look Again: The Strengths Your Family Gave You

Now that you have some insights about yourself (you're a swan, not a duck) and some tools to take you into a more suitable future, there's one very important final step you must take. You must mine your past for overlooked nuggets of gold.

The time has come for the final exercise, an inventory of the valuable assets your family has bestowed on you. If you do this exercise carefully, you will find invaluable strengths you got *just by being a member of your family*. You must acknowledge these valuables, because you will be taking them into the future with you.

Part A. Write a list of twenty assets you got from your family. Include interests, habits, temperament, physical characteristics, and skills.

Don't stop making your list until you've put down at least twenty assets. Don't stop there if you find you're really rolling. Remember to include assets you got from your grandparents and aunts and uncles and important family friends—they may have put something good in the package too.

Don't forget characteristics you might have been criticized for. For example, the criticism "You're uppity like your aunt Alice; you never do anything anyone tells you to do!" can translate into "I'm independent; I have a mind of my own!" Or you might translate the criticism "You're slower than molasses in January, just like Grandpa" into the praise "I'm focused, careful, precise, just like Grandpa!"

Part B. Think of some connections between what your family does and what you want to do. No matter how different your tribe's values are from yours, there are inevitable connections—they did raise you, after all. Draw any parallels, no matter how artificial they may seem. They will open your eyes to strengths you've overlooked.

Here, for example, are some connections Marnie drew between her parents' lives and her own: "My family always made their own way. Nobody helped them buy their bar. That's why I can walk into a new place and hold my own. And scholarship requires curiosity, which I got from my mother, and the kind of quiet stubbornness I saw in my brother. Even some combativeness—which I got from my father."

After you've done this inheritance exercise, you can expect to start feeling stronger. These assets from your family were always yours, and now you have claimed them. This is your legacy. Now you will remember to be proud of it.

A HAPPY ENDING

Marnie eventually did become a scholar.

First she linked herself to the academic world by auditing philosophy, math, and literature classes at a local university. Whenever she got nervous, she went back and did the great debate exercise until she was calm enough to get back to work. Soon she went back to school and eventually published some of her critical writings in academic journals. She also has regular weekly meetings at her house with a group of people who love language and poetry and thinking. This year they're looking at the Bible as literature. They meet and often talk late into the night. For Marnie, it's pure heaven.

P.S. Your family might come around.

Sometimes, after a long while, family members come to see things from your point of view.

Very frequently, once you begin to succeed in your chosen career your family gets so proud, they actually brag about you. They say, "Oh, my son is in a feature film," not remembering they had a fit when you said you wanted to be an actor.

Other families simply never come around. I know people who are very successful, respected and admired by all their peers, but when they go home, their families start pressuring them to change and do the "right thing." How do they protect themselves? One man I know, a theatrical agent from a banking family, just smiles affectionately and remembers that he loves his family and it doesn't matter what they say. Others simply lay down the law: "We disagree. Now, pass the mashed potatoes and let's change the subject."

But most families do come around once they see that you were really onto something and can make a good life for yourself with your own vision.

Probably their pride in you is greater than their need to be right.

Even Marnie's dad came around.

He loves to say, "She's pretty damned smart for a woman."

NINE

Help! I'm Not Ready to Be Born Yet

YOU'VE just graduated from high school or college or you've just finished a training program. Your "real" life awaits you. Today is the first day of the rest of your life. *How come you don't feel so good?*

"I'm too young to die," Ella, twenty-five, told me. And what terrible fate was awaiting her? A job at one of the top law firms in America, that's what. Ella didn't feel too young to die, she felt too young to be *born.*

Somewhere along the way we fall into thinking that school gets us ready for life. Only as we put on our caps and gowns does it dawn on us that we're entering a totally new world.

Anthony, twenty-three, was fresh out of journalism grad school. No newspaper or magazine starter jobs were around that could put a dent in his $30,000 worth of college loans. He would be even more strapped for time and cash as a professional writer than he'd been as a graduate student. When I asked him what he thought he'd do, he said, "I'm considering going back to grad school and taking out more loans."

We all admit it's nearly impossible to go from being a middle-aged homemaker to being a scientist. Why do we pretend it's natural and easy to leave college and start to work? Like that middle-aged homemaker, you're not just moving to the next stage, and don't let anybody fool you—*you're making a radical career change!*

Yes, a career change. Think about it for a moment. You're a trained and experienced student. You've been at the job since you were five years old. You can read academic lingo, do research, take notes, take exams, and write papers. You understand the rules: If you study well you will get good marks. If you study badly you will flunk. At this game you are a pro.

Now take a look at the work world you've just stepped into. Here your success depends on outside forces. Will "they" hire you or reject you? Will "they" give you interesting work or stick you in a backwater? Will your community respect the field you're in? Will your family be proud of you?

Martin never had to please anyone to get A's in school. He just had to do his work. Now he's got to make his supervisor like him or his job's in danger: "At school it didn't make any difference if you looked lousy," he said. "If you knew how to study, you made the grade."

It's hard to believe that school was a temporary experience that you'll never repeat. After all, it's been your whole life. So forgive yourself for being disoriented because *you're having nothing less than culture shock.*

CULTURE SHOCK—HOW TO HANDLE IT

When you leave school and enter the workplace, you might as well be moving from the U.S. to Istanbul. The lifestyle looks all wrong: "You're supposed to work all day, all year, just to pay the rent? That's what you call living? I want out!"

But stop and think for a moment. You're looking at this world of work as only a foreigner can. You can't understand what's really going on in any new country until you live there for a while. This particular foreign visit happens to be one of the most

Help! I'm Not Ready to Be Born Yet

171

important visits you'll ever make, because until you've researched the workplace there's no way to decide what you want from your life. That's why I'm going to make a plea that you try to get a job in one of those big buildings downtown.

I speak from the heart. I'm not a corporate person. In fact, my whole personality requires small, home-based businesses. But I've never been sorry I spent time in big corporations before I decided to work at home. It's impossible to make an informed choice about your own lifestyle until you've visited the corporate culture. *As far as I'm concerned, that puts it first on your agenda.*

I consider this your last year of schooling, because you have some basic skills to learn: how to get up early five days a week, how to pace yourself in an eight-hour day, how to dress like the natives, how to speak the local language. You need to meet people you'd never meet any other way. And you need the self-confidence that comes from learning the ropes, earning your own money, and surviving in this foreign land. You've got to know what you're capable of in this new system even if you ultimately decide to be a beach bum! Think for a moment of the difference between a beach bum *with* earning capacity, and one without. The first beach bum can choose to get out. The second beach bum stays right where he is.

Wait a minute. Am I suggesting a trial marriage? Don't you have to find the "right job"? Yes, I'm suggesting a trial marriage. No, you don't have to find the right job—at least, not yet. I'll show you exactly what I mean in a moment. But first, you have a few things to get off your chest.

Exercise 1: Coming to the New Land—"What I Think of the World of Work"

Divide a sheet of paper in half. On the top left, place a plus mark. On the top right, place a minus. Now start filling in all the good and bad things you expect to happen when you enter the workplace. On the left you might put "make my own money," and on the right you might put "pay my own rent."

Now, let's take a look at that list.

Jane, a recent graduate in sociology, wrote on the plus side: "Look like I have a job when I walk on the street, my family calming down because I got a job."

On the minus side: "Never get hired, get hired but won't be able to do the work, will be unimportant and bored, will be stuck there until I'm an old lady!"

That minus list is a little longer than the plus list, isn't it? Let's take a look at Jane's negatives. They boil down to two: either they won't want her, or they *will* and she'll be trapped! I've talked to a lot of people in her position, and Jane is not at all unusual.

Hillary, twenty-two, went on some interviews and felt they were a disaster. Some of the places just weren't interested in her at all, which felt terrible. Then one place offered her a job and took her on a tour of the offices. "When I looked up and down those halls I felt like I would be entering a prison and I'd be lost forever," she said.

Philip, twenty-four, who had taken off two years to travel, returned and went on only one interview. "That was it!" he said. "Just wearing that damned suit made me feel bad. Worrying, grinning, *begging*—that made me nuts. I didn't want the damned job, but I tried to get it anyway, and then *they didn't want me!*"

Since there's no way around interviews, I'd like to give you some tools to help you deal with those inevitable rejections.

REJECTION

I know the usual pep talk after an interview rejection. "There, there. That's the way it goes. You've got to brush it off and try again." I hated that advice. I knew I was supposed to keep trying, but every rejection eroded more of my self-worth.

Rejection is no fun for anybody, but I'm convinced it's more

Help! I'm Not Ready to Be Born Yet

173

devastating when you're fresh out of school. Why? Because you don't know who you are yet.

Think of it: at your first job interviews, *they* don't know you—and neither do *you.* Will you be an asset to them? Who can say? Businesses try to protect themselves by interviewing many more people than they need, so rejection is an inevitable part of getting into this new culture. You need two allies in your corner to minimize its effects on you: 1) your identity, and 2) your buddies.

First, let's reestablish who you are.

RECOVERING YOUR IDENTITY

Let's start with the past. You had an identity when you were two years old, and if you don't believe me, ask your parents. You saw the world in a unique way, you had a complete set of feelings and exercised them.

At two you weren't even really interested in being good yet. You were trying out the word "no" just in case the adults didn't understand that you were a separate entity who demanded a vote.

Entering kindergarten might have been a shock, but the people in charge knew it was their job to deal with you. The tables and chairs were small, teachers reminded you to go to the bathroom, and they taught you the alphabet instead of James Joyce.

All that consideration for your needs has just ended. For one of the first times in your life, you are walking into an arena that was not designed in any way to accommodate you. You may feel very small in the work world, but the chairs are full size, and you're expected to adapt as soon as possible. Your identity as "child," or "student," has just taken a wicked beating.

Also, your friends and relatives are poised to slap one of two new identities on you: winner or loser.

"My Ella is working for the best law firm in New York. She started at eighty thousand dollars a year!" (Translated: Ella is a winner.)

"My Johnny hasn't quite found himself yet." (Translated: Johnny is a loser.)

Never have you needed perspective more. I want to show you, now, when it least feels true, that *you are bigger than any job you'll ever have.* You need to know this when no interview turns into a job, and you need to know it when you get hired.

The real you is still there, but these challenges to your ego have clouded your sense of yourself. *What you need is an identity recovery project.*

You need to remember it's your life.

I'd like you to back up and take an aerial view of your entire life—past, present, and future. It's going to show you a few things you haven't thought of before.

Exercise 2: Do a Ninety-five-year Plan

Ninety-five years? That's right. You have to start at the beginning of your life and treat all your past years as though you had planned them deliberately: age one—got born, age five—started school, age ten—moved to California. Carry it right up to the present, *and past the present into the future:* age fifty-seven—went to the Antarctic, age sixty-five—grew orchids and wrote the great American novel, age eighty-five—remarried. And you can't stop until you've covered ninety-five years!

Use some accounting ledger sheets for this, or turn a few sheets of paper sideways. Divide them into four columns. Name the first column "Age," and under it write the numbers: 5, 10, 15, 20, etc., right up to 95. (Skip some lines, because you may want to break it down into smaller increments.)

At the top of the second column write "Major Event." That means getting born, starting school, moving, whatever happened —or might happen in the future—that seems important to you. It's a stretch to imagine what major event could occur twenty, thirty,

Help! I'm Not Ready to Be Born Yet

175

fifty years from now, but give this column some effort. You're building the grid that the other two columns will depend upon.

The third column starts getting tough, but interesting: head that column with "What I learned," and write the most important thing you learned or expect to learn at each age. Don't hurry it. This part of the exercise can be a powerful experience.

Now, at the top of the fourth column write: "The most amazing thing I saw." You might not remember the past perfectly, but trust your impulses, they'll be close enough. You'll really have to let your imagination fly when you take this topic into the future, but do it. It's worth it.

Finally, when you've finished the whole exercise, write at the bottom of the last page: "What I would like to tell young people," and proceed to write what this imaginary walk through ninety-five years has taught you about the meaning of life.

Here's what some other people discovered:

Hillary, twenty-two: The thing that knocked me out was remembering what a funny, tough, insightful little kid I was. I used to try to train all the neighborhood dogs to sit up and roll over, when I was four! I don't think I really had any luck, but at the time I thought I was doing great! What a neat little kid! Remembering that made me invent a very adventurous future. I wouldn't have done that before.

Philip, twenty-four: I put in "world famous superb painter," at the age of thirty. Then I found what I want even more than painting! I want to learn to really *see.* I remembered that the only reason I want to paint is because of how it helps me to really see. By the time I was sixty I looked at my life and went back to age thirty and put in things that have nothing to do with painting. I want to live in other countries. I want to know how to build a house. And I want to have my own family, and to love them.

Adele, twenty-nine: The first shock was that I have plenty of time. Too much time. At sixty-five I couldn't think of anything else to do! I wanted to tell young people to quit worrying so much, and quit hurrying so much too.

Jane, twenty-three: Thinking I had ninety-five years made me a lot calmer, because I have so much I want to do: have my own business someday, and then sell the business and travel. And I want to do something that changes the world too, to help ecology and to help people. Now I don't feel I have to choose *between* things. I'll just do them all.

What about you? What did you find out? It's rather important, because you've just given the job description for your whole life.

And that's the point I hope you got: *You've only got one real job you'll ever do, and that job is to live your whole life.* See how full it will be of events, decisions, locations, experiences, projects? Getting turned down at a few interviews doesn't look quite so important anymore, does it? Even rejection is a part of all the things you have to learn.

But you still have to put on your jacket and go out for another interview, and you're going to need more than perspective today.

You need support.

FIRST AID FOR INTERVIEWS

If interviewing is too painful you're going to start avoiding it, so let me give you my favorite invention, the Success Team, which is also discussed in Chapter 10, "Regrouping." A Success Team is a group of five or six people who meet every week and help each other get whatever they need. It's surefire medicine for the miseries of job hunting. Here are the essentials.

Get a buddy—or get six of them.

Companionship is essential whenever you have to do anything difficult. It lowers anxiety, plain and simple. But it's especially useful in a job hunt. Think about it. After an interview, no matter what happened, you will leave the building, go out on the streets, and stand there.

How would you feel right then if a bunch of your best friends ran up, threw their arms around your shoulders, and said, "Come on, let's go get coffee. What happened?" and then praised your

Help! I'm Not Ready to Be Born Yet

177

efforts, sympathized with your mistakes, cursed your enemies. Interviews are tough and you deserve some sympathy, a beer, and a few laughs when you're done.

How do you get that contact? Call your friends and *arrange* it.

Teams are great for everything. You can meet to rehearse upcoming interviews, even read the want ads together. Résumés aren't as hard to create when a friend is asking you questions and doing the typing for you.

One note: A Success Team/buddy system is not the same as a self-improvement group. Self-improvement groups can be an enjoyable and useful addition to all the work you're doing right now. But if you're wobbling between jumping into the world of work and hanging back, self-improvement can be a stalling tactic. Just getting into the real world will improve you by banishing unreasonable fears and making you exercise your skills. Remember, becoming a better person is a lifetime job, so don't wait until you're finished to get down to the business of living.

ACCEPTANCE

Now that we've looked at how to manage rejection, here's the other big problem. What if they accept me—and it's the wrong job, and I'm trapped for life? Why, in a country where you're allowed to change jobs as often as you choose, would anyone be afraid of being trapped for life? I asked around and got the answer from my own kids and their friends:

"We're under terrific pressure to find something right away, and stick with it. You can't just bounce around. You've got to get the right job the first time."

Is that what you think too?

Guess what? You're completely wrong.

You don't have to get it right the first time.

I happen to think it's almost a shame if you *do* get it right the first time. Take a look at that ninety-five-year plan. Even if you don't actually live the whole ninety-five years, you've got lots of time. So why limit your experience this early? I personally think everybody should do a stint in a factory. And then work overseas. And I think everyone should study acting—especially if they ultimately want to be involved with business. I think acting classes can teach you as much about who you are and how to work with other people as psychotherapy and management training programs.

You already know I think everyone should work in a big corporation, even if they have to work in the mailroom. What an opportunity to poke your nose into all the departments and see what they're doing! You'll be amazed with what you'll find. Big businesses have managers, researchers, accountants, product developers, graphic artists, salespeople, electricians and janitors, executives, and temps—and unique cultures.

I hope you get a chance to do it *all*: work in factories and corporations, take acting classes, and work overseas.

Think about it. You're not expected to marry the first person you go out with, so don't let anyone tell you that you have to marry the first job. If your first choice has to be right, no wonder you feel paralyzed! Your school may love to have winner alumni, and your parents may want you successful and independent, and you want to please everyone. But you can't.

The business world today is very different from the one your parents knew. They may be measuring you against a standard from a different economic era, and if you try to live up to their expectations you'll suffer impossible pressures.

The truth is, you're going to have to be a pioneer and move around the business world in a brand new way, getting familiar with a different reality than they ever thought of. *But you're not in any danger.* Reality won't hurt you. On the contrary, it's going to save you.

Help! I'm Not Ready to Be Born Yet

179

THE REALITY SOLUTION

Imaginary obstacles are insurmountable. Real ones aren't. But you can't tell the difference when you have no real information. Fear can create even more imaginary obstacles than ignorance can. *That's why the smallest step away from speculation and into reality can be an absolutely amazing relief.*

Take a small astonishing step—like George did.

George wanted to marry and have children and he wanted to meet the right woman. But his imaginary obstacles made this seem impossible. He was working hard as a computer consultant and didn't have much money. He thought no woman would bother with him until he had enough money to redecorate his apartment, buy a car, and take her to good restaurants.

I asked George when he expected to have all those things lined up; he said he didn't know.

"By October?"

"Oh, no, never by October."

"Maybe in ten or fifteen years?" I said.

George looked horrified.

The truth was, George just had no experience with women and he was scared. We decided to try the Reality Solution.

The Reality Solution means: *Do it before you're ready.* In George's case, it meant: Get into the company of women as soon as possible, before you have any of the things you think you need. (In your case, simply replace the word "women" with the word "jobs" and you'll see why I used this example.)

For George, the answer was to join a church singles group.

He was amazed.

After a few months he said, "There are all kinds of women in that group! And I'm crazy about all of them. I mean, I'm crazy about the fact that there are that many kinds of women!"

"What about the car?" I asked.

"They *all* have cars. They don't mind driving *me*!"

"What do they think of you?"

He smiled. "Some of them really like me a lot."

Taking a small astonishing step means doing something real, *and that can turn your world around.* The moment you engage yourself in a real situation, it blows the fantasy obstacles away.

I don't mean there are no obstacles. To entertain at home, George had to learn how to cook (which he did, and wonderfully), and he learned how to dance too. Then he decided to learn how to drive, even if he never owned a car, because "a driver is a contribution to a group when you go on a ski trip." Where did he get the money to take courses to learn those things? He didn't.

His new friends, many of them women, taught him.

Real obstacles don't take you in circles. They can be overcome. Invented ones are like a maze. That's why you just can't sit around waiting for the information that will finally get you into action. Most of the time, that information can only be gotten by taking small, vital steps into reality.

In this chapter I'm going to give you a group of exercises that will help you get real about work the way George got real about women. I expect to run into some resistance with you. Most people think they have to be more prepared than George, even to take a small step. Don't worry. It's not hard to handle this kind of resistance. It's just necessary to know what's behind it.

And I do.

REALITY IS SCARY

Doing is a quantum leap from *imagining.* Thinking about swimming isn't much like actually getting into the water. Actually getting into the water can take your breath away. The defense force inside us wants us to be cautious, to stay away from anything as intense as a new kind of action. Its job is to protect us,

Help! I'm Not Ready to Be Born Yet

181

and it categorically avoids anything resembling danger. But it's often wrong.

Anything worth doing is worth doing *too soon.* (Just don't risk big things you might need later, like special contacts or money—or your life.) As soon as you realize that the hidden cause of your resistance is *only fear,* movement becomes much easier. This is one place where reason helps you out. As soon as you understand why you're stalling, you can see how limited the real danger is. Then you'll be ready to get moving.

But fear can come in many disguises, all of them stalling tactics. Sometimes people who would rather dream than act justify it by an elaborate process of thinking it through first.

Janet, a young woman who had just finished a hotshot training program, told me she wanted to start a not-for-profit business ethics institute. She wanted to start out as a consultant. "But no one will hire me. I have no experience, no background. People don't even *want* ethics consultants!"

I don't know what an ethics institute is, but I'm prepared to believe that there is or could be one. The important issue was: Did *Janet* know what it was, and would she really like doing it, and could she deliver?

There's simply no way to get answers to those questions by sitting alone in a dark room thinking about it. You have to use the Reality Solution.

I told Janet to get a group of friends together and toss around some ideas on "honor" and "business." Just for starters.

Janet resisted. "Oh, I'm not nearly ready to do anything like that. It's much too soon to actually get a group together, even of friends. I'd have to do a lot more thinking."

"What do you want to think about?" I asked.

"Well, I'd like to have everything be more ready, before I actually get started. It's too, fluffy, you know."

"How do you plan to get ready?"

"Oh, walk around, think it out thoroughly. Spend some time at the drawing board."

"You don't know what you want to draw, yet," I said. "Get some friends together. Order a pizza. Talk about it."

"But I wouldn't exactly know what to say. I have more feelings about it than information."

"Then go to the library. Get information."

"I can't until I know what I'm looking for."

"Well," I said, "you have just proven that it's impossible to get started."

I had her on logic and she knew it.

"I guess I'm dodging. But I really want to do it. Why am I dodging?" she asked.

"What are you feeling?" I said.

"Nervous. Scared."

"What are you scared of?" I asked.

"Just actually doing it," Janet said, thoughtfully. "So I guess I'd better do it."

Here's what Janet did.

Although she felt a bit overwhelmed by the plan, Janet decided to at least do the first step, and she put together a group of friends to talk about ethics in the business place.

Twenty minutes into the evening, her friends had asked a hundred questions, and she was busy explaining.

"What are business ethics, anyway?"

"Does anybody care? I mean, can you get a job in that?"

"Did you invent this?"

Because she was concerned about flying blind in this group, Janet had looked up every article she could find on business ethics and found herself better informed than she thought. She also found herself voicing some passionate opinions.

"Without ethics, business doesn't even work!" she insisted.

Her friends started agreeing with her.

"You know, my father was a decent businessman and there was no place for him in the world," one friend said.

"I saw something in a magazine about how these CEOs are now talking about all of this, scrambling around to keep from

Help! I'm Not Ready to Be Born Yet

183

sinking. As a matter of fact someone donated a chunk of money to Harvard, I think it was, just to give classes in business ethics."

"Well, who's going to invest in stocks anymore, until they trust Wall Street again? I'm not."

"Why don't you design some seminars for corporations, Janet?"

"Why don't you first write an article for a business journal to give yourself some credibility?"

And Janet began her new career.

I'm so convinced that everyone should get started before they're ready that I'd like to suggest you take the *wrong job.* Before you decide I've lost my mind, try out this next exercise.

Exercise 3: Try on the Wrong Job—the Fantasy

Pretend you've decided to take a job. Any job. Place the help-wanted ads, or the yellow pages, or a career directory from the library on the table, close your eyes, turn the pages, and let your finger land anywhere. Whatever career lies under your finger, that's what you're going to do.

Computer sales and supplies, limousine service, chef, or tugboat crew.

I hope your finger landed on a job you know very little about. If it didn't, close your eyes and try again. Pig farmer, electronic engineer, anything. The best job for this exercise is any job you don't know much about. You want a job that would make a decent living, that's not illegal, and *that doesn't fit you at all.* Once you've made your choice, follow the next four steps.

The first step is: Imagine that you've decided to do the best work you can, although it's totally the wrong job for you. Walk through this job, and describe (on paper or aloud to a friend) what the place is like and what you're doing.

Here's how Barb, a graduate in English literature from Yale and the eldest of five, with a habit of teaching, responded to her "wrong job" as floor supervisor at the John Deere tractor factory. "I'm wearing overalls, walking around with a stopwatch and date sheets, watching for the steel delivery, making sure that everything's running, seeing who's sick, getting machines rolling."

Now *the second step is* to ask yourself a question: "What is it like on this job? How does it feel?" Barb thought her job was "Okay. Sort of interesting. But I'm allowed to go home at five, right? And never come back?"

No, you can't leave just yet—not in this exercise!

Because *the third step is:* Imagine you've been on the job for three months. Now ask yourself: What's the job like after three months? How does it feel?

Barb didn't like it so much anymore. "It's stupid for me to be here. I'll never get anywhere. What am I going to do in a tractor factory?"

Now comes *step four,* the "squeeze." The point of the game is, you can't leave this job until you turn it into something wonderful. That's the only door out. If you can't make it wonderful, you're there forever. That made Barb more imaginative.

"The only thing I can think of is that I'd just try to do it really really well. That will at least keep it interesting. And I'll feel better." She was beginning to see that one thing that defined her was pleasure in mastering new things. That was a good beginning.

But you need an even greater sense of yourself, so I want you to make the exercise even tougher. Imagine you've been on the job *six months,* and you're getting bored. Now what? Barb said, "Well, if I was going to be there that long, and I had to make it wonderful, I think I'd try to get promoted. But I wouldn't want to be separated from the people on the floor. I'd like to be communicating with them, but not checking up on them. I'd like to create an environment where everybody felt looked out for and it made them feel proud of where they worked. Wow! Look at that. *My tastes are showing themselves!*"

Barb would never have discovered how strongly her own values would exert themselves, even in a tractor factory, if I'd simply said "What do you think is the right job for you?"

Help! I'm Not Ready to Be Born Yet

185

So what's your solution? If you were in the wrong job and had to turn it into something wonderful, what would you do?

What did you learn about yourself?

Ruth, twenty-three: I picked a job as a management trainee in a large corporation. I can't think of anything I'd like less. But when I had to make it wonderful, I found myself starting an employee newsletter. A really good one! And then turning it into a magazine. I really liked being on the phone pulling the whole thing together and interviewing people.

Candace, twenty: I decided to be a cook in a lumber camp. This is a very bad fit, I want you to know. But within six months I'd opened a crafts shop with wood carvings done by the lumberjacks in conjunction with the local Native Americans. I had them all pulling together, starting a cottage industry, and bringing money into the town. And I was busy turning it into a mail order item. It was really fun. I was the boss!

Do you see how you can find yourself, even in the wrong job? When you're afraid to take anything but the "right" job, you can get paralyzed and take no job at all. I want you to stop being afraid that your first job will determine the rest of your life, because it won't do anything of the sort.

But I don't blame you for thinking that you could be set in a direction that isn't right for you. After all, whenever you enter a new world, that world seems strong and you feel very weak. Who wouldn't? Everyone else has been there longer and knows how to do the job. You are ignorant by definition. *But never confuse ignorance with wrongness, or weakness.* Remember that to yourself, you are and always will be *the strongest element in your environment.* That's why any job, right or wrong, will teach you important lessons about yourself. The truth is that personal development is the real reason you should be working in the first place.

You're already working for a company, and that company is you.

If you can keep that in mind, you'll have the problem beaten.

You are the company, you are the president and CEO. You sell your services, *not yourself.* Every time you get a job, it's like a contract. And every time you learn something, that's your inventory.

You can trust your future if you trust yourself. What does that mean? *You have to trust yourself to know when something's not right for you, and leave it.*

That's how really ambitious people have always done it. They stay at a job as long as it does them good, and when it stops doing them good they look for something else. Until that time, they make sure to do everything as well as they can, and to make every boss wish they wouldn't leave. In every situation, good or bad, they just keep learning.

That's what I want you to do. Not only will it be good for your self-confidence, self-esteem, and durability in the workplace, but it's the wave of the future. More people are becoming free-lancers, carrying their expertise with them as they go from job to job. It used to be that only professionals had résumés; now welders need résumés also. All of us will be gathering expertise and carrying it from job to job, like a bag of tools.

They haven't created the job yet that you couldn't benefit from doing for six months, not if you're a knowledge bandit.

That's why I'm going to make a really outrageous suggestion: Go out and really get the wrong job.

Exercise 4: Getting the Wrong Job—the Fact

Ignore this exercise if you know what the right job is, and you want to try for it. But if you're feeling stuck because you don't know what to do, try this out. It looks radical, but it ends the impasse, because you don't have to figure out what to do at all!

Get the newspapers from ten cities around the country and look through the want ads. Answer anything you think you can get. Just for the hell of it. (It can be a very good idea to live in a couple of places before you settle down. On the other hand, you

Help! I'm Not Ready to Be Born Yet

187

might fall in love and decide to stay, so pick a climate you can stand!)

And if someone wants to hire you, take the job. Yes, that's what I said. Take the wrong job, or at least the job you're not sure is right. School isn't finished yet. Your first few jobs are the real graduate school.

Try out a few jobs if you have nothing better on your agenda. *And remember what each day is for*—not to make your boss happy, not to impress your school chums, but to get knowledge and skills for yourself.

And if your family says, "What on earth are you doing?" Well, it's just another great time to practice autonomy. Just pat them on the head and tell them not to worry, that everything leads somewhere, and experience is good for you. And it's true. Any job is good for you *as long as you remember what you're doing there.*

WHAT YOU SHOULD BE DOING AT THE WRONG JOB

1. Plan your getting-out party.

The first thing you have to do is set a date for leaving and plan a party. Call it your "Getting-Out Party," and invite all your friends (except the ones you've met at your job). Your party date should be about six months from the time you start the wrong job. On that date you're going to either quit this job, or give your friends a good reason why you're not quitting. If you're not quitting, you have to set the date for another Getting-Out Party, six months later.

Planning your party solves two problems. One, you won't feel trapped in the wrong job if you understand that you actually have a cutoff date. Two, your friends won't let you come up with excuses forever, and you'll be ashamed after the third party, so you'll be protected from what I call "job drift."

Job drift: It's a dread disease, and I don't want you to get it. Job drift has happened when someone says, "I just took this job temporarily, but nothing better ever came up. And fourteen years passed!"

What's wrong with that picture? Aside from the horror of the speaker, she made one huge error. She was waiting for something better to come along. If you're looking for varied experience, *anything is better than something you already know*. She should have left her job as soon as it got repetitive.

I know that's not you. You haven't gotten that far yet. I just want you to know that the kinds of problems you run into may not be what you expect. I recently heard a woman say, "I love my job. Great work, great people. But if I could get some interest in this invention I developed, I'd leave. I mean, I've been there a long time, and it's time to move on. But I'd hate to leave. I love that job."

I bet it has not occurred to you that loving your job could be one of the problems. There's a lot ahead that you don't expect.

And a lot of what you do expect *isn't* ahead.

2. Work for yourself.

Wrong jobs can be wonderful as long as you don't forget why you're there. Among other things, that means you learn the business for yourself, not your boss.

You're not there to win hearts or pass tests. You only maintain true independence when you have *your own* tests to pass, not someone else's. It's important to remember that you only have a limited time at this job and you intend to get the most out of it. Make a commitment to learn as much as you can, and don't waste your time. Remember, when you gather knowledge, you gather inventory.

And when you do a great job, you gather referrals.

Don't think the bosses won't spot you. They usually admire ambitious people. As a matter of fact, the biggest pitfall of this plan is that they might try to keep you, even promote you. Promotion is only all right if you'll get the opportunity to learn another job. If it's just more of the same, stick to your guns and get out of

Help! I'm Not Ready to Be Born Yet

189

there. Remember, you're autonomous. You don't belong to any-body but yourself.

Autonomy.

What is it, anyway? Well, if you're not autonomous, here's how you think: The boss (is) (isn't) going to like this report; my family (approves) (doesn't approve) of this job; I can't stand being made to do things that don't interest me.

If you are autonomous, you think things like: *I* (like) (don't like) how well I did this report; if my family doesn't like this job that's *their* problem; *everything* I don't already know interests me.

Of course, if the boss gives you a hard time, you can't help going into a wobble. Just slip outside and go for a walk and let it blow over. *You don't want to get too absorbed by hurt or injustice because you'll forget your autonomy.* After all, you're at this job for your own reasons, you have your own plan. You're here to gather knowledge, because knowledge belongs to you and no one can ever take it away.

Practice autonomy.

Keep a notebook. Call it "Autonomy Notes." On the inside front cover, where you won't forget it, write the date of your Getting-Out Party. Keep a list right there of all the people you plan to invite. Put a check after their names each time you remind them not to miss the party.

On the left-hand pages write down things you felt and did that were *not* autonomous: "I got hurt when the boss didn't appreciate my work," or "I got resentful and deliberately dragged my heels on the filing job." On all the right-hand pages, collect thoughts that will help you remember what autonomy is, like "Knowledge belongs to me," "My life is bigger than any job," and so on. (Try looking up quotes in a book of aphorisms from your local book-store.)

Now, each time you write about a nonautonomous feeling on the left-hand page, search for an encouraging thought that com-plements it for the right-hand side. For example, on the left you might say, "I let my uncle Joe make me feel stupid." And on the right you could put "It's passive to let someone else define you. It's active to not listen to uncles."

Autonomy means you're in business for yourself, no matter who you're working for. Always remember, if you have a slave mentality you'll be defeated every time—*even if you're the favorite slave.* You always have to be your own boss, no matter who you're working for, no matter how happy they are with your work. That doesn't mean you don't do what the boss wants. It means you do what they want *for yourself* because you want to learn it well. And you do more.

More? Yes, I mean that absolutely.

If you're a gifted runner and you have a good coach, you listen to that coach with respect. Not because he's the boss, but because *you* are. Think about it. If you're a gifted runner you aren't trying to get an A in gym. You want to be really good. After all, the coach won't win any medals. You will.

That's why the stupidest thing you can ever do is be resentful.
Resentment is weak and lowers your self-esteem.

It's the most common pitfall of all. You find yourself thinking "I don't want to be involved in this work because I resent it. I'm just going to do the least I can to get by."

That's a complete waste of your valuable time. And it means you're locked into an intimate battle with somebody or some task you don't even like. Remember, this is a foreign country, and you're just visiting. Travel is broadening. Don't let a bad moment ruin your trip.

But suppose they keep giving you the same horrible work, because you listened to my advice and did such a great job of it? They probably will do exactly that. And you'll have to tell them, "I'd be happy to teach someone else how to do this project, but I'd like to keep learning new things. Can you give me something else?" And if they say no, you say good-bye.

Sounds arrogant? Listen, companies know they can't keep good people if they can't challenge them. You're just reminding them of something they shouldn't have forgotten in the first place.

Have you ever heard the expression "taking the bit in your

Help! I'm Not Ready to Be Born Yet

191

teeth"? That's when a horse, tired of being controlled by the rider, takes the metal mouthpiece at the end of the reins into its teeth— and runs twice as fast as the rider wants, in the exact direction they were going. That's what you're going to do. It means you *never* resent a job. You just get totally into it. And *then* if it doesn't improve, you get out of it.

3. *Become a business reporter for* **The Wall Street Journal.**

To keep yourself from forgetting why you're at this "wrong job," turn into an amateur business reporter. That is, learn everything about the entire industry you're temporarily a part of, and the place of this company in it. It will help you develop a valuable attentiveness and give you an excellent education no school can match. What will you do with this information? Don't worry. Information is like money. Sooner or later you'll find a use for it.

4. *Write a novel.*

Sometimes the workplace is so unpleasant to you that you can't stop watching the clock all day. That's a bad way to spend your precious time. In this situation you've got two choices: *You can suffer or you can create.*

Until it's time for you to leave this job, get creative. You'll entertain yourself and learn while you do it.

Start gathering notes for a novel or a movie. Capture what people say, how they look and act, how they treat each other. You don't need a plot yet, just catch fragments, moments, impressions.

This is not only a great distancing technique, it's a wonderful cathartic; you can dump all your frustration by keeping notes on everything stupid or unfair that people do. You'll find yourself actually delighting in dreadful confrontations or overheard remarks. You'll start noticing how the line of command is subtly enforced, or how the top people play politics. And you might even write a novel or make a film someday.

Alan was a very unhappy young lawyer who had to stay in his new firm for at least one year. In desperation he gave novel-writing a try, and discovered that his boredom disappeared. "The tedious talk turned into dialogue." He grinned. "I started looking at the building entrance in the morning, and noticed a kind of yellow marble around thick glass doors, and then I found myself writing about how it looked to me: like the gates of hell. I started writing a pretty good story!"

Let me sum up what you should be doing while you're at the wrong job: 1) Plan your Getting-Out Party, 2) work for yourself, 3) become a business reporter for *The Wall Street Journal,* 4) write a novel or screenplay, and 5) remember to keep writing in your autonomy notebook.

If you will do these five things with some consistency, you'll find your time at any wrong job will be more valuable than you ever believed possible.

That's a promise.

What do you do after you leave the "wrong job"? Well, you've learned a lot more about what you like and what you don't than you learned in school. And you've met a lot of new people, and you've developed a reputation for being a valuable player. You may know exactly what you want now, and who to talk to.

And if you don't? Well, take another "wrong job" in another field that looks interesting and start again. You may wind up with a strange-looking résumé, but it will show the range of your interests and abilities. Don't let anyone make you uncomfortable about the changes you've made. Just say "there's always more to learn. I change jobs so I can keep improving my skills."

Times have changed. The era of cradle-to-grave jobs in corporations is over. Most people will change jobs *and* fields several times over their working lifetimes. Your strange résumé may not look strange, after all.

Meanwhile, one nice surprise about wrong jobs is that some of them can turn out to be the right job. If you keep moving toward activities at work that look interesting, and if the boss lets

Help! I'm Not Ready to Be Born Yet

193

you learn new things, you could find a niche that's just perfect for you.

Just realize that it's really okay that you don't know what you want yet. It's not only all right, it's probably a very good thing. Because I firmly believe you can pick a goal too soon, before you know enough about yourself or the world.

A word about goal setting:

We're so goal-happy in this culture that we try to set goals even if we don't have any information. But if it's too hard for you to work the way I'm advising, without direction, if you really feel you need a goal, there's something you can do, even without information—*set a working goal.*

A "working goal" is a goal that will probably be changed. It's like the "working title" of a movie or book or song. You name your work-in-progress something that's not exactly right just so you can write the thing, and when it's finished you change the name. Well, that works with careers too. Just set your goal—manager, manufacturer's rep, clothing designer—and create a plan to get there. (You might as well pick something that's seems appealing, because you're going to find out a lot about it.) Then follow that plan until you discover something more interesting. I know a couple who started out to study musicology, met some African musicians, and by some convoluted steps, wound up teaching English in Mozambique—and loving it.

That's the best thing about goals—they push you into action. *And that's when happy accidents occur.*

It is also possible to set a direction without goals or plans at all.

How?

Just follow your nose.

Just keep yourself moving *toward* anything that interests you, and *away* from anything dull—even if you don't know why! Like a plant bending its head toward the sun, you'll ultimately find yourself growing toward what you love. You like animals? Find a way to work with them on any level, and remember to do the five "wrong job" steps mentioned above. You could wind up in Hawaii taking care of gorillas! Some people have.

Your interests are a surefire indicator of your talents. There's no way you can know all the things you're talented at, because you haven't encountered them yet. But if you have respect for your curiosity, you'll discover new talents in every job you have.

What does all this add up to? Life is shoving you faster than you'd like to go, and there's no way you're going to avoid moving, either now or later, so I think you should make it now. If you get lost, just pull out this chapter and read it through again, so you can remember who you are and where you are in the big plan.

What you are doing is bigger than your career. To learn how to live on this earth you can't contemplate your navel, you must be engaged in a serious activity. Work is a way of learning who you are in the world. If your personal journey requires that you develop big muscles, you can do that at work. If you need to get organized, you can learn how at work. Work teaches you when to speak your mind and when to shut your mouth.

There may be times in your life when knowing how to work will save you. It can be a haven in times of doubt and uncertainty; the very kind of time you are going through now.

TEN

Regrouping: It's a Whole New Ball Game

Y ou don't have any idea what you want because your life has just changed completely.

I'll bet it never occurred to you during the years you were putting your life together—family, business, home, finances —that one day you'd have to start all over. Like most of us, you probably expected that once you put in your time and set everything rolling, you could dust off your hands, put up your feet, and rest: your family, business, home, and finances would run on their own momentum.

I don't know where we got *that* idea.

Change is not only likely, it's inevitable.

You get laid off (and your entire industry goes under). Or your kids grow up and leave home (you not only miss them, but you're out of a job). Or you retire (imagining you might be on a vacation for the rest of your life, except now your temperament—or your finances—won't stand for it). Or you're divorced or widowed or your spouse falls seriously ill. Maybe you've suddenly become a single parent—trying to be father and mother, homemaker and sole support of your children, with twice the responsibility and half the resources you're used to.

This was never part of your plan, so like any general in the field, when the unexpected happens and the whole operation changes—*you've got to regroup.*

There are all sorts of situations that require total regrouping. Even unexpected good fortune is a big, unsettling change. My friend Barney got completely perplexed when he received a moderate-size inheritance. The money didn't make him rich, but suddenly he had a wide range of new options. "I don't know what to do or how to proceed!" he said. "Should I just travel like I always wanted to, and spend the money until it's gone? Or keep my job and finally buy a home? Or should I invest and quit work, and live—very modestly—on the interest from the inheritance? If I do *that,* what will I do with all my free time? Maybe I should use the money to start a new business. But what if I fail and wind up back where I started?"

If you think Barney's problem is the kind of problem you wish you had, take another look.

It is your problem.

If your life has suddenly changed, *you too have received an inheritance.* Your gift may look more like a disaster to you now, but think about your situation for a moment. Suddenly, you have been given a wide array of new choices—in effect, *a second life.*

And you now have the dilemma Barney had—you don't have the first idea of how to design your new life.

Lorraine, forty-three: Thinking about myself isn't something I've ever done. I've always worked and helped my family. I've been in the automotive industry since I left school, and now the industry's caved in. I might have to leave this part of the country and do something new, but I'm really uneasy thinking about what *I* want.

Rachel, fifty-five: I'm the housewife type who takes care of the children. That's been my full-time job for thirty years. Now I'm ready to do something that I really love but I'm damned if I have any idea what that is. Besides, I'm not trained to do anything. Where do I start?

FEELINGS FIRST

How are you feeling?

You've just been unceremoniously set ashore in a new country. No matter what kind of life (good or bad) you left, a change this big is a shock to the nervous system. At first, the only thing you're able to do is watch with horror as the ship that brought you all this distance turns around and leaves you behind. The loss of a familiar way of life is one of the most difficult losses a person can experience.

It's useless to try to talk yourself out of your dismay, but *you must find a way to avoid getting stuck.* When you're scared or uncertain of the next step, you're in danger of diving into a sense of loss, and although painful feelings are normal at a time like this, finding a way to keep them from overwhelming you is essential. If you know what to do with runaway feelings, your mind will stay cool and clear.

Let me suggest some methods that might help you.

Method 1: If You Always Know What You Are Feeling, but Think It's Not Nice to Complain

Complain anyway.

Whenever I have to go through a big life transition I make it a point to do a lot of whining and complaining, because I'm a lot more scared than I want to admit. So I make myself admit it. Out loud. (Or I write in my special Hard Times notebook.) I go to a private place and allow myself to panic: "If I can't come up with a new life fast, I'll be alone! I'll be on the streets! I'll be broke! I'll go crazy!"

When you're in this mode, all that positive talk you've heard about what a great opportunity you've been given sounds like pure baloney. This doesn't *feel* like a great opportunity, and we're talking feelings right now, not facts.

Method 2: If You Tend to Push Feelings Away

Often you don't know what you're feeling. You may be turned off, or a little tense, and that's all. That means you're someone who is used to handling trouble by holding your feelings down and swinging into action. *But you don't want to ignore feelings just because you know how to control them. If those feelings start to back up, you could be a candidate for panic.* One sure warning sign that it's time to ventilate some feelings is if you notice yourself operating with a short fuse.

To gain access to your feelings you will have to set aside some uninterrupted time to take your emotional pulse. I usually go for a morning walk, since that seems to be when my feelings are most available. If I'm feeling negative, I set aside my stoicism and freely let myself think all the negative thoughts that are floating around in the back of my mind: I think about time and how fast it passes, how everyone I love is getting older, how things didn't turn out as I expected. I use my morning walk to give myself some well-deserved self-pity. And then I go looking for specific feelings.

Going through the list of feelings one at a time—happiness, anger, hurt, and fear—will help you locate yourself emotionally. Think about them and ask yourself: Do I feel happy? Do I feel angry? Do I feel sad? Do I feel fear? Let yourself go and be grateful for any tears or sighs that come, because they're releasing pent-up feelings that need to be expressed or they would cloud your whole view of life.

Remember, *you don't need to be afraid of any feeling.* Feelings are temporary. Expressing them will only do you good. As a matter of fact, once you realize what you're feeling and let out a few "whews" or "ouches," something very nice starts to happen: your feelings start to change. Fear turns from a block of ice in your chest to a light fog, and the next time you look for it, it's gone. Pain lowers its intensity and transforms itself into a soft sadness, a feeling you can live with. Anger often becomes laughter, or just a feeling of calm determination, and, often, many troubled feelings disappear entirely.

When you've opened up all the feelings inside, you can just relax and let them float away. You've done your emotional exercises, and the rest of your day will be better for it.

Of course, if you're in the midst of a very difficult situation you're going to have to touch base with your feelings more often, and sometimes for a longer period of time. For example, if you've had a bout with a serious illness or someone near you has had health or financial problems, you'll need to allow yourself a *lot* of room to feel and express the pain you're experiencing. *But that's why nature made feelings:* to help us process the shocks of life. *When we take in shock, we release it through our feelings.* It's one of nature's gifts to get us through hard times. Repressing feelings isn't healthy and will backfire on you sooner or later. Get the feelings out, and you'll be in good shape to handle the rest of the day.

Method 3: If You Wallow and Sink into Morasses of Bad Feelings

If, after giving them a chance to come out and fly away, the bad feelings won't leave, or if they should show up again when you don't want them, *don't give them a home.* I know a smart eighty-year-old woman who tells her friends when they get too sympathetic, "I only mope on Tuesdays. Change the subject."

Allowing bad feelings to hang around too long can cloud your judgment. When we're depressed, happiness looks stupidly short-sighted. We take the long view, think the long thoughts—looking far into the past and far into the future. We have what I call those "what does it all mean" thoughts. It's hard to remember at those times that your view of reality isn't accurate. No matter how justified this view may seem, particularly if your entire life has been upended, *despair and bitterness are always the result of blurred vision.* While you can't ignore painful feelings, you can limit their time—and their time is up for today. You'll deal with them again tomorrow morning.

Easier said than done? Try out your sense of humor. I think the persistence of big bad feelings caused humans to invent jokes. One of the funniest stories ever written is *Gargantua and Pantagruel,* which the sixteenth-century French satirist and physician François Rabelais wrote to cheer up his sick patients. My son Matthew insists that the Marx Brothers movie *Duck Soup* will cure anything, and, of course, Norman Cousins's medical research appears to confirm this belief. Laughter can shoot you right out of that hole you slipped into.

Prepare each night for a good day tomorrow.

Before you go to sleep, gather your allies around you—in your imagination. This is a Native American practice that can have a powerful effect on your mood the next day. Call up in your memory anyone who is, or ever was, a real friend, and imagine that he or she is watching over you while you sleep. Not only does this establish your sense of being worthy by reminding you of who loves you, but it makes you sleep with a feeling of warmth and safety. And you might wake up free of any painful feelings. You might have to wait for *two* Tuesdays to pass before you need to mope.

CHANGE IS GOOD FOR YOU

After you wave good-bye to your ship by grieving and complaining about your loss, the time comes to *turn around and look at the new land.* You are a total stranger here, but you've faced uncharted territory before and you survived very nicely. A change this radical happened every time you went from being a senior in one school to a freshman in the next. After four years of earning your stripes in high school, you moved on to college or into the work force, and you were a beginner all over again. You've known these feelings of apprehension and uncertainty before. You've been a beginner many times. We all go from most knowledgeable to most ignorant several times in our lives. Now that we're living longer and society is going through a period of rapid change, each generation can expect to make that 180-degree turn more often than the last generation. According to one research firm, 1990 college graduates could expect to hold *ten to twelve jobs in three to five different fields during their working lifetimes!*

Each change is uncomfortable, but it's a part of life and you've already proved you can handle change.

HOW TO FIND YOUR WAY IN THE NEW LAND

First, I'm going to ask you to remember who you are and what you love. You may not have thought about such things for a long time but until you've recovered a sense of your own style, of your innate abilities and talents, you aren't going to be in any position to make good decisions about what to do next.

Figuring out what you really want comes first. Later, you can find out *what's actually out there* for you to do. And with those two pieces of information in hand—what you want and what's available—you'll be in a good position to pick a direction and chart a goal.

And don't waste your time thinking it's too late to go after your dreams. I haven't yet met the person who couldn't do what she wanted if she started now. A friend of mine who just took up ballroom dancing said something simple but profound: You can learn new things at any time in your life *if you're willing to be a beginner.* If you actually learn to *like* being a beginner, the whole world opens up for you.

So, let's start figuring out what you want!

ROUTE No. 1: FOR PEOPLE WHO CAN FANTASIZE

If you can fantasize, it's especially fun and easy to find the keys to what you really want.

Exercise 1: Voyage from Your Easy Chair

I'm not kidding about the easy chair. Get in one. Then get some paper and a pen and get ready to take a quiz. You're going to do some daydreaming. (Be sure to answer the "why" questions.)

1. Who in the world would you like to spend a day with? Why?
2. What famous person would you like to be for a day? Why?
3. What animal would you most like to be for a day? Why?
4. What time and place in history would you like to visit? Why?

Here's how some other people answered these questions:

Rachel, the fifty-five-year-old housewife, said, "I'd like to spend the day with Amelia Earhart. Why? I want to know how she knew she wanted to fly. What famous person would I like to be? Neil Armstrong, the astronaut. I'd like to be the first person to do something no one thought could ever be done.

"The kind of animal I'd like to be? Something adventurous from the jungles, not a cat or dog or anything domesticated. The time and place in history I'd like to visit would be the South Seas, before they were overrun by the rest of the world, when they were still pure, and the people were living in villages and fishing and doing things the way they wanted to."

Hold on to your written responses to this exercise. Believe it or not, your answers are going to take you straight to your goal.

ROUTE No. 2: FOR PEOPLE WHO CAN'T FANTASIZE

A few people in my workshops always raise their hands and say they can't fantasize. They enjoy thinking about some of their leisure-time activities, like fishing or sports, but they really aren't accustomed to fantasy thinking.

Many of these people even resent fantasizing and tell me they're not interested in foolishness, they've got serious things to do. And they're right.

At least, they *were* right.

All their lives, they did what had to be done, and didn't bother daydreaming about alternative lives because they never expected to be free enough to have a choice.

If you're one of these people, you possess two resources that can help you find out what you want to do. The first resource is your memory; the second is your ability to improve on what already exists—without having to imagine things that don't exist.

Let's tap into your memory first.

I'd like you to try to remember some of the things you loved to do at different times in your life.

Exercise 2: What Did You Like to Do at Five, at Ten, at Fifteen, et Cetera?

What pops into your mind that you liked to do at each of those ages? Write that down; don't censor your response.

Here's a typescript of *my* notes from this exercise:

At five, I liked to read picture books and I liked to watch the snow through the window.

At ten, I liked to ride my bike through the fields and sing songs, and read.

At fifteen, I liked to drive around in cars with my friends, and write in my diary.

At twenty, I liked to read and walk on the beach.

At twenty-five, I liked to take the baby for long rides in the car, and write poetry.

At thirty, I liked to go to acting class and pretend I was beautiful and admired and I lived in London.

At thirty-five, I liked to read and write in my journal and be in the country to watch the weather change.

After you've written down what you remember liking at each age, hold on to your chronology. Those early loves of yours may point you in the direction of a bright future.

Now let's utilize your second resource, the ability to improve on something that already exists, to see what information you can find about what you love to do.

Exercise 3: What Do You Like to Do Now?

What do you enjoy most about your present life? Cover *every spare inch of a sheet of paper with everything you can think of that you enjoy.* When you've filled every line with enjoyable things, write in the margins. Include even the little details like "I like a cup of tea and some toast at three o'clock," or "I love finding a lost shoe at the back of the closet when nobody else could find it."

When you've finished you should have a very extensive list of seemingly ordinary things you like to do in your daily life.

Hang on to that list, because you're going to use it in a little while. But right now I'd like to remind you of where we began: You're the person who had no idea what you wanted, remember?

Look how many things you like to do!

Now I'd like you to take a look at everything you *hate* to do—because that's just as important.

Exercise 4: What You Hate to Do

When you begin to design a future for yourself, you must take very seriously the list of things you don't like to do. *You should design the things you don't like right out of your future!*

We can all tolerate a certain amount of discomfort on the way to something we really want, and that's fortunate, since the road to any goal will always have some rough stretches on it. But don't allow things you dislike any permanent place in your goal. Sometimes we're so accustomed to biting the bullet and doing what needs to be done that we forget it's possible to have a life made up of the things we like best. Search your tastes and preferences. If you don't really like to spend much time socializing with your cousins, don't plan to do it. If you don't like keeping books or being a boss—*don't.*

While it can be a good stretch to occasionally try out activities you don't like, *your strongest talents will only show themselves when you're doing what you want to do.* Far from being self-indulgent, putting your best efforts behind activities you enjoy is as smart as planting your crops in rich rather than stony soil.

One quick and surefire way to collect clues about what you really like is to weed out everything you hate. Paperwork, regimentation, too much unstructured time, or too much structured time. So pick up your pencil and make a list of the twenty things you hate most—then cut *this* list until it hurts. I'd like you to end up with three things you hate most.

When you've got your list down to three things, *write down their exact opposites!* If you wrote "cleaning the house," write down what you'd be doing if you never had to clean house again, like becoming a tennis champ or writing poetry or running a home business—or just loafing. If you wrote that you simply hate taking orders, your opposite might be giving orders, or being your own boss.

FINDING YOUR TOUCHSTONE

You have now fantasized some wishes from your armchair, or gathered together all the things you'll need to do a reconstruction. You have sheets of paper covered with your daydreams and preferences, your favorite roles and activities. Now I want you to spread all these papers out on a table and look at them. *The key to the mystery of what you want is somewhere on those pages!* Even if you think you've written silly things, or impossible wishes, or activities you don't even want to do anymore, you can build a future based on what you've written. *You simply have to figure out what is at the heart of what you love to do.* Then you will have found your touchstone.

Your touchstone is the delicious core of all the things you want—the part that makes them truly appealing to you.

All the activities that recur in your fantasies or that you've continued since childhood and anything you love doing that survived the cuts you made to your lists are decisive indicators of a true touchstone.

Here's what happened to me when I wrote my chronology of things I liked since childhood.

Sometimes the repetitions were obvious; my chronology said over and over that I liked to read. Sometimes the patterns were more subtle: I liked to "ride my bike" at ten, "drive around in cars" at fifteen, "walk on the beach" at twenty. Fantasies of London at thirty and spending time in the country at thirty-five made me remember my love for travel and reading and writing.

When I did my personal history of what I loved at different ages, a light went on in my head. Maybe I'd do some travel writing! I tested it out by making myself take notes every time I went anywhere on a business trip, or to the country on weekends, even when I just went downtown—and I discovered that I *loved* writing about even such familiar places. Here was the project I needed to make traveling fun for me!

So pay real attention to what you said in your memory exercise.

Remember Rachel, the fifty-five-year-old housewife who wanted to be Neil Armstrong? She loved adventure and boldness, and that showed up in her choice to be a jungle animal, not a domestic one. And she loved the South Seas. Rachel's choices are speaking to her loud and clear, telling her she's feeling suffocated and unrealized. Until Rachel has her great adventure she may not be able to make a decision about her future. In any event, she should take some small step toward her real wishes. Perhaps a vacation on a small island in the Pacific—even a travel book with wonderful photos can be a good start.

But what if you love something you can't do anymore—or don't even *want* to do anymore? That's not a problem. Because once you've found your touchstone, you can build a dozen goals around it!

Even if you fantasized about or love something you can no longer do—like being a competitive swimmer—ask yourself what you loved best about competitive swimming. Was it being part of the excitement of the race? Was it the possibility of being the best at something? Was it having a focus, a purpose that everyone understood and respected you for? Or did you love having a good excuse to go swimming for hours every day?

Each one of those reasons—and each of the many reasons I didn't think of—can be at the heart of a new goal. Figure out what your touchstone is, and *then just let it rest for a while.* Knowing what you really love best will change the way you look at your whole life. And you'll be needing this knowledge when I take you to the next step, perhaps the most important step you'll take.

WHAT ABOUT OBSTACLES?

Real obstacles.

Every wish has one—or two or three. You might not have the time or the money or the credentials or the know-how or the connections to do what you want to do. You might say you're the kind of person who doesn't stick to things, or who's just not confident enough to plunge right into a new life.

I'm going to make a suggestion now that could change your view of what's possible in this world for the rest of your life. I'm going to suggest that you get yourself the one thing that can surely help you surmount obstacles, the one thing that is the real secret to all success.

Your own Success Team.

Isolation is the dream killer. Your boss makes you come to work, and your teacher makes you do your homework, and your family makes you bring home the bacon. But when it comes to dreams—nobody makes you do them. If you never write that novel or visit South America or learn to play guitar, nobody is going to care. So nobody is going to push you. And all too often your dream goes unfulfilled.

And I'm not a believer in trying to develop all the character that's required to make us push ourselves. I just don't have it. I not only don't stick to things that are hard to do, I don't even remember I was supposed to do them after a few days. That's why in 1976 I put together the first Success Team, full of my friends, and said to them, "You'll tell me your wishes, and I'll tell you mine. And I'll help you and nag you until you've gotten your wish, and you'll help me and nag me until I've got mine." A Success Team is just a buddy system in which everyone helps each other go after their dream.

There are very few ideas I've had that make me as proud as the Success Team idea, though, really, it's the simplest idea in the world!

Now, when you have to start your life all over, you need a support system like you've never needed one before.

How will you get yourself galvanized to do all you have to do? You won't have to. Your team will do it for you.

Whether you're talking about homework, cleaning closets, or getting the best lawyer in town, you need two things: support and information. A team gets them faster and better than you can possibly get them on your own. Your team will buy into your dream, like stockholders. They will want you to make it.

It's a whole new world. No will of iron, no grinding self-discipline. That's Teddy Roosevelt's way, Arnold Schwarzenegger's way. This is the warm way; strong, patient, thorough—people looking out for each other and finishing what they start because it's based on love. Not grandiose love blazoned across the sky, just daily, reliable love, like when you help a kid with his homework or take a neighbor to the hospital.

There's nothing as exciting as going after what you really want and getting support for doing it. It's like being born rich. Of course, it's a little scary to get all that help when you're not used to it, but it turns your life around.

And we all need it. When it comes to our dreams, we're all orphans.

This is no time to be a loner. You need your own buddy system to give you the courage to poke your nose into all those new doors.

You need people who are genuinely interested in how you're doing, people who will cheer you on when you do well and sympathize when things go wrong—and who will tell you to keep trying.

Don't even consider staying home and trying to figure out your future by yourself. That's too hard on you, for one thing. You'll get discouraged or overwhelmed. And it's not practical. Too many opportunities will pass right by if you sit home alone. There's a lot going on in this world and you're not going to know about it unless you get out where people talk to each other.

If you're in a new town and don't know anyone, join organizations or put ads in the paper, something like "Self-Help Support Team starting—let's get together and help each other find new jobs." The YWCA in most towns has a full-time counselor on staff dedicated to helping displaced homemakers get a new start. Their services are inexpensive or free. Don't let yourself fall through the cracks by trying to do everything on your own. I created my Success Team workshops after many years of being a loner, and when I began to see what a difference it made in my work life to have friends behind me, I only regretted I hadn't created Success Teams years earlier.

ONE MORE EMOTIONAL PASSAGE: MID-LIFE

All this talk about finding touchstones can be very exciting, but you'd better get ready for an emotional reaction. Simply zeroing in on what you really want out of life can bring on something like a mid-life crisis even if you think you've already had yours. After all, this may be the first time since you were a teenager that you thought about living your life for yourself—*your* way, according to *your* wishes.

You can forget until mid-life that only part of you is a provider and a parent; the other half of you is just—*you.* Inside every one of us is a unique spirit that belongs only to us. This spirit doesn't bring home wages or take care of anybody, and it's completely free to want fantastic things—to run the four-minute mile, or to be a mystic.

This spirit has been shut up in a soundproof box for many years.

Most of us get caught up in a kind of benign servitude when our kids are little, when, for years, we hardly have time to look at a magazine.

Even when our kids grow up and their real demands have ended, we don't always remember how to stop serving or how to fill the new time we've been given. We lose track of the years until one day something happens that jolts our sense of sameness and wakes us up to the realization that we've been drifting: a friend dies unexpectedly, our first kid goes off to college and we realize we were working so hard we forgot to be around while she was growing up, or we just realize that we've reached the pinnacle of our career and there's nowhere else to go.

That's when the free spirit in you gets loose and starts saying, "Didn't you know there were two of us? There's the workhorse. And there's *me!*"

That's the day you might go into a panic about how little of your time you've devoted to getting what you really want.

It's not that you should have run your life differently; we all need to take up responsibilities at a certain age, to love and care for people besides ourselves, or to build our careers. But one day it's time to give up some of those long-time responsibilities and begin a second life.

This might be the first chance you've ever gotten to learn who you are.

* * *

This wonderful revelation, this new focusing on yourself, should feel delightful and luxurious. The first thought will be "I should have done this years ago." But the second thought can stop you dead in your tracks. "What have I been doing all these years?" you might say. "Did I think I'd be young forever? Did I think the kids would be kids forever? How could I have been such a fool?"

Sometimes these regrets are so painful that rather than admit them, we turn away from our new freedom. We don't want to start our new life.

Deborah K. had spent years building a successful computer consulting business. She had six responsible employees and all the work she needed. Down deep she really wanted to travel all over the world, and the way her business was structured, that was completely possible. But Deborah spent most of her free time trying to find "the right guy."

"I've dreamed of taking three or four months at a time and doing some real traveling, to Africa, to Asia, everywhere. But I was waiting to get married. I didn't want to go away until that got taken care of. Now I don't feel like waiting anymore. I figure if I'm going to find someone, I'll find him while I'm traveling. And if I don't, well, that's okay too. At least I'll be seeing the world."

But Deborah didn't look very happy, and she wasn't rushing out to her travel agent to buy plane tickets. What was her problem?

"This is hard to face," Deborah said, "but I wasted a lot of years."

I checked my impulse to talk Deborah out of this painful viewpoint because I knew she had to go through some regret before she'd really be free.

People have to face regrets. Becoming mature means learning to accept what you cannot change, facing unresolved sorrows and learning to love life as it really happens, not as you would have it happen. And part of loving life is admitting your regrets.

Don't let the prospect of feeling regret dismay you. We can all look back at things we wish we'd done differently.

But I don't think any of us could have helped ourselves. We were all trying to make things come out right.

Working with the knowledge and the needs we had at the time, how could we have done differently? As a friend of mine recently said when he was asked why he had wasted so much time on an obviously lost cause, "I was misinformed."

We were all misinformed. We don't start out wise. We become wise by making mistakes. And there is good news. Once you have what you want, you won't regret the past nearly as much. *But you have to regret the past to get what you want*—so why don't we take a good look at what you deprived yourself of, and use it to build a better future?

The only cure for regrets is to face up to them. Dare to look at the empty spaces in your past even if it hurts. And then promise yourself *today* that you'll fill those spaces from now on! Regret can't hover for long in the company of determination.

Now, what were the empty spaces? If you had been twins and only one of you had to fill your obligations to get educated, to succeed in a career, to raise a family—and the other you was free to do *anything*—what kind of life would the other you have chosen to live?

Exercise 5: Just the Two of You

This exercise has three steps to it, so take up your pen again. I want you to write the life story of someone who never got the chance to live a life: *your other half.*

Step 1: *Write the life story of your imaginary twin.*

Deborah wrote: My twin would have had a ball. She wouldn't have worried so much if she looked right or acted right for men, she wouldn't have spent so many years trying to make inadequate relationships work. She'd have said, "I've got places to see and things to do!'' She'd have traveled through Russia and Mongolia and the Gobi desert and China.

Step 2: *Where would she be today, this twin of yours?*

Deborah wrote: She'd be an expert on travel. She'd have friends and photos from all over the world, and she'd have read great, unknown travel literature. She'd have written two, three, maybe four books! She wouldn't have crippled her progress by putting her own dreams on hold and using so much of her time on men.

Step 3: *What are you going to do about this?*

Deborah started to smile. "I guess I'd better buy a camera and go see my travel agent. Time's a-wasting."

After you've processed your regrets, a light goes on. You start looking at your past differently.

Deborah said, "Well, of all those years, really only the last five are a waste. I fooled around an extra five years when I knew it was time to move on. But I was afraid to admit I'd made a mistake. I needed to build up some courage. I really couldn't have dared to begin until now."

Deborah knows what she wants and she knows where to find it, but not all of us are in her position. Many regroupers need jobs and aren't sure where to begin looking.

WHAT'S OUT THERE?
(HOW TO FIND OUT WHAT'S AVAILABLE)

Let's be realistic—you can't go after what you want if you don't know what's available.

"Lack of information is the single biggest problem we run into," says Anita Lands, who teaches retirement classes at New

York University's School of Continuing Education. "Our main focus is helping people start discovering what is really out there."

Except in our own areas of expertise, we're all woefully ignorant of actual jobs that exist in the world.

"These days I travel all over the country selling music to radio advertisers. Would you believe I was in the business thirty years and never knew about that side of it?" a songwriter told me.

How can you find out about things like this if you're an outsider?

You need to get inside.

The best way to get inside is to pull in that buddy system of yours and ask them to help you *network.* Networking will give you new ideas, let you know what's out there, and turn you into an insider.

You absolutely must get into the mainstream and that means joining organizations. I'm not a big joiner myself, but I learned the hard way that if you're sitting off by yourself you'll never know when and where the party's going to be. You find out about parties by checking in with your friends to see what's going on. That goes for finding jobs too. I'm not talking only about classic networking, where you go to a business conference in a three-piece suit with your business cards. You may not be ready for anything so formal. Informal networking is the best kind for now, and that means hanging out with different kinds of people, getting to know them, finding out what they're up to. This may sound unfocused, but when you're not sure what you want, you don't really know what to ask for anyway. I think not knowing what you want can be an asset. It makes you feel less opportunistic and less self-conscious.

But where *are* all these people? Well, you've got to turn into a "joiner" to find them. Start out with affiliations you already have: your church or synagogue has social meetings; your alma mater has alumni activities. Then move to your interests—and I mean *any* interests. You might find out about a job building boats if you join the ASPCA! There are hundreds of organizations to choose from. Just ask the local librarian for the *Encyclopedia of Associa-*

tions. Take a big pad of paper with you and allow a few hours. Write down the information about whichever associations seem interesting to you. You'll be amazed at what's available.

I believe the best way to network at this moment in history is to get a computer and go on-line. I wish everybody had a computer and knew how to get involved with telecommunications. Local electronic bulletin boards are inexpensive and they act exactly like an old-fashioned coffeehouse or a neighborhood bar. You can always find somebody who's willing to help you when you go on-line. I've never encountered so many generous, supportive people as those I've met on my computer screen. Maybe the anonymity makes everyone feel safe enough to share, and *do they ever share!* People ask for the names of good dentists or good furniture movers or honest mechanics—and they always get lots of answers. I've seen insider jobs posted many times, saying something like, "If anyone is looking for a pasteup job, one just opened up in my office. Give me a call."

You're not computer literate? Neither was I. A friend came over to my house and set me up, and now all I have to do is click my computer mouse a few times and I'm looking at messages someone left for me, or notes about good books people are reading, great places to eat, even celebrity gossip.

If I can telecommunicate, so can you. Ask around until you find the friend of a friend who's willing to come set you up. (Telecommunications mavens are very good about welcoming a new person into the world of electronic bulletin boards.) If you don't know a soul, walk into a computer store and ask for some information about a computer user's group, or buy a computer magazine and see if they have a listing. If you own a Macintosh, find a Mac user's group; if you own a Kaypro, go to a Kaypro user's group; and so on for any other kind of computer. The people at user's groups help each other with technical advice, and they're always very knowledgeable and willing to help.

Wherever you go to network—computer screen or local church—be friendly! To a natural joiner this may seem so obvious it doesn't bear saying, but I had to learn it, and you might too. If you've gone to meetings and been too unsure of yourself to say a word to anybody, and then left determined to never go back, you have to let yourself have the experience of some initial discomfort. You'll learn it doesn't last long. Once you start meeting people, your discomfort will disappear.

Part of being friendly means that you tell people about yourself, including your present situation. If you're shopping around for a new kind of career, let people know about it, and be sure to ask them what they do, and how they like it, and how they got started. My friend Pamela says, "Whenever I need anything, I tell everybody I know, and it works. I get on the grapevine and I keep asking until I get it."

PUTTING IT ALL TOGETHER

When you have some idea about what you love, and after talking to lots of people have discovered what's available, you are all set and ready to go. Now you can create a job that's just right for you.

I believe in creating your own work world the way you create a house, brick by brick. There's a plan for getting into every kind of work, just as there's a plan for building every kind of house. Whatever you want, no matter how little you know about it, you can set up a step-by-step plan for it.

Once you've been out in the world meeting new people, you'll see possibilities that never occurred to you before.

Now, I know what you're probably saying—*Forget what I want. Who's going to want* me?

All this nice talk about finding what you want doesn't go very far if you're afraid you won't be able to get *any* job: "A lot of us need any kind of work we can get, and we don't have the luxury of figuring out what we want."

Do you need a job right now? There's really no conflict, you simply have *two* projects: a short-term project of getting a paying job as soon as possible, and a long-term goal of finding work you really love. Simply take the long-term goal-getting system you just learned and apply it to your short-term goal. Network for information, make a step-by-step plan with the information, and get a Success Team for support. Once your job-search project is rolling, you can start working on your long-term goal: finding work that's right for you, so you can pay your bills *and* enjoy your labors.

If you can't find work that's right for you, don't worry. There's a very good chance that you can create it.

How do you create what you want if it's not readily available?
Moonlight.

Get a day job; start your own business at night.

Alan managed a printing business. He said, "I'd really like to be a portrait photographer. I'd like to take pictures of people's faces. But I can't give up a money-making job to be a photographer."

How can Alan be a photographer when he has a full-time job? He just takes out his camera and shoots pictures whenever he's not working. This is a good time for Alan to get involved with other photographers so that by the time he's ready to make a move, he knows what's going on in the world of photography.

That's how most people get their start.

By hanging around an airstrip in the Catskills, June became a professional flying instructor. By going every weekend to a stable to help exercise the horses, Morton wound up on a ranch in Australia, breeding Thoroughbreds. By attending an academic conference on a literary subject that interested me, I became the original editor of what is now a well-known scholarly journal!

Trust this system. It produces miracles.

A SUCCESS STORY

Norman looked at his present-day likes and figured out a great new job for himself.

Norman, part Native American, grew up in Washington, D.C. He was a computer programmer. And he was curious about his Native American heritage. He read books about it, attended lectures, watched documentaries, looked at Native American art. Taking his vacation in the Southwest was an initial goal he set for himself. He had six weeks of vacation coming and he'd saved enough money to go, but then his car died. He had to use all his money to get himself a new car. He had no money left.

So he asked his friends for help; he invited them to his place to help him brainstorm ways to beg, borrow, steal, or barter his way to the Southwest.

They asked what skills he had. "I don't know how to do anything but teach English," he answered apologetically.

"Teach English?" his friends said.

"Yeah, English as a Second Language, I'm certified."

His friends said, "The Bureau of Indian Affairs must be crying for teachers! Call your senator!"

Norman called his senator. The senator put him in touch with the right bureaucratic group at the Bureau of Indian Affairs, and the Bureau of Indian Affairs said, "We want you! We need eight weeks!" Norman only had six weeks vacation coming.

So he got his friends together again and said, "I only have six weeks."

Everybody said, "Too damn bad, go anyway!"

And Norman said, "You know, you're right."

He asked for and got two more weeks (unpaid) vacation from his job and went to the Southwest. While he was there, he lived with a Native American family and had such a wonderful time that he returned home, quit his job, and moved to the reservation. He's now teaching on that reservation.

Now you can see where all this wishing leads. Deborah and Norman and Alan have found a way to turn their wishes into new careers.

No matter how impractical it may seem, finding out what you like best is the most practical thing you can do.

YOUR NEW VITALITY

At workshops full of regroupers, I'm often asked what I have to say to people who simply don't feel ambitious anymore.

"I'm willing to believe I can still be a success at everything I ever wanted, but what if I don't want to anymore?" George, a retired college professor, said.

To George and everyone like him, I say, "Congratulations. You've moved beyond the drive that fueled your youth and you're ready to start living. You're past wanting the world to give you the praise you weren't able to give yourself. And now, finally, you can do what *you* want."

Was there something you wanted to do when you were younger that you *still* want to do? What stopped you? Prestige? The need to conform? Well, take a look around you. Those obstacles are gone.

If you want to be an actor, lie in your hammock, go to college, or feed the hungry—*now* you can do it.

Each age has its own gifts. You can see the difference in older people—they have a passionate interest in the world but they lack the endless hungers that drive young people.

George is sixty-six. He retired three years ago.

"At first it was very tough for me," he said. "I can't believe how much I wanted to be back in harness. I just couldn't believe anything else could be any good. And then I started looking around me and I simply fell in love with everything: my wife, my grandkids, reading, the change of seasons. I've never felt more alive."

That's what starting over can be like.

Not too bad, is it?

ELEVEN

I've Lost My Big Dream— There's Nothing Left

ROTTEN luck exists.

It's popular these days to say there's no such thing as luck, to say you make your own luck. Americans are particularly susceptible to this kind of thinking because our focus has always been on potential, rather than on tradition. We Americans have a tendency to say we're completely responsible for everything that happens to us.

But:

When you pursue what you want and you get it—a top-notch executive job, or a great marriage, or a chance to play basketball for the Los Angeles Lakers—then suddenly, because of something completely out of your control, you lose everything, that's what I call *rotten luck.* Your company is taken over and your division is sold off—without you—or you're suddenly widowed, or you miss competing in the Olympics because of an injury. You play by the rules, you do everything right, all your hard work pays off, then some force outside you—a change in the economy, a freak accident, or just age—reaches into your life and snatches your dream right out of your hands.

Rotten luck can take the heart right out of you and leave you with no goals. You don't know what you want anymore, because you don't want anything you can possibly have. You only want the past to come back.

Rotten luck is the end of an era.

You can't bounce back. And you're doomed to frustration if you try to treat what happened to you like a mere setback.

Rotten luck needs a different kind of attention.

The first thing you must do is to clear away any notion that your misfortune is your fault. Even if you're growling "I know damned well this isn't my fault," deep down you may secretly blame yourself for what's happened. You may try to catch yourself on some dumb detail, like "I shouldn't have gone into the office on a Thursday." You'd rather think there was something you could have done than face the fact of your helplessness.

And you lose confidence in the system. When you've trusted your own ability and determination, worked hard, been rewarded, and then lose the reward for no good reason, your trust in yourself and your belief in just rewards goes into a major wobble.

Let me give you some examples.

Bill M. was an extraordinarily gifted athlete with a great future. From boyhood, he excelled at every sport, but baseball was his game, the game he *loved.* Like many kids, Bill dreamed of playing big league baseball; unlike most kids, he had every talent and support he needed to achieve his goal. A major league team drafted him right out of twelfth grade, retrained him as a pitcher, and brought him up carefully through the minor leagues.

One beautiful spring day when he was twenty-one, he found himself in Florida sitting on the bench of a major league ball club, side by side with a two-time Golden Glove winner and other players he knew of and had long admired. "It was heaven. I couldn't believe I was finally there," he remembered.

Then his first week in Florida, during a full-team workout, another player slid into Bill and broke his pitching elbow. The injuries to his ligaments were inoperable. He had never pitched a regular season big league game—and he never would.

I met Bill ten years later. He was working as a salesman in an auto parts store and the only thing he liked about his job was that he didn't have to put any energy into it.

His life was like being in Dante's Limbo—without pain, without joy. He *thought* he'd gotten past the loss of baseball. He *thought* the only reason he came to see me was he was bored at his job. He told me that for a few years after the baseball injury he'd been depressed. He wasn't depressed anymore, he just wasn't cheerful. The years were sneaking by and Bill hadn't found any work he cared about to replace baseball. And he didn't know why.

Is that you?

Ask yourself: *Does your past look a whole lot better than your future?*

If it does, you aren't ready to plan tomorrow because you can't stop thinking about yesterday. And no cheery affirmations will convince you that the future can be as good as the glorious past.

Well, you're not alone.

John L., an executive vice-president of a Fortune 100 company, very good at his job and loved by his staff, got laid off in his late forties during a particularly tight crunch in his industry.

Nan, fifty-one, a homemaker and mother, watched most of her beloved world disappear when her youngest child left home for college; the rest of her life went up in smoke a year later when her husband died.

Like Bill and John and Nan, you may also have given your best and devoted yourself to your dream. And when you lost it, you were left without a fallback position.

The people around you don't understand. They say, "Get back on your feet and into the game," or "Dust yourself off and get back up on the horse."

What game? The game is over.

What horse? The horse is gone.

For you to start again you'd need to be a different person with a different goal. Not all former singers want to teach music. Not all former athletes want to coach. That's not you. You loved exactly what you had.

If someone suggests you try a total change in careers, it can feel like an insult. It's the same as saying, "We're sorry you lost your mom; we'll get you another one."

Some things aren't replaceable.

You're not going to be able to get that dream back, but you can get your life back.

MAKING A COMEBACK FROM AN IRREVOCABLE LOSS

You can't talk yourself out of a major loss. Your heart is too independent and too smart to listen to you. It knows what it feels, and it feels grief.

You must grieve, or you can never get beyond the past. This fable might help explain what I mean:

There once were two monks, a young novice and an older monk, walking on their way through the countryside; they were observing vows of silence until sundown. The monks came to a stream where a woman stood on the bank, helpless to get across. Another vow of their order was never to touch or make any contact with women. Yet, without hesitation, the older monk picked up the woman, carried her to the other side of the stream, set her down, bowed and continued on his way. The novice was stunned. He could hardly wait until sundown to ask his questions. Finally, the sun set, and the words came rushing out of the young monk's mouth: "How could you do that? How could you pick her up like that?!"

"I put her down on the other side," said the older monk. "You are still carrying her."

The lesson? You can't put something down unless you've picked it up. You can't put tears behind you until you've wept them. You can't let go of the past until you've grieved for it.

"What good will grieving do?" you may ask. "It won't bring back my past." No, nothing will do that.

But grieving will bring back your future.

Unexpressed pain keeps you a captive to the past. Once you have let yourself cry about your past, you can become free to look to the future. The past will still be alive to you, but you won't be paralyzed by it.

Wounds of the spirit heal like wounds to the bone: in biological time. You can't tell a bone how fast to mend, you just let nature do its work. You can't hurry the process. All your broken bone needs from you is some bedrest. The same is true of emotional wounds. All your hurt emotions need from you is to let the tears come. You're not going to be able to jump right into optimism about your future yet.

And there's something you may have to do first—even before you let yourself grieve.

If you feel rushed by friends telling you to forgive your enemies, forget the past, get your chin up—*and it irritates the hell out of you*—if you find that suggestions to look at the bright side make you think that you're surrounded by morons, you'll probably have to deal with bitterness.

You're not ready to forgive and forget.

THE TRUTH ABOUT BITTERNESS

You have plenty of good reasons to be bitter. Friends who tell you to "carry on" don't understand. All the same, bitterness isn't as authentic as it looks. Believe it or not, one of the reasons we choose to feel bitter is because it's easier than feeling pain. It makes us feel tough. Being bitter gives the illusion that you're fighting, that you're not taking defeat lying down. But bitterness is a log jam. It won't let you get moving.

Let's dynamite it with a good, healthy tantrum. If you think you're past bitterness, try the next exercise anyway. It might surprise you.

Exercise 1: "Don't Tell Me to Cheer Up, You Jerk"

Imagine someone says, "Now, my dear, you have no reason to be unhappy. None at all. Just cheer up and carry on." Does that create a little negative reaction in you?

On paper (or into the tape recorder) let yourself roar back at those chirpy positive thinkers, no holds barred. The trick behind this exercise is to write until you can't think of anything else to say. No one's listening, so have a good time.

One more thing: Keep this exercise going until you can't stand to do it anymore. Then do it a little longer. *Do not stop until you're bored sick with the topic.* Otherwise, your bitterness will be back in a few hours and get in the way of what you have to do next. (If you find some part of you saying "What's the point of this stupid stuff? It won't do any good!" that's only your bitterness trying to get out of a little hard work. Salute it for its deviousness, and keep on writing.)

Here's an example of how to do this exercise:

Olivia, forty, was a television anchorwoman ousted by corporate politics. When her network changed hands, the new bosses brought in their own people and threw everyone else out. No jobs on Olivia's level were available at any other major network. She was clearly out of the game. She opted to write her bitterness exercise into a notebook. She told me, "Writing out my bitterness took *four days!* I took the notebook everywhere I went. I stopped in a restaurant for coffee every time I thought of something else I wanted to write. Every time I thought I was finished, I remembered another thing I was mad about. I went into about twenty restaurants. I had so much coffee in those four days I was nearly crazy!"

Well, crazy or not, Olivia did her bitterness exercise and it worked. "I called *everybody* down," she reported. "I went through every single detail. I cursed every miserable person who did me harm, and half the ones who didn't—because they didn't help! I cursed evil, I cursed fate, I cursed my birthday. Then I started all over again. It was grand to pull out all the stops."

Olivia brought me fifteen bitter pages to read. She thought she was finished, but I insisted she write fifteen more. "It's losing its punch," she complained, but I insisted on more. Finally, she threw the notebook down, and said, "Enough! You win. It's boring me!"

She was ready to move to the next phase: remembering what was wonderful about what she lost.

Exercise 2: Praise Your Past

Write a letter, or an essay, praising your past. Tell about the best times in your old life. What *did* you love about that time? What were your favorite moments? Run your mind over your past lovingly. What did your work look like, smell like, taste like? How did it feel in your bones to be doing it? What do you remember loving most of the day-to-day experiences? *You were in love with your life,* so remember your delight in the small things too.

REMEMBERING THE GOOD TIMES

Olivia remembered, "Walking full speed up the ramp at the airport with my assistant following me at a run taking notes. I looked like a million dollars. I was like a commercial about success. I loved having secretaries to help me, being liked and respected, that was heaven. And thinking up great story ideas with my producers, working with those people. That was fun!"

"I used to wait until everyone was at work or school," Nan remembered, "then I'd plow through the messy house in two hours and turn it into a picture book, with flowers in the vases, *everything.* And I'd sit down by the window and have a cup of coffee in a beautiful cup. At two-thirty I'd miss the kids and go wait for them at school. I loved seeing the kids pour out of that school. Sometimes I'd go really early, and read a book in the car."

John, the executive vice-president of marketing in a Fortune 100 company, said, "I loved helping my people. I knew how to listen. I liked going over to their desks, anticipating what they needed. Even when I had to call them on something, there was always a way to help them out. I liked being easy to talk to, which I was. I had a reputation for it. It was the best part of my day when I could help somebody solve a problem or resolve a conflict."

Letting yourself describe every lovely detail will give you back something you lost, a precious time you put out of your mind because it was too painful to remember. When you remember that time by praising it, you'll have rescued it. You'll have pulled it out of the corner where you threw it a long time ago. And you'll be able to take your past with you into the future. *You must take it with you because you'll never consent to go without it.*

RESCUING YOUR PAST

Something inside you is too loyal to permit you to turn your back on everything you loved and simply walk away. No matter how many times people tell you to let the past go, it's never possible. You'll never move wholeheartedly into your future unless you take your beloved past with you.

And that's exactly as it should be.

There's no reason to turn your back on a happy past. Sometimes we try to turn away from the past because we feel it somehow betrayed us. It's as though we loved our past, but our past didn't love us. So we go on strike and pretend we don't care, as if to punish fate for being unkind. Fate never cares, of course, so we only hurt ourselves.

Once someone I cared for deeply did something very unethical, so I tried to totally revise my feelings about him. "He's not a good person," I said. "I don't know how to love him anymore."

And a very wise woman told me, "Your love belongs to you. You mustn't let anyone touch it, not even him. You can keep away from him, but don't try to destroy your love. That love is yours. Keep it." And I did. It's one of the good things I gathered in my travels.

It won't really break your heart to remember something that got snatched away from you. It may *feel* that way. But sometimes *feeling* that your heart's breaking is good for you.

LETTING YOUR HEART BREAK ALL OVER AGAIN

Bill felt as if he'd been hit by a truck the whole week he was writing about his climb to the major leagues, but he said, "It was a relief to give in and remember it. My memories were there all the time anyway, bothering me. I know that now." In Bill's essay of praise, he remembered being welcomed by the other players, being taken in as part of the family. He remembered the lights at the night games, and the loudspeaker announcing his name, and walking out onto the field chewing gum.

"Being in the majors, you can't know what that means to a ball player. You're the best. It makes you feel calm when you walk around. It makes you want to smile," he said.

Some of Bill's favorite memories were actually fantasies, wildly exciting hopes he once had—maybe he'd get into the World Series, maybe he'd become most valuable player. The possibility that he might get to the top of the top exhilarated him.

After he praised his past, Bill felt oddly better. "I can look at the sports pages more easily for some reason," he said. "They're not so irritating." Realizing that he still grieved for his lost career was a revelation to Bill. And realizing that there is honor and necessity in grieving for a loss allowed him to respect his sorrow instead of disparaging it.

What about you? What was your big dream like? You may have noticed that the more you described what you loved about your lost past, the more difficult it became to continue your description. It can bring up emotional pain to look back and see what you will never have again. It's hard to look through picture albums at people we loved who are now gone; it hurts a little to hear our favorite songs from junior high school. We all fight sorrow as if it would harm us. The opposite is true. Sorrow can heal us. Letting your heart break can be good for you. I think most of us fear that if we unleash a great sorrow it will flood over us and drown us. Any feeling, delayed too long, feels huge and endless. Remember how you feel when you're very hungry? Just as a normal-size meal can end a great hunger, a decent period of grief can end a great sorrow.

Bill might someday consider devoting a day of celebration every year for the "Late Great Game of Me and the Major Leagues," where he shows pictures and newspaper clippings and tells stories about famous ball players he knew. Like a mourner at a wake, he can share his stories, laugh, and bring all the glory back to life for a day. But he'll have to deal with those hurt feelings first.

You, like Bill, will have to admit that fate beat out your best efforts. Bitterness always hid that fact.

HEROES AND GRIEVING

Grief is especially hard for leaders. They usually have a stoic streak and take pride in being a buffer for the people who depend on them. They know how to keep a stiff upper lip, how to take it on the chin, how to bite the bullet. That's often why leaders are leaders, after all, to take the blows from stockholders, to quiet fears when an industry goes up and down, to protect other people from hard times. If you were a mother, you absorbed your children's woes and fears and your husband's worries, and when your family was fine, you tended to keep on taking care of people by looking out for your friends.

Well, that was okay then. But being a hero is a burden you no longer have to bear. And you don't want a burden right now because you're about to take a trip—and you need to travel light. You're going to gather up those beloved memories of yours, signal the protective part inside you that it's safe to turn your back on the past, and take the first step in the right direction—toward the future.

Your first step in the right direction is to end your resentment toward your present life.

FORGIVING YOUR PRESENT

If you've lost a big dream, you may not like your present life at all.

"I walked into the first place that would give me a job," Bill said, "and I took it. And I hate it."

Well, it doesn't do you any harm to have a life you're not madly in love with. But, if you're like most of us, you probably spend too much energy cursing the way things are. I'd like to talk you out of that.

For one thing, your life looks much worse than it is because you think it's permanent. Thinking it's permanent makes it feel intolerable. But it only looks permanent because you've never recovered from your great loss. When you have, you'll see that this time in your life is just a way station to a better life.

For another thing, being at war with your present is using up too much concentration, to say nothing of energy. It's exhausting and distracting, and the present isn't important enough for all that. You're going to need that energy and concentration for building your future.

Finally, it will do you good to realize that this phase of your life is actually your friend. Maybe not the greatest, most scintillating friend in the world, but a true friend who feeds and houses you. Your present life is like a raft that came along after your ocean liner sank; it may lack most of the qualities you really want in a vacation cruise, but it will keep you out of the water.

GRIPE AND GET OVER IT

If you need a gripe session about your present life, go to it. We can't always will away our negative feelings, and we don't have to. Complaining is a healthy, natural way to get past negative feelings, as long as the complaining is done the right way. So, if you need to, take ten minutes by the clock and say the vilest things you can about your life. Ask your friends to listen and applaud you. Be obnoxious. Snarl and whine. Have a good time.

And then stop it. Because you've got more important work to do.

Exercise 3: Forgiving Your Present

Write a letter of forgiveness and apology to your present. Name everything in it that you're grateful for, and try to remember that the alternative would have been to be in deep water, far from land.

Here's what Bill discovered: "Some people I know have to smile at people no matter what mood they're in. I don't. I get to sit at my desk in the back room and do most of my work in privacy, and be real.

"I like the low pressure of this job. I always know what to do next and it's never anything that tears your guts out. It's an honest business, straightforward, no tricks.

"A lot of this is because of the boss, who is an easygoing guy, not much older than I am. Sometimes I think he's the perfect manager: invisible, approving, available."

Bill went on like that until he actually let himself like his work situation a little.

"I wouldn't have believed I could feel better about this job," he said. "The truth is, I was operating under old habits of thought I simply hadn't looked at. There was no passion behind my dislike of my job. I had just let my opinion rest the way it was first formed."

By the way, you can expect to experience some new feelings once you're not shaping your life with resentment. And one of those feelings is a peculiar emptiness. You had a drama going about your current life, and that drama was fueled by anger. When the anger melts, the drama melts too. It wasn't a pleasant drama, but it gave your life some meaning. When the drama's gone, your life may look like it has no meaning at all. Your life won't feel terrible, but it will feel shapeless.

That's okay, believe it or not. Better than okay. Because open space is a great place to grow a future.

But as anyone who stops drinking, drugging, round-the-clock exercising, dating maniacs, debting, or fighting in a war knows, the change from high drama to even-keeled peace is huge. Even if you *want* to make this change, you may feel as if every organ in your body only knows how to process the life of drama. If that's the case, you may need to do one more exercise before you can proceed to think about your future.

Exercise 4: I Refuse!

Just write it twenty-five times: *I refuse to like this stupid, lack-luster, dead-end* [you fill in an adjective] *present life of mine.*

Yes, this is another Hard Times session. Turning your life around after a big loss is like turning the *Queen Mary* around in a harbor. You have to do it bit by bit, slowly, and you have to correct your position over and over until you get turned around. Don't worry. You'll get used to having small, contained temper tantrums. You're moving heavy freight within yourself. Your insides are bound to feel tender.

So, just write it twenty-five times. And *mean* it: I refuse to accept my mediocre current circumstances! I refuse. I refuse.

Finished?

Okay, let's move on.

YOUR FUTURE: FACING A BLANK

The first thing you're not going to be crazy about is the realization that you don't know very much. *When you were angry, you knew everything.*

When you admit you don't know a thing about what's coming, you put yourself in a position to do some learning, which is exactly what you need to do. It's not easy to let go of the illusion of knowing it all, but there is one very peculiar benefit to losing everything and having no chance of getting it back: You learn that you don't *have to* know it all. When fate takes the reins out of your hands, you're put in a position you've never been in before. For perhaps the first time in your adult life you get to experience a completely receptive state. John, the former business executive, spoke to me about this:

"The effect losing my job had on me really surprised me. I was still in a lot of pain, but something brand new started to happen. I finally felt like I wasn't the smartest thing in the universe, and instead of feeling bad about that, I just became curious about what was coming next. I don't exactly know how to explain it, but for the first time I didn't feel alone. I felt like I had something important to learn."

John was really onto something.

When your worst fears have come to pass, something very unexpected and valuable takes place. Being confronted with your limitations opens you up to a new level of learning. You begin to believe that information about how you're supposed to live will be provided to you. And it will be.

If anyone deserves to relax and stop feeling responsible for everything in the world, you do.

FALLING IN LOVE AGAIN

Now, after you've cleared away a lot of internal debris about your past and present, you'll naturally want to fall in love with a new future.

The thing about you is that you have a great capacity for love of your work. If you loved your first career, you will love another career the way people who loved being married a first time love being married again.

I know three possible routes to a future, and one of these should be right for you.

1. You can use your past affiliations to create your future.

If you're an ex-sports figure or businessman, everyone thinks you should go into sportscasting or consulting. Everyone thinks you should use your old job connections and reputation to get yourself a new life. And maybe after you've grieved for your past, you'll find you *do* want to get a new life this way.

Suzanne Farrell, a principal dancer with the New York City Ballet, one of choreographer George Balanchine's great muses, abruptly stopped dancing after a second hip replacement operation. As it happened, Suzanne Farrell *did* want to do what everyone assumed she'd do. She did want to build her future out of her past practices. Soon after her surgery, she started teaching ballet and staging George Balanchine's works.

And I know another ex-ball player who's not like Bill. Steve loves baseball as much as ever and loves young people. He used his reputation to help him get a job as a college coach.

2. You can use a touchstone from your past to create your future.

Bill didn't want to coach. And John tried being a consultant, but hated being a transient person in a corporation, hated not being someone everyone could count on.

If you're like Bill, John, or Nan, I can show you a technique that uses your past to created an entirely different life that you *can* love.

Exercise 5: Finding Your Touchstone

Get out the essay praising your past.

Pretend someone said you could have three elements of your old life back.

Make a list of everything you loved and start crossing off items, one at a time, until you absolutely can't cross off another. You're going to have to shorten the list until it hurts; only then will you realize what the *most* indispensable elements from your old life are for you. Underline the ones you must have. Those two or three things are your *touchstones*. Those are things you can build a new life on.

Here are some examples of touchstones:

- Bill: a sense of mastery; being outdoors; being a star.
- John: having a special place in a community; having a sense of moral purpose; problem solving.
- Nan: making a pleasant and orderly home; watching children grow; having my husband nearby.

Now, *if you could build a new life with your touchstones, would you want to?*

This is an interesting question. The answer is not as obvious as it may look. Nan didn't want to build a life on anything from her past.

But the touchstone technique was the right one for Bill.

After he resolved his resentment toward his job and realized he liked it all right, Bill had a pretty good year. He decided to stay at the sales job for the time being. As his heart lightened, he started doing a better job without really trying; he started coming out from the back room more, started becoming friendlier. One of the other salesmen invited him over for a family dinner and they found they shared a love of old cars. And after a year, Bill began to feel his energy returning. The sales job was no longer any problem. The path was clear for him; he began to want to put his heart into something again. At that point he had to start searching for what that something would be.

He found his touchstones, and he decided he didn't want to deal with one of them: being a star. "I'm leaving that behind," he said. "Or, rather, I'm carrying it with me, right here." He patted his heart. But he used his other touchstones—his pleasure in the outdoors and his love of mastery. He wanted a continued sense of excellence in his work. Mastery over a skill was of deepest importance to him. He had to find something he could do that would give him the same opportunity for discipline, for a private sense of increasing mastery, that baseball had given him.

Bill became a photographer. He started by taking pictures of kids playing basketball on an outdoor court, and soon the technical aspects of photography absorbed his interest. He was on his way to a new big dream.

John went back to college and studied philosophy. There he hoped to find a special place in a community, where he'd have a sense of moral purpose, where he'd consider and maybe even solve some human problems. He'd always been interested in issues of what's morally right, but he'd never had the opportunity to explore his philosophical interests. Although he was looking forward to college, he was shocked by the sudden change in his life and had a hard time adjusting.

"There I was, an old guy among kids—I maybe had no right to be there. Here nobody knew my name or cared that I was there; certainly nobody wanted any help from me. Nobody said 'Good morning, John' when I came in, and nobody typed my papers. I turned from somebody into nobody. It was a real eye-opener. I knew I was going to have to find something meaningful to hang on to, and I didn't know where to look."

After two semesters, John moved across the street to the theological seminary.

"There I found my people," he smiled. "And my new career." John's now studying for the ministry.

What about you? Now that you know what it is you loved most, would you like to build a new dream around it? If you would, it's possible. At this point you might want to review Chapter 10, "Regrouping: It's a Whole New Ball Game." And take your touchstones along with you.

In your past are many passions you put aside to pursue your big dream. By remembering your past, like John, you now may decide to pursue them. When Nan remembered her past, she was surprised by her flood of affection for an old, forgotten milieu. She said, "I loved the jazz world before I was married. In college, I played jazz piano, and I was a small-time impresario, a booking agent. Then I got involved in my family and home and almost forgot about it."

Nan created a new touchstone, using what she loved long ago. And she got involved in the jazz world as an agent—an increasingly successful one!

But, if you've lost a big dream and grieved over the loss, there's a third possibility for your future.

3. You can relax and smell the roses.

My friend Joyce called me from South Carolina and said, "I've decided to become a goal-free person." She had made a wonderful life for herself as a teacher, yet she never could stop trying to improve herself in one way or another: lose weight, learn a language, save more money.

Now she says, "Every day that I wake up and have no goal is a triumph. I've spent my whole life trying to improve myself. I'm through with self-improvement." Because she was always rolling up her sleeves to take on another task, she never had time to look around and enjoy the view. Now she's part of what I call "The Wisdom Factor."

THE WISDOM FACTOR

You had a great contentment when you were doing your best. I'm talking about the perfectly focused, perfectly quiet moment you had when you were right in the middle of what you loved most.

According to physicists, it's mathematically impossible for a batter to see a ball leave a pitcher's hand and have enough time to swing the bat and hit the ball. So how does the batter hit the ball?

Everyone who achieves excellence knows about the magic in every moment of peak performance. They know that they must let go of their will and *trust* their training. They know how to discover each moment as it comes, instead of trying to manage and control it.

Well, now you have a chance to let your whole life be like those wonderful moments. You're someone who has already learned how to let go of the controls and trust yourself. Wise people take this knowledge with them when they leave the winner's circle and go to smell the roses.

Now you can open yourself up to the weather, your dog, the small, perfect gestures children make, fixing your car—life.

Your new situation is like that of a grandfather who said to me, "I wish I'd been this relaxed with my own kids. Now that I'm not responsible for seeing that my granddaughter turns out right, I can just enjoy her. I wish I'd known that before."

Now that you know you're not responsible for everything, you're free to enjoy life.

Loss is a great teacher. Life can be seen as a series of weanings, starting in infancy. Each loss puts a dent in your narcissism and makes you realize that the universe does not revolve around your wishes. Being self-centered, goal-centered, was necessary, but it made you miss so many moments, people, beauty, feelings, so many opportunities to learn wonderful things, so many good times. Now, life stretches out for miles all around you. Once you are no longer blinded by your own plans and projects, a fascinating world shows up, just waiting for you to open your eyes and see it.

TWELVE

Nothing Ever Interests Me

"NOTHING *ever* interests me," Chris told me sadly. He was twenty-eight, a restaurant cashier with a college degree. He said, "Sometimes I see something that looks a little interesting, and then I say, why get started? I won't really love it. *Nothing* has a real spark for me."

Chris was speaking *the language of chronic negativity.* You hear it whenever someone says things like, "When life looks good, it's not real, but when everything looks pointless, *that's* the truth." You're using it when you say "always," as in "It's *always* like this," or when you say "never" as in "Things *never* turn out right for me." This language also is full of phrases of regret and self-blame like "Why did I?" and "I should have known" and "Now it's too late."

Whenever you use this kind of language, you can be sure your view of reality has a bad cold. As hard as it may be, you've got to promise yourself you won't trust this kind of thinking for a minute.

Because it's all wrong.

Someone's thinking gets mixed up in this way for a lot of reasons, and this chapter is going to take a hard look at them. But first, we've got to bump that negative language out of your head.

FIRST AID FOR CHRONIC NEGATIVITY

Chronic negativity is no joke. It casts a shadow over the sunniest day and makes the smallest decision painfully difficult. The language of chronic negativity comes from a spirit that is weary, even despairing.

Chris came to see me one day waving an article from *Time* magazine. He said, "Look at this article! It's about 'Men and Depression,' and it says that lots of depressed men are sarcastic, like me. They put everything down, they don't think they can be helped, et cetera, et cetera. Do you think I'm depressed?"

I said, "Sort of, Chris. You've at least got chronic negativity."

He said, "Okay, I'm listening."

So I told him three things anyone should do when they've been in a negative mood for too long.

1. Look for a physical cause.

Although your unhappiness may be triggered by actual events in your life—a recent loss, or a difficult childhood—your emotional situation can eventually affect you physically. When any feeling gets overworked, it throws off your body chemistry. If you lived in a constant state of terror, for instance, your adrenal system would eventually start misbehaving. Your body chemistry may also be off kilter for other reasons we don't understand. So I always advise that you look for a physical cause in any chronic emotional ailment—no matter how purely emotional the trouble may appear.

Medication can often make a difference, especially with low-grade chronic negativity.

"I just couldn't bring myself to take a drug," Rick said. "I don't know why." He thought about his life for a moment and said, "You know, it's hard to believe, but I think it's been fourteen years since I've had one really happy day."

I must have looked appalled, because Rick decided to swing

into action. He went to the public library, read more articles, and came back to see me with new information.

"You know," he said, "I may have that problem where some people get depressed when they don't get enough sunlight." Rick works on sound stages in big, dark studios where films are made. "Sometimes when I can't get outside for lunch, I start to feel horrible. In the winter when the days are short, I get even worse."

If you have clues this strong, it's time to talk to an expert, and that's what Rick did.

He went to a specialist, who confirmed his suspicions and explained that Rick probably had Seasonal Affective Disorder (appropriately called SAD). The doctor recommended light therapy; now Rick sits in front of a high-intensity light unit every morning before he goes to work.

He's lucky. He found a physical cause for his problem right away; he needed more light. Rick was grinning the next time I saw him. He said, "Help me figure out what I want, quick, before this good mood goes away." (His improved mood *didn't* go away —and he *did* find a project he loved. Read on.)

You should do some research too. It's worth it. Look up recent articles in magazines and newspapers and see what the latest word is on the treatment for chronic low-grade depression. Become as knowledgeable as possible about the latest medical developments.

Once you're more informed, you may want to get yourself some help. Talk to your family doctor or contact a psychopharmacologist and see if they have any suggestions.

Trying to pull your mind out of a long slump with nothing to help you but that same mind *is too hard!* Medication can be like someone throwing you a rope.

With that in mind, I give you step number two.

2. Exercise. Now.

When I quit smoking about ten years ago, I was hit with the heaviest early morning misery I have ever experienced. I couldn't stand the feeling and I wasn't used to it, so I did something very radical—for me. I went jogging.

I hate exercise. My idea of paradise is to sit at a computer and write, sit at a table and talk, sit under a tree and read. My favorite high-energy exercise is to stroll slowly around New York looking at everything. When I work up a sweat I feel like something's wrong with me.

But the morning I was driven to go jogging, my misery was so strong it seemed even worse than working up a sweat. As a desperate measure, I went running every morning for a while, trying to outrun my dreadful feelings. Running worked. I didn't feel heavenly when I got home, but I didn't feel terrible anymore. And by afternoon my blues always lifted.

The next morning when the low mood returned, I'd run again. And the exercise would help again.

That lasted seven months. I remember the first morning I woke up feeling sunny again. Then there were two good mornings in a row. Then the bad time was over.

(I immediately stopped running and went back to strolling.)

I had the same experience one more time, a few years later, when I decided to cut out coffee for a few weeks. (I really have to quit cutting out things.) This time I tried running with a headset tuned to music. Hot music. The kind that would wake up the dead and make them dance. And that made me come home from my run feeling sensational!

Legal mood-altering without a prescription, that's what exercise with music is, and I strongly suggest you try it. It's an over-the-counter way to improve your body chemistry. Give it a try. Play that music and get moving for at least five minutes. It works even in small doses.

You'll never feel like exercising less than now when you need it most—but do it anyway.

Now that your motor's running, you've got to get some forward motion going. Right now, you're not good at creating your own momentum. Hence, I give you number three.

3. Pick a goal—preferably involving other people.

"Pick a *what?!*" you might be saying. "The whole point is that I *can't* pick a goal."

No, the whole point is that you can't pick a goal that you *love.* You *can* pick a goal you don't much care about.

Since your desire is not working well at this point, you are not going to be able to pick a goal you really want. Even if you do pick one that you want today, you won't want it tomorrow. You know it, I know it. So find a project and do it. It's of no great importance what it is. I suggest you pick something that you think you might like if you were in a good mood, since *you're going to have to do it whether you like it or not.*

Why do I want you to do that?

It's good for you, that's why.

Remember, this is first aid. We're not working on your life plan yet. We're getting you back into running order first; so redo a room in your apartment, or try to become a good tennis player, or teach somebody how to read.

If you possibly can manage it, get other people involved in your goal. Pulling at least one other person in on your project will keep you on track and give you added energy.

You've got to get moving. And you've got to keep moving.

"I've picked up projects before—and put them down because they all become pointless," you say?

Well, this time you're not going to put it down.

It's time to disconnect your discouraging "it's pointless" feelings from your behavior. *If you can stop acting on those feelings, you can start the process of finding what you want—even in a negative mood.*

Before those negative messages go away you're going to be involved in a new project, and that project will help drive those messages out of your mind. So pick the best goal you can come up with and get started. Remember, you don't have to *like* this project, you just have to *do* it. No more internal debates about whether or not it's worth doing. You're not in the proper mood to assess the worth of any project right now.

And if you start thinking "Why am I doing this?" (which you will, every ten minutes), just answer yourself by saying, "Because I said I would." And that's settled.

As soon as your negativity realizes it can't stop you, it will detach itself from the project and leave you free to become more involved. It takes some time, and you may continue to feel negative when you're doing nothing, but after a while you'll find that *you don't feel bad while you're working.*

And the process of healing will begin. Working on a project when you're feeling demoralized is like exercising a weak arm or leg: the more you exercise, the stronger your morale will become.

If the project you've chosen looks overwhelming, break it down into small steps, set small subgoals, and break those subgoals into even smaller steps until you've finally got something you can do today. Then write every step in your calendar. They are now appointments, and you must keep them. Woody Allen said that 80 percent of success is just showing up, and this is what he meant.

Try to get a buddy involved. At least discuss your progress with her on a regular basis. Your belief system is wobbly right now and a buddy can help stabilize it.

Candace, forty-four, an assistant clerk in a doctor's office, another chronically negative client of mine, got involved with a group of ecology-minded neighbors who were cleaning up small city parks. Candace decided she was going to claim the group's goal as her own, whether she really felt enthusiastic about it or not (and she didn't—at first):

"I wanted to learn how to do two things: I wanted to learn how to make a decision and stick with it, and I wanted to learn how to live with a little frustration.

"I decided to show up every time and practice wanting that damned park to be clean. I know this goal looks small, but following through on it was a whole new world to me. Sometimes I'd think it was the most meaningless, stupid thing a person could do. But sometimes I'd get indignant if someone left a mess in *my* park! It changed everything. *I stopped feeling that I was waiting for life to happen to me,* and I could make things happen on my own!"

Candace uncovered something very important. When you're chronically negative you are *passive.* You're waiting. Getting into action can kick-start your energy and turn your life around.

One more caution. Have another project lined up before the present one ends. *Leave no gaps. Overlapping goals are essential until your mood turns around.*

DISABLED DESIRE

Now that you're applying first aid to your chronic negativity, let's take a good look at the bigger problem—your ability to *want* seems to be disabled. When nothing ever interests you, life looks like a beach full of broken rowboats; you feel stuck on the shore with no way to travel. Meanwhile, other people with the mysterious gift of enthusiasm keep pushing those same boats out into the water, climbing in, and rowing away with no problem. How do they do it? What's their secret?

It's normal to occasionally run into a wall, a "down" period, when nothing really looks very good. A big disappointment can cause that. Sometimes we even feel let down after completing a successful project! Our systems seem to need some emotional "down time." After a while we feel better, then we get interested in life again.

That's not the same as never being able to stay interested in anything. Unless there's a chemical reason for it, this odd lack of enthusiasm points to an early source. *You could be someone whose ability to desire got injured when you were very young.*

This whole book is about blocked desire, but a person who is never interested in anything almost certainly became blocked in a dramatic way: someone or something tampered with their desire mechanism and threw it out of kilter.

If you're someone who believes that nothing interests you, I'm really glad you're giving it another try (by reading this book) because there's more to this problem than you think.

You Were Born to Desire

Whenever you find someone who's not interested in anything, genuine despair is at the bottom of it.

Yes, I said despair.

I know that's a big word, but I don't think we should underplay what's behind your lack of interest. A grave sorrow is in you. Where does it come from?

People who despair have lost a great happiness, maybe greater than the rest of us. Their disappointment is so extreme that their dream must have been sublime. If that's you, it's essential that we put a tracer on your happiness. You must find out when you last had it, where it went, *why* it went.

If you can't pinpoint an event in the last few years that started your negativity, if you think you've "always" been this way, I have some news for you. *You weren't born uninterested.*

You were born loaded with curiosity and brimming with desires. Nature *likes* us to want things. Desire is the first thing that drives us: desire for warmth and closeness and food. Curiosity follows fast on the heels of desire. As a baby, you investigated anything your eyes fell on. You reached for anything you could get your hands on. So *what happened to you?* Where did your desire go? What happened to all that enthusiasm?

You hid it away for safekeeping. Your enthusiasm is intact. As tiny children we instinctively protect what we prize most. When danger shows up, we might hide our intelligence and our originality, and *if necessary, we hide our desire.* You may not know how to get access to your hidden desire right now, but it's inside you. It's whole, rich, unique, and ready to emerge whenever the coast is clear.

Apparently the environment got very dangerous for your desires when you were a child, so to protect the precious stuff from danger, you hid it wisely and well. As an adult, you're ready for your rich appetite for life to reappear, but now you can't find it.

Don't worry. There's a way to track it down.

Let's take a look at how your desire went into hiding in the first place.

When you're young and enthusiastic, if someone repeatedly sticks a pin in your balloon, deflating you and making you feel defeated, after a while to protect yourself you try to remember not to be happy. You learn to control the situation by sticking a pin in your own balloon first. Every time you start to get enthusiastic, you stop yourself—*and you do it with the language of negativity:* "This is stupid. This is pointless." Even if no one ever actually said those words to you, if you've been disappointed too often, you'll invent them.

Protecting yourself by stopping your own enthusiasm is unavoidable. No one can take endless doses of hurt. Unfortunately, stopping your enthusiasm can get to be a habit.

One of the difficulties with the brilliant survival tactics we create as children is that they take on a life of their own. They become a part of our operating style, even when we don't need them anymore. When we grow up and go out into the world, we can leave behind the dangers of childhood, but we rarely leave behind our survival tactics. *People who aren't interested in anything are people who can't stop protecting their enthusiasm.*

What made you hide your desire?

What is the source of this pattern of yours?

Once we know what the danger *for you* was, half your desire-recovery work will be done.

Adults can deflate a child's dreams in several ways. Let me run a few examples by you to see if they stir up any memories.

Story No. 1: Criticism.

Jackie, a brilliant young woman from Idaho, got a scholarship studying geology in Moscow. She had a wonderful time. When her studies were over, she returned to the United States and found a job doing geological surveys for an oil company, but something had changed. Her love of geology disappeared just when she was getting ready to enjoy a fulfilling career. After a few months, she quit her job. She held a series of unsatisfying administrative jobs all over the country. She's never been enthusiastic about any work since she returned from Moscow, and she can't figure out why nothing interests her:

"I don't know if I really liked science. Maybe it was just an opportunity to get away from home and be in grad school. I loved being with the teachers and the other students, and they all loved me. But when it was time to get a job, I felt like I wasn't really interested in science. I started feeling the same depressing way I always felt at home.

"These days I feel kind of cynical when I get offered other jobs, like they *look* pretty good, but I figure there must be a trick to them. If I look closer, I'll see that they're not really good at all. I kept thinking, this job's not good enough, or that job doesn't pay enough, or that job isn't respectable enough or reliable enough. Sometimes I wonder if I was ever *really* interested in anything."

Jackie was raised alone by her mother in a small Arizona town. Jackie's mother had a hard life, and was extremely bitter about it. She was also relentlessly critical of everything Jackie did. "My mother never opens her mouth without reproaching me," Jackie said. If Jackie did something well, her mother found what was wrong with it. If she sounded happy, her mother called her selfish. "When I ask why she can't ever say anything nice, she insists she's trying to help me avoid a bad life. Talking to her is just hopeless." Jackie shrugged. "She always snaps, 'You want me to be sugary all the time, to lie to you?' "

In the mystery of Jackie's lost enthusiasm, her mother's endless criticism is the culprit.

That criticism is what made Jackie become a demoralized adult.

Here's how that happens: Whenever a child has been assaulted by too much criticism, she switches from her natural inclination to learn about the world into a pure survival mode. Like a country in wartime, the criticized child leaves aside the pursuit of a constructive life and directs all her energies toward the enemy.

Story No. 2: Witnessing criticism.

There's a kind of person who was *never* criticized, but who watched a parent systematically belittle an older brother or sister and decided to hide so the same thing wouldn't happen to him. Unlike the child who gets caught in the middle of the drama, a younger child has the "advantage" of watching the conflict and deciding on a survival strategy.

The child who has watched this painful situation gears himself for only one thing: staying out of trouble. His security is more important to him than even the smallest adventure. He has decided not to get involved in life.

When he grows up and leaves home, he doesn't heave a sigh of relief and finally begin to live. Like those Japanese soldiers who wouldn't come out of their foxholes after World War II, he doesn't believe the war is over.

Chris, the restaurant cashier, was the baby of his family and spent his infancy watching his angry father criticize and belittle his older brothers and sisters. At five years old, Chris decided he was going to stay a baby forever; keeping a low profile seemed the only smart thing to do: "I decided to not want anything. I saw my big brothers and sisters get verbal abuse for having independent thoughts and desires. I never wanted that to happen to me."

Time out for a word about *anger* and *depression:*

The people in stories 1 and 2—the overcriticized kids and those who witnessed emotional, psychological, or physical violence—have in common a childhood trauma that's widespread and worth special mention.

Too much anger in the home.

"My childhood was really okay, I think," some people say. "The only thing was that my parents just couldn't stop being angry at each other, not at my brother or at me. We were used to hearing them fight. But we knew they loved us."

Unfortunately, I'm afraid these people are guilty of wishful thinking. If you take a closer look, you see that no one walks away from any angry household without being profoundly affected. Anger is frightening and feels dangerous to small children —even when it's not directed at them. Eventually, waves of anger in the air create an underlying unhappiness in a small child. Sometimes this unhappiness doesn't appear until adulthood, when all the childhood fantasies of creating a happy life have failed—and such dreams usually do fail, because *unhappy children have unrealistically high expectations of life.* A couple of disappointments are enough to make them hopeless and depressed. Depression is a survival trait, keeping small animals out of harm's way by causing them to crawl into a safe, dark place and go to sleep. If we could bounce back to a positive state when the danger was gone, depression would be a great asset. Unfortunately, depression is hard to shake.

Was Jackie's mother angry?

Jackie's mother may have convinced herself that she was only teaching Jackie how to grow up—but there's a dead giveaway that this wasn't true; her criticism was unkind, not encouraging.

When someone attaches unkindness to criticism, *she's angry.* Angry people need to criticize as an outlet for *their* anger. That's why you must always reject unkind criticism. Unkind criticism is *never* part of a meaningful critique of you. Its purpose is not to teach or to help, its purpose is to punish. When Jackie gets off the phone with her mother she feels punished. And her feeling is correct.

But anger isn't the only thing that can affect your natural enthusiasm.

Story No. 3: On being interrupted.

Loving parents sometimes unintentionally harm a child's ability to develop desire, because they interrupt their child too much.

These parents would do anything for their children. Except leave them alone.

They drag their children off to interesting or "beneficial" activities, assuming a child needs constant entertainment. Sometimes I think they feel uneasy or guilty when their child spends any time thinking private thoughts or playing alone—as if that means they're neglecting their duties as parents.

But there's a natural flow of thoughts in our heads when we're alone. You can see a rhythm in the impulses of children when you watch them at play. When a toy catches a child's attention, he'll get involved for a while and then look out the window and think for a while, and then go looking for someone to play with. All this activity is essential to develop an interest in the world.

When we leave infancy for childhood, our attention span lengthens. We find ourselves spending hours fixing a bike or reading a book or playing with our friends, and these activities feel important to us.

But whenever Candace played by herself as a child, her mother would swoop in and start talking. After years of this, Candace became tense and easily distracted. She forgot how to tune in to her private thoughts.

When she came to see me she had a pattern of never following through on anything: "I get interested in careers, but the second I think about picking myself up and actually doing something my interest disappears. Going after the job, preparing a résumé, making calls seems like such a huge project I get worn out just thinking about it."

Why does Candace lose energy? Because energy is fueled by desire and Candace's desire never got an uninterrupted time in which to mature. We all need to develop a private, inner self, and when families don't respect our autonomy they create a violation of ego that throws us off balance. We get accustomed to focusing on *them* instead of what interests us.

Whenever somebody thinks your life belongs to them, no matter how warm and generous they may be, they're bullies. Being a loving bully is an easy error to make. When your children are small, their lives do sort of belong to you: you're responsible for what happens to them. And as they grow up you're *supposed* to butt in now and then to teach them your values.

But if you don't learn how to respect your children's "otherness," if you get too involved with their private time, their games, their schoolwork, their friends, they won't know how to stop defending themselves from your potential interruption, even after they're fully grown.

Story No. 4: Broken promises.

Some parents cannot resist enticing their children into wonderful fantasy trips. A child's enthusiasm *is* a delight, and grownups can sometimes lift their own heavy spirits by getting children excited. As long as it's clear that the adult is only pretending, no harm is done. But a child's heart is too sincere to tolerate any trickery for long. It's wrong to make promises or even intimations you don't intend to keep.

When Sandra was a child, her father would say "We're going to go to the jungles of Peru this summer!" or "Come on, get the brochure, we'll go to Disneyland." But they never went anywhere.

Sandra's father routinely got his kids so excited they could hardly sleep all week; and just as routinely, by the weekend, he'd forget what he promised, or he'd be busy. If Sandra or her brother started to cry with disappointment, their father got furious. Several Saturdays, he stomped out of the house and was gone all day, taking the family car with him.

A lot of people create fantasies for children, but I've always felt a little uneasy about the people who blur the lines between make-believe and promises. Some people who are supposedly great with children are playing a hurtful game by creating expectations, then not delivering. Parents should simply never make promises they don't intend to keep.

Many of the things Sandra's father promised could actually have been done. He just didn't do them. He probably went fewer places with his kids than anyone else in their neighborhood.

So Sandra lived in fantasies. Her difficulty with reality showed up in her work life and in her personal relationships. She built a good business as a consultant in industrial fabrics but didn't respect the work; she thought it was stupid. She wasn't interested in "ordinary" men but got involved with glamorous, insincere men for short periods of time—then suffered terribly with each break-up, fearing she'd never get married—a humiliation too terrible to contemplate. Her constant fantasizing and disappointment as a child made her desperate to finally have one dream come true—in the shape of a magic prince who would transform her life.

She was one of those people who fantasize because they find reality a disappointment. Some people assume that this is normal, characteristic of all of us, but that's not so. We don't all prefer fantasy to life; we don't all find life a disappointment. If you do, it's very important to take a careful look at the causes for your disappointment. Finding out what happened to you will wake you up.

Revelation is the first and the biggest step to changing your life and reviving your interest and desire. The rest is mop-up.

When Light Falls . . .

When light falls on the dark corner of our minds where we keep our oldest assumptions, our whole world looks different. Just understanding what troubles us, realizing that each of our difficulties has a name, a cause, a logic to it, is liberating. Nothing can make you feel as helpless as ignorance, and the truth *can* set you free. Here's how knowledge led directly to problem solving for these people.

Jackie: I knew I hated my mother's criticism, but I never connected it with my problem. I didn't know why I was always in a bad mood even when I hadn't seen her for months. Now I know I was doing my mother's job on myself!

Chris: I felt like such a loser for being so cautious, without initiative. My brother and sister were the ones who caught hell from Dad. I forgot that I decided to disappear so he wouldn't find me.

Candace: I thought I was *lazy,* but now I see that I always expected to be rescued. Taking care of myself actually made me feel terrible, like I had been abandoned.

Jackie, Chris, and Candace are fortunate because they can see what happened to block their natural instinct to desire. They've now taken the biggest step in breaking free of their habit of negativity. I hope their stories have helped you do the same. *But even if you can't figure out exactly what caused your enthusiasm to go underground, you now know that its disappearance is no mystery.* Something happened to you, plain and simple.

So let's see what it takes to get your natural enthusiasm for life to come back on the scene.

Making the World Safe for Desire

If you want to coax your hidden enthusiasm out of its hiding place, understanding why it's hiding isn't always quite enough. Your past packs a lot of power, so you need to develop a strategy to take away that power.

Strategies will differ slightly depending on what threatened your desire, but there are a few things everyone can do. Jackie, Chris, and Candace each used some of these simple strategies to change their lives.

Solution No. 1: Give in to the criticism.

If you're like Jackie and you can't seem to get untangled from a negative relationship, you need a strategy to keep from being pulled into any games. One of my favorites is this: If somebody tries to convince you that you're no good, *agree with them*—and watch them drop the ball with surprise.

"The struggle itself is your enemy," I told Jackie. "If you can't win it, you'd better temporarily lose it. Relax and be unhappy. Get a job, go about your business, and let your mother win. I think you'll be surprised at what happens."

Jackie was furious at the idea of even pretending to agree with her mother's criticism but finally gave it a try. The next time she talked to her mother on the phone, she stopped saying things were fine and took away her mother's chance to knock her down. Instead, she told her mother things were terrible: "I'm no good. I don't really have anything. I haven't accomplished anything."

At first her mother responded in a habitual way, saying "It's your own fault, you ruined everything," but Jackie stopped herself from taking the bait and engaging in the old battle.

"You're right. I did ruin everything," Jackie said. "I don't know why I'm so stupid. I've always been stupid."

Her mother was thrown for a loop. "Well, you were never stupid," she said hesitantly—*and the game turned around!* After a few phone conversations Jackie's mother actually began to encourage her. "You're *not* stupid. It's your boss's fault. Don't let him get to you."

"For the first time in my life she's not criticizing me," Jackie said. "What is this?"

Jackie had jammed her mother's circuits. Her mother was resentful of this "lucky" child because her own life had been so hard, so every time Jackie tried to impress her mother she only set herself up as a target. The minute Jackie laid down the bat and let the balls fly by, the game was over.

Solution No. 2: Write odes to your defenses and "shortcomings."

Your defenses are what's causing your trouble. Your defense against criticism or interruption was to become passive, indecisive, or inert. Well, for once, let's give these tactics the respect they deserve—they kept you alive, after all, and protected your precious ability to desire from the falling bombs of criticism and anger.

Exercise 1: Praise Your Defense Mechanism

Part A: It's time to start admiring that defense mechanism, which tells you not to move. Praise that mechanism for being so clever at keeping your desire from being brutalized. Write your praise in the form of a sonnet or a limerick, a country-western song, or an aria. I know this may seem odd, like praising your brakes for locking on you, but remember—your defense mechanism kept your passion intact inside you all these years; it deserves your praise and gratitude!

Part B: This is another way to quit fighting your critic. Write a tribute to whatever you were criticized for. For example, if someone called you stupid, write "A Tribute to Stupidity."

Example: Stupid people are gentle, funny, kind, generous. They don't hurt other people or make them feel bad about themselves. They are often good listeners. (And they aren't so stupid. They're just smart enough to keep their mouths shut and their minds open.)

If you were accused of being a show-off, or too shy, write your love lyrics about aggressive people, or superstars, or loudmouths, or quiet people, or wimps. Write an ode to people who start a lot of things and fail. (What imagination they have! What courage!) Or write an ode to people who can't hang on to money. (How easygoing, generous, relaxed, what good values, how unlike people who put money above everything!)

The next time someone makes you feel stupid (or loud, or vain, or selfish), remember that tribute and say it aloud. "I kind of like stupid people. They're kind, funny, etc.," and listen to the phone line go dead. Your critic might think you're a little strange, but you've taken his biggest weapon out of his hands—you *don't care* what he thinks!

You are, in effect, saying "So what?"

When you say "So what?" you're turning the spotlight on your critic and off yourself. You're exposing the fact that *he's calling you stupid because he's angry; he's not angry because you're stupid.* You're actually saying, "I don't have to fight with you just because *you* want to. Have it your own way."

Chris, who watched his father ridicule his brothers when he was a child, became fearful of the slightest criticism. That is, until he learned to say "So what?"

And then something very interesting started to happen. He found himself more accepting of his life. He stopped telling himself he wasn't happy, stopped letting his stomach churn over another day of failure, and began to take the days as they came.

"I went skiing the other day, and had a good time," he said. "I've had good times before, but when I got home I'd wipe them out by saying, 'Sure, but I don't have a career I love, a woman I love, a life I love.' Nothing counted unless I was in total bliss. This time I didn't do that to myself. I just thought about what a fun day I'd had, and went about my business. *I'm beginning to realize that my life isn't as unhappy as I thought.*"

Life isn't supposed to be an all-or-nothing battle between misery and bliss. Life isn't supposed to be a battle at all. And when it comes to happiness, well, sometimes life is just okay, sometimes it's comfortable, sometimes wonderful, sometimes boring, sometimes unpleasant. When your day's not perfect, it's not a failure or a terrible loss. It's just another day.

Solution No. 3: Oz your parent.

If, even after you shine a light on your problem and give in to your criticizer and write a poem or a love song about your character flaws and say "So what?" you *still* can't enjoy your life as it is (Sandra couldn't), then you have to do something I call "Ozing" your parent. Remember the scene in *The Wizard of Oz* when Toto the dog pulls open a curtain to reveal that the Great and Powerful Oz is only a nervous little man?

You have to take away your parent's overrated power by realizing what he's really been up to. This exercise is an eye-opener, I guarantee it.

Exercise 2: Know Thy Enemy (Role-play Your Critic)

Pretend you're the person who has made your life so tough. Then take a pencil and paper and write down *your* story. From the critic's position, explain *why* you've been so critical or why you never followed through on promises.

Why would a person make fairy-tale promises to children, then renege on those promises?

Sandra thought she knew a lot about her parents' lives, but her information came together in a new way when she role-played her dad. (She used the information her family had given her—and faked the rest, which is a perfectly okay thing to do in this exercise.)

Sandra's dad speaks:

"In the twenties when I was a kid, my father [Sandra's grandfather] was rich, and we all had a carefree, dreamy existence. We started out with yachts and garden parties and trips to Paris. But Dad made bad investments and lost everything in the Crash. I never forgave him for that. I stopped being a dreamer and became hardheaded and practical.

"I thought I hated dreamers. But somehow I fell in love with a very impractical woman. She was more beautiful to me than all the practical women I ever met. At first I liked being the practical one and taking care of her, but by the time we had kids, the charm of my wife's dreaminess wore off, and I got impatient with her.

"My daughter, Sandra, was a dreamer like I had been as a child. Part of me loved that. I loved to see her eyes light up when I'd tell her some wonderful thing we were going to do, like go to the circus.

"But when the circus came I'd get angry. I'd think, 'Circuses are stupid. If we spend our time going to the circus, we won't do the serious things that need to get done. And my daughter will grow up to be a bubble-head like her mother.' Whenever Sandra asked my permission for anything frivolous, like a movie, I'd get irritated and say, 'Just exactly what is the the good of that?' and 'What good will that do you?' It makes me mad that she's not practical—and it scares me."

Sandra was shocked when she role-played her father. She

said, "He's fighting himself when he fights me! It's a case of mistaken identity. This is weird!"

I assured Sandra that mistaken identity—also known as projection—is very common in parents.

Once she understood that the cause of all those broken promises in her childhood was her father's fear of being a dreamer—and had nothing to do with her—she started to create a real life. She decided to stop looking for glamour and try to find a decent man to marry. She moved to a singles complex and met as many of the people as she could. She hung out at the pool, went to barbecues, and even threw a party at her apartment. She began to see what nice guys were like.

"At first, I hated it. I didn't like normal, practical men. I was sure they'd drag me down into an ordinary, uninspired life. But, really, they were doing a lot better than I was, and they deserved respect," she said. She worked at learning to respect her new boyfriends. And she worked harder than ever to improve her consulting business. She even used her gift for daydreams instead of letting it use her by joining a theater group and designing sets.

"The key person I had to learn how to respect was myself," she said. "When my business got better and I got a good review in the newspaper for one of my set designs, I started feeling that in the real world I counted for something. After that it got easier to respect other people."

Sandra's not the only one who compensates for disappointment by setting her sights unrealistically high. The whole concept of happiness could use another look.

HAPPINESS

It's possible to want too much happiness.

This isn't always a fashionable thing to say, and I am a great believer in making your days as good as they can be. But I get

suspicious when I meet someone who is discontented with anything less than total bliss.

When I first met Jackie she'd tried a dozen jobs. "I want a job
that makes me radiantly happy!" she insisted.

I said, "You're so *un*happy, how about starting with a job that
just doesn't make you unhappy? We'll move up to radiant happiness later."

"No!" she insisted. "I want to be happy!"

When will I be happy?

*Chronically negative people seem to expect more happiness
out of life than ordinary people!* You'd think a chronically down
person would be satisfied just to feel okay, but often he's not.

He doesn't seem to know that *most of us don't walk around in
a state of bliss every second of the day*—and we don't have any
problem with that. I was intrigued by Jackie's insistence on "radiant happiness."

We had to take another look at Jackie's story. She was locked
into a struggle with her mother, remember? Well, *happiness was
what they were fighting about.*

"Did your mother want you to be *unhappy?*" I asked.

"No, but she hated to hear that I was happy. She resented it,"
Jackie said.

And, of course, this dynamic was obvious, but I'd never quite
noticed it before. Take a look at any overcriticized or overinter-
rupted child and you'll often see the same thing. The parent is
actually disturbed when the child experiences independent happiness. How could this be true? Surely no parent begrudges her
own child's happiness!

But some parents do.

Parents are as capable of irrational thoughts and feelings as
anyone else:

- "If she's happy, she'll go away and leave me."
- "If a kid is too happy, it's bad luck, something terrible will
  happen."
- "If my son is happy, he's being selfish; what about me?"

(Or, as the American novelist Richard Ford put it: "Angry words are all alike. They all mean, 'What about me?' ")

Without consciously acknowledging it to themselves, many parents do have a negative reaction to their children's happiness.

No wonder so many chronically negative people *insist on joy, rather than simple contentment.* They were locked in combat with their parents and they needed great happiness as a defense against the tremendous parent-driven force for unhappiness— constant pleasure seemed the only refuge from constant discontent.

Lovingly teaching parents to let go is the grown child's job. Instead of being their child, you now have to be a kind but firm adult. *You owe them that much.* They helped you to be unafraid to start school; now you help them to let go of you and get on with their lives.

Candace very gently began to wean her mother. She started sending more greeting cards and making fewer calls and visits. *When she talked to her mother, she made her mother talk about herself.*

"The habit was always to grill me, to hear about everything I'd been doing. She was so sweet, I hated to deprive her of the information she wanted, but I developed a technique. *I really practiced it,* and she didn't exactly know what was happening.

"If she pressures me, saying 'When are you going to get married?' I say, 'Did you know you were going to marry Dad when you met him?' and she's off and running on the story of her life. I know it's a trick, but it's a merciful one, and I'm not the type who could hurt her by clamming up completely."

Now you've got some techniques that will make your world safe for desire. Nothing is left but to convince your enthusiasm that it's safe to come out of hiding.

How to Take a Chance

You were very wise to save your enthusiasm for better times. *Well, these are better times.*

You're going to have to let yourself get interested in something again. Yes, this will open you up to the possibility of disappointment, criticism, or ridicule—at least from yourself—but you have the right to do what you love, no matter what anyone says. This is what living with risk really means. Not Evel Knievel stuff, but daring to want something you've talked yourself out of since childhood. Daring to try. Daring even to be a fool.

A WORD OF PRAISE FOR FOOLS

The worst thing that can happen to you as an enthusiastic adult is that you could appear foolish to people who need to criticize. Let me assure you—enthusiasm is worth this risk. If you allow yourself to be enthusiastic, you'll be so full of wonder, you won't care what people think.

Isaac Bashevis Singer tells a story about a wonderful "nar," a foolish person, which I'd like you to think about:

One day, the village nar and his wife are visited by their friend. The friend says, "You've got to go outside! There's a cow walking up the outside of your house."

The nar stands up and says, "Really?"

The wife says, "He's tricking you again. You *know* there's no cow walking up the side of this house."

But the nar runs to look.

When he returns, the wife says, "So, was there a cow walking up the side of the house?"

Sheepishly, the nar says, "No."

The friend is laughing his head off.

"Why then did you do it? Why do you *always* do it?" the wife says.

Smiling softly the nar says, "I knew there was probably no

cow walking up the side of the house. But what if there were? I wouldn't want to miss that."

In life, as in literature, great lives are the ones ruled throughout by unabashed and childlike eagerness—and a readiness to take chances, even to look foolish if necessary.

Mozart and Shakespeare were willing to be downright silly, and they led great lives. If you're willing to make your life safe enough for your enthusiasm to reappear, you too can have a great life.

As the Good Book says: Hope deferred maketh the heart sick: but when desire cometh, it is a tree of life. (Proverbs, 13:12)

THIRTEEN

A Rage Against the Ordinary

D o you live beyond your means, financially, emotionally, or some other way? Do you have a big dream or two that never quite come through? Do you make promises you can't keep?

Are a lot of people mad at you?

Are they tired of helping you? Do they want you to pay your own bills, and take care of your own problems, and do the ordinary things that everybody else has to do? Do you either ignore these people or feel furious and misunderstood?

If your answer to these questions is yes, you have a strong resistance to running your life the way everybody else does, because you're reserving yourself for a special fate. *You're in a rage against the ordinary.*

PORTRAIT OF A RAGER

Unlike many other people, a rager can state his goals in a second: "I want to make money from my designs," "I want to get a job in a band that's worthy of my capabilities," "I'm a fabulous (artist, investor, manager, woman, man) and I want the world to give me my rightful (fame, fortune, recognition, knight in shining armor, angel of my dreams)."

If you're in a rage against the ordinary, you don't want to be a painter; you want to be *the greatest* painter. You don't want to be a powerful businessperson; you want to be *the most powerful* businessperson. Glory is so important to you that you're impatient with the chores and details that make life work. You avoid anything that hints at the ordinary on your way to glory, which results in a terribly precarious existence. You deserve a big hit, and you want it *now.* You don't have time or inclination to build the foundation of skills and know-how that would actually get you a hit.

By the way, there's nothing wrong with a rager's dreams. They're magnificent and well worth going after. But a rager's dream comes with its particular pitfalls. One of these pitfalls is that anything less than the top feels pointless. Starting at the bottom, apprenticing his way to becoming a master at his craft is intolerable; a rager needs to feel he's a master before he really is —and this is a recipe for frustration and rejection.

Big, troubling feelings gnaw at a rager's insides most of the time.

The pressure of his precarious lifestyle, his frustration at being unable to get the recognition and rewards he thinks he deserves make a rager irritable, defensive, impatient, or fearful much of the time. If you're a rager, you may try to cover up these feelings by criticizing others or being cynical, so you probably have difficult relationships. You often quarrel with the very people who can help you get your dreams. These conflicts always feel like the other guy's fault. People just won't see it your way. Everyone's angry with you and *you're* angry with everyone—and you're angriest of all at fate.

So if your dreams are bigger than the rest of ours, your disasters are bigger too. Or at least that's how it looks and feels to you. To everyone else it looks like a rager is hopelessly unrealistic and causes himself a lot of unnecessary pain and trouble. He's *always* on the brink of disaster; he's routinely making hairbreadth escapes.

A rager's position as an overlooked genius, combined with his near disasters and thrilling getaways, sometimes serves to enhance his already considerable appeal.

Ragers are among the most charismatic people in the world. When he's frightened or in trouble, a rager's raw need pokes a hole through his attractiveness; then he seems manipulative, even selfish. But when a rager is happy, he's utterly enchanting.

It's this charm that makes people want to be around him, even after they've been repeatedly pulled into his problems—and ragers always have lots of problems. They don't have money for the rent, or they don't have time to type a paper that's due tomorrow morning, or they need to borrow your car or your best clothes—and this doesn't happen once or twice, it's a way of life.

Ragers don't want to take care of the details.

They think they're trying very hard to be successful in their real work, whether that's acting, real estate, finding a spouse, or designing computer programs, but when it comes to the practical side of making things happen, they just won't take care of business.

This is a tragedy, because these are often exquisitely talented people.

Ragers mystify nonragers. How can they stand to live such cliff-hanging lives? What fuels their incredible tolerance for near disasters when all they'd have to do to avoid disaster is think ahead a little bit? Why don't they want to take care of themselves? They're so capable and smart; they really don't *have* to use other people. They don't have to blame the world for their plight either. Their behavior is a great mystery to their families and their friends.

They aren't lazy either!

Ragers are hard workers.

As a matter of fact, they require themselves to work harder than other people, because they have a double effort going all the time. They're constantly working on—or thinking about—their designs, their projects, their inventions. And they're constantly avoiding one crisis or another, coming up with new and fantastic schemes to get other people to help them, working as master salesmen—wheedling, bargaining, or making glittering promises —to get out of whatever mess they're currently in.

HOW TO LIVE AN EXTRAORDINARY LIFE

"Just a minute," you might be saying. "What about Michelangelo and Muhammad Ali and everyone else who ever accomplished *extra*ordinary things? Did they settle for drab, workaday lives? Big winners need to take big risks, don't they?" Am I suggesting we waddle passively, like lemmings, into an abyss of mediocrity?

Of course not.

But ragers have made a serious miscalculation. They've missed the difference between raging against the ordinary and *being extraordinary.* An extraordinary life, a life filled with great accomplishments, is also filled with a myriad of very mundane details, hard work, and patience. Famous scientists have to pay their electric bills and walk their dogs. Successful actors have to stand on line at the supermarket. *Everybody's day-to-day life is ordinary.*

Extraordinary people don't waste any energy raging against the ordinary—they don't even care about what's ordinary and what's not. They're too busy taking one small step after another. You may be a prodigy, born with a whole range of talents, but the more gifted you are, the harder and longer you must work to create something that matches your vision. *Talent plus patience will allow you to master your craft—and mastery is what gets you your dream.*

"So many people less talented than I am are getting the jobs I want," the rager says. "It's all who you know. It's all whether you're willing to be a butt-kisser or not! Don't talk to me about mastery!"

Whether or not there's any truth to this rager's thinking, if you scratch the rager's surface *you'll almost invariably find someone who isn't as accomplished as she ought to be and isn't working hard enough to get that way.* I once asked a raging actor, "Are you as good as you ought to be?" She got uncomfortable and said irritably, "Maybe not, but people no better than I am are getting jobs." If it's hard for ragers to work on their craft, imagine how they hate taking jobs they consider "beneath" them, just to earn their expenses.

Everybody who ever tried to achieve a dream knows it's frustrating to take time out to do boring necessities, like paying bills or taking a paying job. I worked as a waitress for years to pay for college, and I *never* enjoyed it. My feet hurt, the cooks were nasty, the customers were inconsiderate. And I wanted my time for studying.

Nobody likes to work like that. But every time I picked up my pay I knew it was worth it. I gave myself the gift of a college education. I knew where the next semester's tuition was coming from. I was tired, *but I was never afraid about money.*

Most people complain about life's necessary chores, but they do them anyway because the rewards are so clear.

If you're in a rage against the ordinary, you aren't like most people. Doing life's necessary chores isn't just unpleasant for you —it's unfair, humiliating, outrageous. *These painful feelings make you refuse to take care of your life; they force you into immobility.* And because you don't want to plant seeds or tend your garden, *you never know where the next crop is coming from.*

"I'm special," you think—and there's a good chance you're right. But something fishy starts to happen in the next step of your logic.

"I'm special; therefore I shouldn't do anything but what I want. *If I do, it takes away my specialness.*"

This logic requires a careful look.

Here's how your thinking goes: Any ordinary jerk can take some kind of job to support himself. If I do the same thing, it means I'm no better than he is. It means I'm an ordinary jerk too.

You may look busy, you may be painting or building models or sketching new inventions all day and night, but you aren't doing the crucial preparation and follow-through work that would get your paintings into galleries or your inventions in front of important people. You might never get anywhere because you can't stand the "grunt" work, and you know it.

Whenever you have the opportunity to earn money for yourself by doing ordinary work, you feel absolutely terrible.

- "I felt totally humiliated last month," said Yona, a twenty-nine-year-old caterer who had trouble paying her rent. "I tried cooking for another caterer, just for the summer, to earn money. It almost killed me. I'd rather beg on the streets."

- "You say you won't crawl to get what you want. What do you mean by crawl?" I asked Sylvia, a thirty-two-year-old sometime opera student.

  "I mean get a demeaning job."

  "What is a demeaning job?"

  "Any job."

- I once asked Patrick, a forty-five-year-old sculptor, "What would it cost you—emotionally and psychologically—to be just a guy who builds whatever your customer wants and can pay the rent every month?"

  "It would be like asking Coco Chanel or Yves Saint Laurent to work as a tailor," he said.

  "But why can't you be a great designer *and* a tailor," I countered. "After all, designers do know how to stitch and pin—they can do it all. Most of them started at the bottom."

  Patrick's face flushed red and he shook his head in short, determined jerks. "I shouldn't have to do that," he said with absolute sincerity.

Contrary to Patrick's idea, all geniuses aren't as sensitive as he is about ordinary work. Einstein worked in a patent office for his paycheck and didn't find his day job at all humiliating.

As long as you're raging against the ordinary, you're losing every chance to attain your real dreams. In spite of your powerful desire to achieve, you are systematically *preventing* yourself from an extraordinary life. As George C. Scott said to Paul Newman in *The Hustler,* "There was a point when he decided to win and you started making excuses."

How do I know all this?

Let's get better acquainted with Yona, Sylvia, and Patrick.

RAGERS I HAVE KNOWN

Yona: All Work, No Play

Yona was the caterer who refused to take a supplementary job as a waitress although she was always short of money. Her best friend, Patricia, worked in a restaurant. Although Patricia worked hard and was often tired, she still came over to help Yona finish cooking late at night because she felt so sorry for her. She often loaned Yona money, although Yona was very reluctant, even angry about taking it. "Yona works harder and earns less than anyone I know," Patricia said to me once.

Patricia earned $600 a week. She put away $300 and lived on $300. She did that for years. As a result, she bought her own apartment. Also, she received hospitalization coverage with her employer, and several times got a month's vacation leave at full pay. When I met Yona she hadn't had a vacation since childhood.

Sylvia: The Raider

For a while, Sylvia lived her life as if it were a Noël Coward play. Everything she did was bathed in glamour. She wore mink, flashed exquisite jewelry, sipped champagne at elegant parties, studied opera in Europe, and never worked a day in her life. But she always had a pack of hungry creditors howling at her door and a landlord forever threatening to toss her out on the streets. This was hard on her nerves, but she refused to try to find a steady source of income. Whenever she got too deeply in trouble, she called friends and family in a frenzy of desperation to bail her out.

How did Sylvia manage to live like a jet-setter while flirting with financial ruin? *Because she could talk anybody into anything.* She was attractive, electrifying, and utterly self-absorbed. She would convince just about anyone—lovers, friends, parents, the mailman—that something glorious was just moments away, or something disastrous was about to happen to her, and they would continually rush in to provide money for the great opportunity or the rescue, even after promising themselves they'd never get suckered again. When her charm or powers of seduction failed her, Sylvia would resort to outright coercion. She would throw herself at people's mercy, *make* them help her, call them up and say "You *have* to do something or I'll be out in the streets." It seemed to her that all the "ordinary" people she knew were somehow responsible for helping to rescue her. Not for a minute, of course, did she consider getting herself a job.

I met Sylvia when, after exhausting her entire repertoire of scams and histrionics, she *had* been evicted from her apartment. She'd used up her welcome with every friend and now actually did have homelessness staring her in the face. It didn't take long to size her up.

"You are a raider," I told her. "You live up in the mountains. Down in the valley are farmers who are growing fields, building nice homes, and living responsibly. But you can't stand to farm— it's beneath you. So what you do is, when the crops are ready, you sweep down and raid. You take all the food and swipe the candlesticks off their tables and run back into the hills. Then you live up there like a big shot with candlesticks made out of silver that belong to other people—people who *earned* them by working their tails off on the farm. Don't you feel guilty about taking what other people worked for?''

"No. If they didn't want to help me they wouldn't have done it," she said.

"And you'd rather *die* than be a farmer yourself, wouldn't you?''

Sylvia looked at me for a moment.

"You're damned right," she said.

Patrick: Looking Back in Anger

Patrick was the surly, discontented son of a Midwestern millworker. He had sent himself to art school but dropped out after one semester. He was a supremely talented sculptor; he was also arrogant, wildly temperamental, and, like Sylvia, about to land himself on the street. For years, he floated around New York City where, like so many other artists, he came to be a darling of the downtown crowd. When he could, he lived off a succession of women—who obligingly put him up, on their couches or, at times, in their beds. Only menial jobs were available to him because he wouldn't train for better jobs. But Patrick refused to work at menial jobs, refused to sweep out offices or work behind the counter in a hardware store. He felt such jobs were beneath his abilities (which, of course, they were), but the money from those jobs would have paid for the materials he needed to do his artwork and kept him afloat until he was able to build a reputation. Occasionally, he took on a construction job, but more often than not, he quarreled with his clients, insuring against repeat business.

When Patrick came to me he was living on his own in a wretched tenement in New York's Hell's Kitchen. He was two months behind in his rent. But just as his landlord was about to slip an eviction notice under his door, the cavalry came in the person of a building manager who was redoing the lobby of a suburban apartment condo. The man needed a sculpture for the condo lobby. (One of the few clients whom Patrick had not totally alienated had given Patrick's name to the condo manager.) The man knew exactly what he wanted and showed Patrick a few drawings that his board had okayed. He was willing to pay enough money to cover about four months' worth of Patrick's rent.

Patrick took on the job—but a funny thing happened on the way to the sculpture. The more he spoke with his client about specifics of the structure, the more he felt anger rising within him. Based on past experience, Patrick knew that before long, things would turn ugly. He would argue bitterly with the manager, and there would be a screaming match, spiced perhaps with desk-pounding and foot-stomping. He would lose the job and probably his apartment. And he'd already run out of friends, old and new. Before this oncoming disaster could hit, Patrick sought help.

WHAT'S REALLY GOING ON WITH A RAGER?

Look again at the kind of things ragers say. What is their subtext? What are they really asking for?

What Do They Really Want?

Sylvia: I've got a special gift for singing and somebody should subsidize me, and I mean it. I'm meant for something special. I can't just give up and start being some kind of stupid nine-to-five secretary.

Patrick: Most of the jobs I can get are demeaning. I'm not going to work at some laborer's job until the world decides to wake up and buy my art. I've got fabulous ideas. I deserve a grant.

Yona: I'm a *great* cook, a true chef. It's bad enough that I have to cater church socials; I won't fry eggs in a greasy spoon to pay my rent. I'd rather starve than cook for people who don't appreciate my cooking.

Do you hear a repeated plea? I do.

The message is: *Someone is supposed to rescue me.*

But *why* is someone supposed to rescue them?

After you've known a rager for a while, you begin to suspect that what's behind his confusing behavior is that *he is trying to settle an old score.* He's trying to right an old wrong. And he's trying to achieve this vindication with a big rescue. (Until he gets one, he requires endless small rescues, but small rescues will never really satisfy him.)

If you're a rager, you probably don't understand why you're living by these self-defeating rules; you might not realize why you're trying to settle an old score. You only habitually think. *Ordinary jerks can walk; genius is supposed to fly.* Meanwhile, you feel deeply uneasy because, in your mind and heart, you know perfectly well that you're too old to get rescued.

Yona almost lost her catering business before she pulled herself up and started changing her patterns.

"I created that business—and I did all right but I couldn't really get it going. I hated to get up in the morning and wouldn't look for new clients. Once I was almost bankrupt. I really just hated taking care of myself.

"*I felt that if I took care of myself it only proved that I didn't deserve to be taken care of!* If you were first class, people didn't make you work. They treated you like a princess. To me, being capable was the booby prize. The idea that I could create my own world was totally counter to all my fantasies."

STORY TIME

Years after she'd been cured of raging, Sylvia told me, "When I was living like that I always thought, 'This time something wonderful is sure to happen. I'll never have to worry about ordinary problems again.' I was absolutely counting on a fairy-tale ending.

"All I could think about was being discovered or winning the lottery," Yona told me.

Does the hope of a big rescue sound familiar to you?

Let's take a closer look at exactly what kind of glorious rescue you secretly want.

Exercise 1: What's Your Fairy Tale?

Part A: The tale.

You already know what your dream is. Now, close your eyes and savor your favorite moment of that fantasy. How exactly do you want this moment to happen? What is the climactic scene in your life's movie?

When you've sufficiently enjoyed the fantasy, open your eyes. Jot down a few words about what you saw.

Here's how some others saw their fantasies fulfilled:

Yona: A rich, handsome foreigner marries me and takes me all over the world with him. Sometimes I cook wonderful dinners for the two of us, but I never have to work for, cook for, or serve anyone else ever again.

Sylvia: I get a letter in the mail saying someone heard me sing at a party and wants to pay me fifty thousand dollars to sing at La Scala.

Patrick: The Museum of Modern Art sees my designs and says, "Bring this guy here, now! He's a genius! We want his sculptures in the garden!"

But wait just a minute. These are pretty nice fantasies. Everybody has that kind of fantasy, don't they?

Sure they do. But there are some very important differences between the casual daydreamer and the people who desperately need a fairy-tale ending.

Let's take a closer look.

Part B: The analysis.

Look again at your happy ending. Ask yourself the following questions.

1. Does your fantasy always require the act of an outsider for it to come true?
2. Is the end some kind of rescue or reward that comes only to special people?
3. Do you get "found" or "discovered" in your fantasy?
    And, most telling of all,
4. Is your life pointless without this happy ending?

If you answered yes to these questions, you've got your life set up for disaster; you must *wait* for astonishing good luck for your life to work out at all.

You're prohibiting yourself from going out and getting what you want. For some mysterious reason you feel that *if you have to do it yourself, everything will be ruined.*

"I shouldn't have to fight my way to the top," Patrick told me once. "Any lackey can do that."

Patrick's ideas about how to get his dream had put him in a trap. If you're a rager, some pledge you've made to yourself prevents you from lifting a hand on your own behalf, from making a living, finishing your projects, taking care of essential details. Somewhere inside yourself you have a hidden agenda. If you live by a rager's rules, you watch everybody else go out and get what they want, but you have to stay where you are and wait for it— and curse fate if it doesn't come.

You've put yourself in a straitjacket.

As long as you are passively waiting, you can't give your dream a fighting chance. As long as you live this way, you're missing out on this life (and I'm not convinced we can depend on reincarnation).

If you're a rager, you've been told more than once that there's no excuse for your behavior—and maybe there is no excuse. But there is a *reason.*

There's a reason for everything.

You're making your life difficult for a reason that may surprise you—you're avoiding getting your dream by your own efforts because you don't want to destroy the hope that someday someone will rescue you. *And you actually want to be rescued* more *than you want your dream.* To be rescued will prove once and for all that you are a worthy person. The rescue will do one other thing that is very important to you: it will undo an old wrong and make things finally come out right.

How can you be sure this "wrong" is an *old* wrong, an injustice from your early years?

Because your behavior is the behavior of someone who got stuck in childhood.

YOUR UNDERSTANDABLE BEHAVIOR

How could anyone allow herself to get in such an unenviable position? Always in some kind of trouble, always discontented, always making other people angry at her? Always living for a fairy tale while real life passes her by?

Does this sound like a case of arrested development? *Well, it is.* When an adult acts this much like a child, something went terribly wrong in his childhood and he has hung back to fix it. The something that happened still constitutes the major drama of his life.

Someone or something left ragers stranded, exposed to the elements at an age when they should have been protected. Some sad circumstance left them prey to a paralyzing lack of confidence and self-esteem that they're covering up by imagining themselves as gods.

Everyone's first experience, everyone's earliest lesson, is that somebody chose to be responsible for us. As babies, we're so lovable that somebody feeds us, keeps us warm, hugs us, smiles at us. The sensation of being taken care of while we're small shapes the way we see everything for the rest of our lives. As we get older we know we have to let go of our dependent position, but if we were pushed away from babyhood too suddenly (by the birth of a younger sibling, by adult responsibilities that came too early, by the loss of a parent, or by some kind of abuse), we become like a dust-bowl farmer being pushed off his land with bulldozers—we chain ourselves to the house.

Against all reason, we refuse to leave childhood. *Ever.* Years later, we may not remember the original reason we chained ourselves to childhood, but the chains remain nevertheless.

For instance, if you've been deprived of a parent at a crucial age—through death, long-term illness, or neglect—or you had to watch a parent be rejected or humiliated in some way, the child you were has been injured badly and, in a child's mind, unfairly. Somehow that injustice must be undone. Reparations must be made in the form of great rewards *given* to you, not earned by you. Now you *have* to be a star and you have to be "discovered," not because you're gifted—although you are—but because *it's only fair.*

You go through adult life feeling that you were robbed as a child and now the world owes you something special. Or you feel that by reaching great heights you'll somehow reshuffle the terrible cards fate dealt to your father or mother.

If you're a rager, you belong to a group of people tyrannized by the tiny child who lives within them, *making them live a life no adult would consider living.* You are trapped, because taking charge of your life would create a deep sense of despair in you. If you got an ordinary job and experienced some security, that child would feel buried alive.

And you can't just tell the child to disappear.

First of all, no one knows where she ends and you start. Second, you ignore her determination at your peril. This child inside you formed her plans at an age when the ego is so single-minded and tenacious that it has no concern for the cost. Have you ever tried to argue with a tired two year old? Don't ever do it. With a child that young, you must back down and have some real humility, or try using your superior brain power, because a battle of the wills is out of the question. A two year old doesn't care what happens to him. He must have his way.

The child inside you is like that two year old; she wants some things really badly. She wants what you want: love, fame, and glory, whatever your dream is. But she wants you to get it *her* way. *And you can't get your dream her way.* You can only fail if the child continues to run your life.

This tyrannical child in you is no joke. She means serious business.

Because of her you're fighting old or nonexistent battles and *your life's energy is going into the past even when you don't know it.* You may be absolutely certain you're using 100 percent of your energy to get ahead, but you're really using it to work out an old drama. Every action, every setback or accomplishment, is seen in the context of that drama. If you don't win a big foundation grant, it proves the world is unfair. If you do, it confirms your right to the glory and prizes. After playing out your ancient drama, you have no resources left over to take charge of your present life. Unless you can find a way to leave that drama and pour your energy into what you want *now,* you'll never be able to get anywhere.

"Say what you like, I can't change," Sylvia said. "I can't and I don't want to. That brat inside me feels like all of me. *It felt bad to use my parents and my friends, but when you feel like I do, you can't help it.*"

Patrick, who has since changed his ways and become a full-time, regularly commissioned and exhibited sculptor, said the following about his past: "I had gotten addicted to manipulating. The need to get whatever I wanted at any given moment was so overpowering that I was willing to sell out my friends, even though it got to be very uncomfortable when I was in the middle of going through my old manipulative number. I could hear the machinery creaking. I could see the sucker biting. I could even see the future when the shit would hit the fan because I'd still be too broke to pay back. Even so, I had to have that shot of help right now."

Children don't have a sense of consequences. Your inner child isn't counting the cost of her stubborness. But you're stuck with the mess.

How much are you willing to pay to meet the demands of your inner brat?

If only we could just forget the past, and move on. Easy to say, hard to do.

But there is a way to reduce the power of the past enough to make a real difference—*trace the child's feelings to their source.*

Tell the story of the big rip-off.

THE HEART OF THE MATTER

It took some doing to get to the source of Sylvia's ruthless acquisitiveness and discover why the mere thought of paying her own way plunged her into a bitter depression. Though she clearly wanted to change, she often acted like an unfriendly witness at a Senate probe. I pressed lightly, asking a series of gentle questions about her school days and family life, most of which met with terse "nos" and "yeses" and steely "I don't knows." When the velvet touch failed, I took the gloves off.

"Quit ripping off your friends, Sylvia," I told her. "It's unethical. Get a job and pay off your debts."

That really teed her off. "I will not!" she snapped, sounding like a preschooler. "Why should *I* have to get some lousy job? What do you want me to do, go waste my life in some cubicle? Or maybe you'd be happy if I became a damn waitress, so I can be someone's servant all day and get treated like a lower form of life."

If you agree with Sylvia—if the idea of earning your own keep makes you livid, or sad or resentful—go to the desk and pull out a pad and pencil. We're going for a little trip.

Exercise 2: Jet Clarity

Close your eyes and pick a job. Any job—the more repulsive, the better. Imagine you've gotten up, made the dreary commute, and you're there, with an entire eight-hour day staring you in the face. Really experience it, take it all in. How does it feel? Outrageous? Unjust? Frightening? Let the feeling become strong.

Now think back to the first time you ever felt that emotion. How old were you? Jot down the first age that comes to your mind. Now, pencil in hand, *go back to that time and that feeling and write a description of all the surrounding circumstances.* Don't edit yourself, just let it all flow out, in a stream of consciousness narrative. Where were you at the time? At home? In school? Who was with you? Your parents? A teacher? A group of friends? And, most important of all, what's made you so upset? Summoning up painful memories doesn't always go that smoothly; be prepared to meet some mental resistance, but try to use the images that come to trigger the details of these memories.

Jet Clarity is a powerful and efficient way to clear up the mystery of troublesome feelings left over from your past. It helps you express those feelings *in a context where they have meaning.* If you don't cry about the thing that really made you sad, you'll cry forever, and you'll cry about the wrong things. You can feel the truth of this when you take any overreaction or chronic feeling back to its source. Suddenly, the feelings become very hot, very intense for a few moments *because finally they are at the right place.* Feelings that haven't been expressed attach themselves to every part of your life and make you view reality in a biased way. But you'll find that once you express your feelings about the *real* issue that caused them, *you will actually change.*

If you did the exercise, you probably arrived at some liberating—and surprising—insights into your behavior. Here's an excerpt of what Sylvia remembered:

> I was two, two and a half. It was when we were living in Canada and my mother took sick. We were very close, she and I, and almost every night—it's funny, but it always seems to be summer when I remember it—almost every night we'd lie on her bed with the exhaust fan on and she'd read me all about Winnie-the-Pooh and Tigger and

Eeyore, and then she'd sing some funny song, and I'd fall asleep in her arms.

But there came a night when they wouldn't let me in my mother's room anymore. They kept the door shut most of the time. Sometimes my father or one of my aunts or uncles could go in, and whenever they did I'd try to run in and they'd throw me back out—once I ran in and climbed on top of my mother and I'll never forget how she smiled a sad, sweet smile at me. But they ripped me off her like I was a leech or something, and I went *bananas,* crying and kicking and screaming—the whole thing. Finally, they told me I was too bad to live at home anymore and they packed me off to my Aunt Alma's in Quebec.

I couldn't know it then but my mother had Lou Gehrig's disease, and she was dead within a year. I never saw her again until they brought me to the funeral home and—I don't remember doing this but my father says I did—I tried to climb up on her one more time, and of course somebody smacked me on the ass and dragged me straight back home.

As a two year old, Sylvia had been robbed of her rights. She felt badly used by her family and abandoned by her mother at one of the most tenacious ages for children, "the terrible twos"—an age when a child deprived of anything is likely to shriek for hours. So what she did was carry that two-year-old tenacity into adulthood to collect the debt she was owed.

Because she was so busy trying to get reparations for this ancient wrong, trying to take back what she felt was rightfully hers, Sylvia never developed any real self-esteem. She had no idea what it feels like to take pride in an accomplishment, because she never fully developed any talent or project of her own. She did love to sing and would occasionally apply herself to learning her craft—but then she'd always stop, unless some immediate reward beckoned.

By taking her feelings back to their source, Sylvia found her hidden agenda, the unfinished business left over from her child-hood: She felt the world owed her a glamorous life because of the loss she'd suffered as a two year old.

When Patrick tried Jet Clarity, he awakened his feelings by imagining cleaning offices every night for a living. Fury showed up at once, and Patrick traced the fury to its source—when he was seven. As he wrote out his memory, he became visibly agitated.

Here's what he came up with:

> I'm in Indiana, in the house where I grew up. In the living room—flowered wallpaper, mauve with roses. Hand-me-down Victorian furniture. My mother's there. Pam, my little sister. And my father with his head turned downward. He's talking and his voice is broken. He's saying, "They sunk me. Smitty, Bud, Cy—all of 'em." It was about the mills. My father was running for president of the union—the local. He was favored—and he should have been. He was honest and fair and everybody knew it. It was all he ever wanted out of his lousy life. But he hadn't finished junior high school, and some of the others thought he was bad for their image—for their bargaining position with management. A few of them got together and formed a coalition, put a big voting block behind another guy—a young radical foreman named Dennis who was going to night school. They spread a lot of lies, that Daddy could hardly read and such—which was crap. So he lost—not by a lot, but by enough. The bastards betrayed him—even Jack Wade, one of his oldest friends.

"What did your father do then?" I asked Patrick, after reading his story.

"What could he do? He swallowed it. He had to work with them, you know—he had nothing else. But it broke him—at home, that's where he showed it, looking downtrodden, hardly speaking sometimes. He's a sweet soul, very modest, and he doesn't have a lot of faith in himself. Other men might have fought back, or gone to school—he was still young then—and he could have gotten a supervisor's job. But that was it for him."

"And how did all this make you feel?"

"I wanted to kill them," Patrick said. "All the people who hurt him. I still do sometimes."

Patrick realized he had spent his time trying to rescue his father, trying to undo the humiliation that had broken the man he idolized. Patrick was going to do something grand with his life, then he was going back to Indiana, take his father and his whole family to the top of a hill, and build a palatial home—to shove it down the throats of the people who had ripped off his daddy thirty-five years before.

Patrick felt he had to start at the top because working his way up from the bottom was too slow. But of course no one would hire a new man for a top position, so the world was defeating him as it had defeated his father. By becoming nothing more than an honest workman, Patrick felt he was somehow betraying his dad. So whenever he was confronted with a task that was less than grand—even if it brought him money he badly needed—Patrick unleashed all the anger and hatred that should have been reserved for Smitty and Cy and all the other workers who had conspired to keep his father in his place.

After you trace the feelings to their source, you know *why* you have trouble helping yourself in ordinary, effective ways. You can also expect to feel calmer. You've had an insight connected with a long overdue emotional reaction, and much of your intensity has expressed itself.

After her rage had subsided a bit, Yona was able to explain: I resented being forced to be self-sufficient. My parents were really inept, and I was taking care of myself since I was six years old. I was self-reliant too soon, I guess, and I didn't like it one bit. I really felt it proved I didn't deserve to be loved. I've always felt so cheated.

Sylvia: I run up credit cards because I feel that it's outrageous that I should suffer when I already suffered so much as a kid. I feel that somebody did me harm, and *they* should pay for it, *I* shouldn't!

Patrick: The world crushed my family. Well, I won't let them crush me. I'm not going to be somebody's slave labor. I'm too good for that.

Tracing your problem feelings to their source won't get rid of them forever, but the hidden drama that created them will be clear to you. Suddenly, you can see *why* you're unable to go in a simple path toward what you want. You can see *why* your life is so complicated and difficult. Only when you understand what's driving your impulsive behavior can you ever begin to get free of it.

What's *your* hidden agenda?

What's the real reason you'd feel so bad if you took care of yourself?

AFTER THE FALL

Once you've figured out the old purpose behind your present-day raging, some good news and some bad news await you.

The good news is *you can have whatever the adult in you wants.* You can have a great job. You can do what you love, become well-known, accomplished, respected, have joy. You can make grand things happen, see foreign lands, find a mate, have a family, be a star. Every magnificent adult dream you can dream is possible for you.

The bad news?

You cannot have what that child inside you wants. You can't get the villains to undo the wrong they did so long ago, can't fix your parents' sorrows, can't win love that wasn't willingly granted to you in your childhood. You can't make your sick mother well. Even if you could get the love you wanted as a child, you can no longer absorb that kind of love. You're never going to be able to make an ancient drama come out differently, or right an ancient wrong.

But there is more good news.

Once you've uncovered the old drama and let your feelings finally be about the right incidents, those feelings will loosen their grip on your present life. You won't interpret present problems as a representative of your past. Your inner brat will be getting ready to let go of you. And there's something you can do to help her give up the old fight.

Praise her.

Exercise 3: Praising Your Inner Brat

You've got to admire that stubborn kid inside you. She caused you plenty of trouble, kept you from leading a comfortable life, and slowed your progress, but she never would capitulate to the enemy. She refused to forget the past and was fiercely determined to settle your old debt. She's pretty amazing. *She has integrity!* So before you take another step, I think it's time to admire her, to write a paean to her.

A paean (pronounced PEE-uhn) is a song of praise, designed to heal you. The name comes from Homer's *Iliad,* and refers to Paean, an Olympian physician to the gods. Later the name Paean was given to Apollo as the sun god, the healer.

I learned about the healing power of a praise song when I put together a "bad habit workshop," designed to help people who couldn't stop smoking, biting their nails, or being hopelessly disorganized. In the workshop, they were hard on themselves, saying things like "I don't know why I do it. I'm just killing myself. I just hate myself. And I can't stop." Their self-criticism suddenly struck me as very peculiar, although I do it too. To say "I hate myself" is very odd. You're being two people. One is being bad; the other is scolding the first one. No actor would play a villain that way. If an actor is going to play a villain with any insight, he has to stop hating the villain first. An actor understands that no villain wakes up and decides to be a bad guy that day. To him, his behavior is justified.

So I told the "bad habit" group to take this "bad" smoking or nail-biting or sloppy character they were scolding and assume the troublesome guy is convinced he's doing the right thing.

Admit that your inner brat was always trying to protect you. Now you have to thank her.

You have to say, "There's a child in me who refuses to quit smoking (or refuses to start paying bills, or refuses to stop quarreling with my colleagues) and this child won't give an inch. She doesn't understand the harm she's doing. She has simply held on to her principles and picked a corner from which she will not be coerced and will not be compromised."

You can do this exercise about anything you wish you didn't do—pick the wrong lovers, fall asleep when it's time to do homework, say yes when you want to say no—*anything.*

Get out a legal pad and pencil and interview your "bad" kid about her "bad" behavior. First, review the facts. She won't let me get a job, be reliable, etc. Then ask questions until you get the answer to *why* she's doing what she's doing.

Then *you have to thank her.*

Here's a sample interview from the anti-bad-habit workshop. We had these discussions by using the Fritz Perls two-chair technique—moving from one chair to another as we questioned our inner selves.

Q: You're the smoker inside Cheryl. Why aren't you quitting?
A: I don't want to.
Q: Why don't you let her quit?
A: I don't want to.
Q: Why not?
A: She's always doing what everybody wants. *Just one time, she's not going to.*
Q: Are you mad at her?
A: A little. But I'm trying to help her. Trying to help her tell everybody to go to hell.

Q: You're really on her side, aren't you? You deserve some
   appreciation.
A: She's got to do something bad and not get talked out of it.

After a smoker praises his inner brat, every time he picks up a
cigarette his resistance to quitting is less. *The conflict is gone.* If
smoking is your way of saying "Screw the world," and you *know*
it, smoking starts to feel a little silly. And you have actually taken
a step toward quitting smoking. (If, incidentally, you can't stop
your bad habit right away, you might replace it with something
that won't hurt you as much but will still say "Screw you!" to the
world. I know a woman who stopped smoking and started reading trashy novels instead of literary ones.)

Okay, now take a look at *your* interview. What do you notice
there?

"She's got a lot of guts," said Yona about her inner brat. "She
knows what's right for her and *nothing*—no amount of anger or
scorn—will budge her. She knows what trouble she has coming.
But rebellion was the only way to keep my mother from neglecting all of us when I was a kid. And that brat is still trying to make
sure I don't get neglected."

There's one more thing your feisty inner child needs from you
to help her admit the pain she's suffered and realize that the game
is over. You should give her an understanding adult—an angel—
in her corner.

Exercise 4: Break the News to the Kid

Pretend you have gone as an adult to your childhood home to
visit the child you once were. Walk into the house and notice the
furniture in the living room, notice the kid's room and all her
clothes and toys. Where is she? What is she doing? Watch her for
a while. What's her mood? If you came upon a child like her
today and you could say anything to her—what would you say?

Then say your answer out loud.

Yona said, "She looks so sad! She's fat. Sitting in an armchair, eating Oreos, and reading Nancy Drew books. She's unkempt. Her hair's in a tangle. If I could say anything, I'd tell her the truth: 'You are a lovable kid in a bad situation. It's not your fault nobody's taking care of you.'"

Sylvia said, "She's climbing out the bedroom window in the middle of the night, not dressed warmly enough, looking for trouble. In the morning, her aunt will scream at her. She'll be exhausted. Her homework won't be done, so the whole school day will be painful. She's lonely climbing out that window, looking for a friend, looking for a thrill. I want to tell her, 'You deserve to sleep in your own bed and get kindness and companionship from your family. You shouldn't have to put yourself in danger to get what you need. *It's not your fault you're doing this.'*"

This child inside you has always been misunderstood and scolded—even by you. After all, you're supposed to be an adult and she's been making you look and act childish. But misunderstood children get very tired. They want to rest, and they can't rest until someone sees them as they really are, with some compassion and understanding.

When the child within you gets a sense that her grievances have been heard and respected, chances are you'll both cry a few tears and take a nap like a baby does—and wake up feeling better. Then you can begin to walk away from past injustices and get on with your life.

RUNNING ON EMPTY

Now that your inner kid is starting to let go of her preoccupation with injustice, you should feel wonderful. But at first the feeling isn't all good. You've grown accustomed to your hurt, your resentment—you've been living with it most of your life. Without your hurt, you're different. Something's missing. You feel empty.

"Look, I tried to change. It felt horrible," a client said to me once.

When the lifetime drama of righting an ancient wrong and the daily drama of never-ending disasters in your life is gone, it feels very strange.

Patrick said, "I used to be frightened all the time, at the mercy of my creditors and my few remaining friends, but life had so much meaning. When I finally told my friends that they weren't doing me any favors by loaning me money, everything got worse, not better. I'm glad now that I changed, but at first it was rough."

After she'd taken an imaginary visit to her childhood, Sylvia said, "I really liked that child, and when I let myself feel kindness and understanding toward her, my defensiveness vanished for a few minutes. As soon as it was gone, I felt so sad."

Face it—it's tough to even *want* to grow up.

And when you first begin it feels like a great loss. When your fairy tales are gone, the hard truth becomes too clear: you're in a world where no one feels obligated to dedicate their life to you, and where things aren't always fair.

In one important way, an adult is always alone; he gives up the illusion that parents, teachers, grown-ups in general are devoted to him, and he loses the notion that things always turn out right. It's a trade-off, and ultimately it's a beneficial trade-off, because whoever makes that trade gets to be a grown-up. Only an adult has the power to carve out a good life for herself.

SAVED BY ALTRUISM

To move from childhood to adulthood, we all have to learn a hard lesson, over and over: to give up Center Stage narcissism, bit by bit, until we become true members of the adult world, in partnerships, living and letting live, giving up our need to manipulate and control.

If you're a rager, this lesson is going to be particularly rewarding for you, and it's going to be particularly difficult for you, because you need to do some tough "counter-narcissism" work.

Ragers are frightened people. When you were raging, you were so wrapped up in yourself you couldn't see anything else, and you couldn't build a stable life for yourself. No amount of help from other people could fix that.

I'm going to suggest something that might surprise you. *The best way for a rager to begin to see and to stabilize is to bail out someone else!* The minute you can look out for somebody else you start to develop a pontoon—a boat that can't tip over and become unstable.

Exercise 5: Saving Somebody Else (or He Ain't Heavy— He's My Brother)

I'd like you to practice being a rescuer on paper before you actually go out into the world and help someone. So pick up your pen again. You're going to fix someone else's problems.

In your narcissistic raging days, you may have forgotten that your friends and family members have their own crises and sorrows. It's time to wake up to the world that's bigger than your own problems. Remember, *helping someone else isn't penance, it's perspective.* Seeing the world as larger than your own problems will help break the hold that narcissism has on you.

Pick someone you know who's in serious trouble, not of her own doing. A close friend who's lost her husband and has children. A sick aunt who's about to be evicted from her apartment. Or a friend whose career is going nowhere, who needs someone to help get her back on track.

Now, draw up a scenario in which you are closely involved in this person's problem or project. Devise strategies and solutions for them, offer them a helping hand and a shoulder to cry on. But whatever you do, *never* allow your central focus to be yourself.

Sylvia chose to help her father. His hardware business was failing, a casualty of depressed conditions in Edmonton. Compounding matters, her father's second wife had left him, and he'd started to drink. Sylvia had always had a volatile relationship with her father, but she loved him and he'd provided her with staunch financial support over the years. Still, when he cried out to her for help managing his business, she balked at first. The idea of going back to Canada to be trapped in some drab, ordinary job enraged and terrified her, and he *was* the parent who had allowed her to be tossed out of her mother's sickroom and packed off to Montreal. *He* owed *her.*

But she was able to realize that letting her father down wouldn't right the wrong she'd suffered as a toddler. She went back to Edmonton, where she volunteered to work full time without pay as manager of the hardware store. Once there she used her gift for sales and problem solving on behalf of her father instead of herself, and she discovered that no business is dull when you make it your own. Not only did she save her father $20,000 a year by working without a salary, but, because she was such a monster of energy when she wanted to be, she actually turned his failing business around. She was wonderfully creative (to her father's initial dismay) and started "Women and Carpentry Week," the culmination of which was a group of women in hard hats putting up a house frame, with the local TV station filming every move. Her father's business nearly doubled that week.

Most importantly, Sylvia was generous with her feelings as well as her labor. She provided her dad with much needed moral support through his personal difficulties, nudging him into joining an over-fifty singles club.

Does altruism seem too simplistic a tactic to you? Just try it and you'll change your mind. How do you begin? Look around you. Is there a hospital that needs volunteer help in the children's ward? A neighbor who could use help learning to read? Somewhere in your life there's a way to help others that will be right for you and will enrich your life.

Yona, who opened a one-day-a-week soup kitchen and social hour for pensioners in a forgotten part of her town, said, "It gave me back my heart. I quit feeling sorry for myself. Now I like my life. I've stopped wasting my time being resentful."

Patrick started giving art classes to inner city kids. "I feel like a good guy, for a change," he reported.

Becoming generous, carrying someone *else* for a while, does amazing things for your self-esteem.

Selfishness—even in the name of an injustice—lowers your self-respect and creates shame. One of the reasons you had so few ways to save yourself was your shaky self-esteem—it caused your resistance to jobs you felt were beneath your dignity. It takes a strong ego to take any job and remember you're still yourself; you didn't have that kind of an ego. *If you feel defined by any job, your self-image isn't solid enough.* But if you change your theme song from "I was robbed" to "I did some good in this world," your self-image will change right along with your song.

The French novelist André Gide wrote about Constructive Altruism in his Nobel Prize–winning journals:

> Each one of these young writers analyzing his suffering from . . . mystic aspirations, or from unrest, or from boredom, would be cured at once if he strove to cure or to relieve the *real* sufferings of those around him. We who have been favored have no right to complain. If, with all we have, we still don't know how to be happy, this is because we have a false idea of happiness. When we understand that the secret of happiness lies not in possessing but in giving, by making others happy we shall be happier ourselves.

BEAUTIFUL DREAMER

Well, now you've got a handle on your rage against the ordinary. Does this mean that those dreams of yours were nothing but attempts to fix the past? Should you forget them?

Absolutely not. Those dreams came from the core of you and they were good. You strapped a burden to the back of your dream when you used that dream to right an old wrong, and that burden didn't belong there.

Your dream is too good to be carrying the burden of fixing your unhappy past—especially when that burden prevented you from getting your dream *and* had no effect on your past.

Now the past will begin to let you go. Now your dream is finally free to come true.

You're a great dreamer; now go for your dream the right way. Give your dreams a fighting chance. You've proven that you can be unstoppable. Now make some unstoppable progress. How? *Be a farmer, not a night raider.*

Be as responsible and hardworking as a farmer. Go out and get a steady job and earn some money. You need to teach yourself that you have the power to fix your own life; you need to understand that money, skill, and wisdom accumulate bit by bit, over time; you need to learn how to delay gratification.

You need to acquire a real craft and quit flying by the seat of your pants like a special person who doesn't have to obey the rules. You need to learn to plan and enjoy *going after* what you want instead of waiting for it to come to you. *You have the right to go out and get what you want.*

AFTERWARD: THE POWER AND THE GLORY

Changing is hard work. But, let me quote Gide again:

"How often have I directed my attention, my study, to this or that fugue of Bach . . . precisely because in the beginning it discouraged me . . . guided by that obscure feeling that *what thwarts us and demands of us the greatest effort is also what can teach us most.*"

Yona is on the staff of a new cooking school in North Carolina. She writes a cooking column for a newsletter that goes out to gourmet clubs, and the column may soon become a book!

Sylvia calls every year to update me on how wonderful everything is. The shift from narcissism to altruism brought about drastic changes in her life. The longer she stayed with her father, the more she remembered what she loved about living in Edmonton. And she began to sing again; one day, she started taking voice lessons in earnest. Six months later, she was offered a part-time faculty position in the music department of a community college. That was two years ago.

Once Patrick understood the real source of his anger, his outbursts and his quarrels with clients subsided. By tracking down some old leads, he met a number of contractors who were also painters, photographers, and writers who did construction work, and he learned from them that construction is never pedestrian to an artist. Of course, he had to take on some low prestige jobs, but his artistic coworkers showed him how hard artists work at their art, and he was touched by something quite new to him: humility. He accepted that, for all his native talent, there *were* some things he didn't know, techniques and shortcuts that experienced professionals used every day to make their lives easier. For three years two nights a week, he went back to square one, sitting side-by-side with people half his age at the School of Visual Arts, until he was ready to work on his own.

It took almost three years for Patrick's old patterns to disappear and the new ones to surface, but they did. "I used to walk around lost inside a house of mirrors and now I'm out here with everyone else, paying attention to stop signs and traffic lights."

Like Patrick, Yona and Sylvia have left center stage and entered the real world. Now for the first time they're feeling pride in taking care of themselves and being compassionate to others. What has happened to their magnificent dreams?

"I've learned something totally new to me," Yona said. "It's called 'patience.' The opposite of rage has turned out to be patience. I'm patiently developing my career, for one thing."

Patience with the ordinary. It has a nice ring. Patience with the ordinary is taking Yona, Sylvia, and Patrick closer every day to actually attaining their magnificent dreams. And to living extraordinary lives.

FOURTEEN

The Red Herring, or Trying Hard to Love Something You Don't Really Want

I T T O O K a lot of probing to get Lee, a burned-out photographer's rep, to admit the truth.

Lee had come to see me saying she wanted a radical career change, and we had both been frustrated for weeks because she couldn't settle on any goal that really satisfied her. We knew what Lee loved. She loved gardens, music, and comedy writing. But even when we pulled these loves into what should have been a fascinating life plan, Lee still looked very unhappy.

"You're going to have a hard time writing comedy in that mood," I said.

"I know," she said.

"You really love this stuff, right? You love gardens, music, and comedy writing?"

"Yes, I really do," she said.

"That's the truth?"

"That's the truth."

Finally, I played a hunch.

"Lee, is it the *whole* truth?"

"What do you mean?"

"Pardon me for getting personal, but how's your love life?" I said.

Lee started to cry.

The truth was: Lee didn't really want any career on this planet. She was *trying* to want a career. What she really wanted was Steve. Steve was a gentle and shy mathematician she'd been seeing for two years. He had recently ended their relationship when he was transferred to a new town.

"Why did you hide that? Why wasn't that top on the list of what you wanted?" I asked.

"Because it's impossible," she said. "He doesn't want me. Anyway, I feel like a wimp for caring more about some man than my own career."

I had played the right hunch: Lee's search for a new career was a red herring. (The phrase "red herring" comes from the pranksters' practice of drawing a smoked herring across a track to throw hounds off the scent. Nowadays, it means any false clue deliberately planted to mislead or divert attention.) Lee wanted to throw herself off the scent, because she was embarrassed that she wanted a man more than she wanted a career. She was trying hard to have a politically correct heart—which is impossible. If you're as apologetic as Lee was about wanting love more than a career, let me remind you of a couple of facts we all know—and we all keep forgetting.

Fact one: You cannot tell your heart what it wants. Your heart will tell you.

When you try to force your feelings to submit to your mind, it's like throwing away the map to a happy life.

It's a terrific way to get totally lost.

Your heart is the center of a million-year-old survival system. If it's longing for love, there's a good reason.

So, if you're having a hard time getting to work on what you're *supposed* to be doing because something else keeps distracting you, you'd better put down your tools, quit trying to work, and *start listening* to the messages from your heart.

To Lee—and to many of us women—the forbidden wish is for love. "Love" feels like part of the old "women were born to love, men were born to get out into the world" training that our mothers got. And that old propaganda did a lot of harm to women who longed for meaningful work, who wanted a chance to get into the game they knew they'd be so good at. We're smart to avoid falling under the spell of the old propaganda. But we shouldn't let ourselves get confused; the right to meaningful work does not cancel out the need to love somebody.

No *man* would consider it wrong to want to love *and* to fulfill himself—not for a moment.

Of course, some people are perfectly content to live alone. I'm happy that the time has passed when our society felt that a woman—or a man—without a mate was an incomplete or pitiful thing. We've seen through that myth now, and none too soon. Yumie Hiraiwa's story "Lady of the Evening Faces" ends when a woman leaves her husband in what one reviewer called "the classic act of liberation": "She was indeed lonely, but she was free. From then on, she would be able to live just for herself. She noticed that the men and women walking about town thinking the same way were surprisingly numerous. They all strutted triumphantly along the chasms of the city wearing the elegant expressions of the single nobility."

If you feel like this woman, you don't need to read this chapter. But if you think solitary people are wasting a wonderful opportunity for connection, if you're somebody who has a genuine gift for good relationships, *you will not be happy alone.* If you want love, then love is what you must go after; you must at least give it your best try.

Fact two: If you go after the thing you want the most, you'll be in a much better position to go after anything else you want.

Get your priorities in line. Do first things first. If your stomach is empty, get something to eat. If your mind is empty, go back to school. If your heart is empty, get your love life straightened out. Getting your love life in order can be the most efficient thing you do toward getting a great career.

After all, when you succeed in getting your love life in running order, you're going to need something else to do. You won't just say "Whew! Gotcha!" and fall back on the couch for the rest of your life.

If love is what you want, you must try to get it. Having love will make your work life better.

YOUR LOVE LIFE

Let me enlarge our definition of "love." In a red herring situation, "love" doesn't always refer to romantic love. You might be longing for *anything* you think you can't have, and using the career search as a red herring designed to distract yourself. Take Celia, for example: Celia devoted over ten years to becoming an opera singer. She found the perfect teacher and studied singing diligently and intelligently; her career was within her grasp. In another year, she would be ready to audition in front of anyone.

So I was shocked when she made an appointment with me to work on a career change. My surprise must have shown on my face because the first thing Celia said was, "Singing is over. I don't want to discuss it. Help me find something else."

Obeying her orders, I began to ask the obvious questions: Did she want to stay in music? She didn't think so. Did she want to go into business? She said no.

Finally I said, "Celia, what's going on?"

"My teacher dumped me," she said, and she started to cry.

A few days earlier, out of the blue, Celia's teacher shut the piano and announced that she would no longer be teaching Celia, or anyone else. She said she'd had enough and had to get on with other things. She didn't want to teach anymore. Teaching was over, the decision was final, and that was that. Celia tried to plead with her teacher, even offered her more money, but the teacher was adamant. Celia went to bed for two days, unable to stop crying.

"I hate being so weak. I've just got to get over this," Celia said.

"You might be moving a bit too fast," I suggested.

BEFORE YOU GIVE UP ON A DREAM . . .

There are two things you must do before you give up on a dream.

First, check for a heartbeat—your dream may still be alive. If you're feeling terrible about abandoning something you want, take a second look. It may be premature to declare your dream a hopeless case.

Second, *quit trying to be a Spartan and learn how to be a mensch.* A Spartan knows how to live with deprivation. A mensch dares to ask for what he wants. A Spartan has a special kind of courage: he or she can endure terrible pain and privation without a whimper. A mensch—loosely defined as "a real person, someone who does what is right"—has more courage than a Spartan: a mensch can put away pride and speak his heart.

Before you turn your back on a dream, you must have the courage to speak your heart. It's the right thing to do.

Exercise 1: Tell the Truth about What You Really Want

This exercise is simple and fast (but not always easy). Take a large piece of paper and with a broad marking pen write the following words on it: "I want _____, and I'm not ashamed to say it." You fill in the blank.

Now tape that piece of paper to the wall.

Good God, where is your pride?

You've just admitted that you want somebody who has rejected you. And why would I ask you to do a thing like that?

To remind you that your love belongs to you.

Even if it turns out that you cannot—or should not—have a relationship with someone you love, *that doesn't mean you don't love them anyway.*

Your love is not in someone else's hands. It belongs to you. It comes from your affectionate nature, your imagination, your best impulses to know and be known by another human being. If that person doesn't want you, even if he doesn't really deserve your love, you still won't be able to kill that love, *and you shouldn't try.*

You have to keep away from people who don't love you back or who can't be trusted with your love. But there's no reason to turn your feelings off. There's nothing wrong with your love, just with your beloved.

When you're old and wise, you'll be very happy to think about the gallery of rogues and angels you allowed to touch your heart.

Love isn't a competitive sport. You don't have to play pride games. Even if the worst happens and you are undeniably rejected, there's great dignity in saying: "I loved her and she didn't love me. That's a damned shame, isn't it?" Pride is a thin substitute for sincere, openhearted dignity. This kind of behavior may *feel* risky, but it reflects an inner strength that is admirable—and is quite different from the clichéd warning about not wearing your heart on your sleeve.

WHERE YOU ARE NOW

Let's take a coolheaded look at your situation.

Did you take "no" for an answer too soon?

If, in your sober moments, you know that the other person really doesn't want a relationship with you, you have to back off. You know perfectly well if you're concocting a private fantasy. I'm not encouraging fanatic obsessions. But most "red-herring chasers" are perfectly stable people who *prematurely* assumed there was no hope. It wasn't in their sober moments they decided they weren't wanted, it was in their hurt moments. When you're hurt, you lose your good sense. You just want to crawl into a hole and pull it in after you. You only want to come out from time to time to mumble bitter comments about how hopeless life and love can be.

When you say "What's the use? I guess I'm not supposed to have what I want in this life," that's hurt talking, not good sense.

You know you should try at least one more time to get your heart's desire, but you can't help wanting to protect yourself, and you need to vent some frustration at the same time. There's no point in trying to reason with yourself right now because feelings are more powerful than reason. Why don't you let the hurt have its say and clear the air?

Exercise 2: Twenty Reasons Why There's No Hope

Make a list.

That's right, write down twenty reasons why you can't have what you want. Twenty? Yes. If you run out of reasons at six, just keep writing until you've hit twenty, even if you get as petty as "I love sushi and he hates it."

Don't be afraid of the negativity. You won't get stuck there, I guarantee it. I love a good complaining session, and I like it loud and ludicrous. It's usually a good idea to push negativity until it's ridiculous, exaggerated, self-indulgent. Give it a try and watch the thunderclouds roll away.

Take a pencil and write the first line at the top of the page: "I want X, but I don't have a chance because . . ." and let it rip. Here's what you might say:

. . . "her parents hate me."

. . . "I don't make enough money."

. . . "he told me he could never forgive me."

. . . "she said she doesn't think she can marry again."

Now push it to its extreme limits.

"I'm a louse and I deserve to be shot. She's totally right."

"He probably has twenty-five models over at his house right now. What does he want with a dud like me?"

There, feel better?

A gripe session gets that negativity out where we can see it instead of letting it lurk around inside where it has too much power. Now shake off the negativity like a dog shakes off water, because it's time to make some plans.

PLANNING A CAMPAIGN

Here's what happened with Lee.

At first she protested my suggestion that she try to get back together with Steve.

"But he told me he doesn't *want* a relationship," she said. "What am I supposed to do, *make* him marry me?"

"Doesn't he love you?" I asked.

"*He* does. His family doesn't. We're really happy when we're together. That's why it's so terrible."

"Lee, is it possible he's just scared?"

"Sure, it's possible. But he's made up his mind."

"How many times did he tell you it was over?"

"Once. But with him, that's enough. It's final. I don't have another move."

"I have an idea for one move," I said.

"What?"

"Move to his town."

Lee just stared at me. I explained that if she moved near him, they could visit and have some time to see if he would really stand by his decision. She'd let her job in New York languish anyway, so she had nothing to hold her here. She could sublet her New York apartment and live on savings for a few months while she checked out her number one priority: Steve.

Lee agreed to sound him out. She called to tell him she thought she'd like to move to his town and asked if he'd help find her a place to live. If he hadn't said yes, she would have had to respect his wishes, but he agreed very quickly.

She packed up her cat and her typewriter and moved three hundred miles to the apartment he found for her—right down the street from his house. Within a few days she joined a group of writers and began to work on her comedy writing.

Steve couldn't stay away from her. He'd been missing her terribly, but he too had been justifying his decision to separate with all kinds of reasons why they couldn't be together. After a while Steve's fear passed and he asked Lee to marry him. They've been married for ten years and neither one of them has ever regretted their decision. In the last few years Lee has completed two novels and is working on her third.

Celia's story wasn't over either.

After Celia finished telling me her sad story about being thrown out by her singing teacher, I asked her, "What are you going to do about it?"

"Do? What can I do? She said she's finished teaching, loud and clear."

"Did she look reasonable?" I asked. "You know, was it carefully thought out? Did she give you some notice? Did she give you some advice on how to continue?"

"No! She just threw me out. Without warning!"

"Don't you find that curious? What could have upset her like that?"

"I don't know. But I told her I needed her. I needed her or my career would be set back for years! For good! And she looked even angrier!" Celia said.

"Is she the kind to get herself in a situation where she does a huge amount of giving, more than you expect? Teachers can fall into that rather easily."

"Oh yes, that's her all right," Celia said. "She's incredible. She makes every lesson a major wonderful event. There's no one like her."

"Ah. Then I know what to do." I smiled.

"What?" Celia asked.

"Bring her a dozen roses," I said.

Celia's teacher sounded and behaved like someone who had been both overworked and underappreciated and badly needed some appreciation.

The next day, Celia bought a bouquet of flowers and knocked on her teacher's door. She was inspired when she talked to her teacher that day. She hardly knew where the words came from and she meant every one of them. She said she'd never appreciated how tough a teacher's life must be. Especially a teacher who was so brilliant and gave so much.

"I'm not asking you to take me back as a student, because you have every right to your decision not to teach. But I want my chance to do something for you," Celia said. "I'll balance your checkbook, or clean your house, or do your cooking, or answer your correspondence. You've given more to me professionally than anyone I've ever known. I feel lucky to have worked with you. I want to help you now."

Her teacher melted. Like most teachers, she had no way of telling anyone that she was worn out and a bit wounded at the unthinking demands of her students. She admitted it was hard always being on the giving end. When she saw Celia's honest regret and her sincere concern, the teacher no longer felt taken for granted. Her energy reappeared, and she took Celia back as a student.

"While I was talking, I realized that I really would have helped her even if she wouldn't teach me anymore. She wouldn't have let me, but that's not the point. I used to think of her as a giving machine, not a human. I'll never take her for granted again."

You really can change people's minds if you don't let yourself give up too soon!

Lee and Celia avoided what could have been heartbreaking and unnecessary tragedy.

Wounded feelings and a false sense of helplessness had knocked Lee and Celia off track for the moment, but they were able to straighten themselves out and continue their lives as they should have—going after what they love.

You can't do exactly what Lee and Celia did, because your situation is sure to be different. You're going to have to design your own specific plan of action.

PLANNING *YOUR* CAMPAIGN

What should *you* do? You're going to need to do some fresh thinking and generate some new ideas. The best way I know to do some fresh thinking is to gather friends together and let them help you.

Exercise 3: The Idea Storm

Chances are good you won't have much success coming up with really fresh thoughts by yourself. Most probably your head is filled with obstacles you're very emotional about, and it's hard to sort out the real obstacles from the unreal ones. Now is the time to have an idea party.

Here's how to organize the party: Call your friends and tell them you need their excellent minds at an idea party. For some reason, everyone sort of knows what an idea party is even if they've never heard the term before. And almost everyone likes being a part of an idea party. Ask your friends to bring a guest or two if they can. In my experience, strangers are often extraordinarily valuable brainstormers, bringing you surprising insights and information. Also, ask everyone to bring food. People relax and break the ice when they have to mess around together in the kitchen, unwrapping food or looking for pots and dishes.

Potluck is a great way to warm up a group so they'll feel comfortable about contributing ideas. And potluck creates a comfortable chaos. Everyone relaxes and feels he has part ownership of the evening, and everyone's raring to put his good feelings to use.

Start the brainstorming part of the evening by simply explaining what you want and why you can't seem to get it, and ask for suggestions. This beginning creates a leisurely conversation and makes your situation very clear. However, limit this first idea exchange to a half hour. It probably won't produce truly innovative ideas. After a half hour, move on to the following game. This game involves thinking at a lightning pace, too fast to censor the ideas. Here's how you do it.

Step 1: The idea storm.

Elect a note taker who can write very fast, or turn on a tape recorder so you can catch every comment, and get a kitchen timer ready. Have everyone sit in a circle focused on you as you name each of the obstacles to your goal, one at a time. You might want to think of this as tossing each obstacle in the air like a ceramic target and having everyone try to shoot it to pieces. Sometimes we even use the gesture, tossing an imaginary object into the air and saying, for example, "I'd have to sublet my apartment and my lease won't allow it!" while everyone points their imaginary slingshots and rifles at the object and calls out as many solutions as they can think up in one minute. "Sublet it to your mother!" "Get married!" "Let it sit empty!" "Ask your landlord to change your lease!" "Stay there!" etc., etc.

Let everyone "shoot" at each obstacle for one minute.

After one minute, toss up your next obstacle and repeat the process. When you've gone through the whole list of obstacles, you'll have a piece of paper or a tape full of ideas on how to overcome each obstacle, and you'll be ready for the next step.

Step 2: Working the list.

Your list will contain more ideas than you can ever use, but you have to process the list with another exercise if you want any of the ideas to be useful. Right now the list is composed of ideas that weren't given the benefit of careful thought. Don't be fooled by appearances. *Every single idea on that list can be useful.*

That's a guarantee.

First, you have to *make* yourself find some genuine merit in each idea. It may not look that way at first, but there is no idea without merit.

For example, if you needed to advertise your home business but you had no budget for advertising, someone might say, "Call the local news and tell them you're going to burn your house down if you don't get some business soon." Where's the merit in that idea? The free publicity. Now you have to find a better way to get it.

As soon as you've found some genuine merit in the idea, address the other side of the idea, the side that you know just won't work—but address it as another obstacle to be overcome, not as a reason to give up. Using the above example, you'd say, "It's great because of the free publicity, but what do I do if I don't want to burn my house down?" and a new round of brainstorming will yield less radical ways to get free publicity.

As you go through this exercise, one of the new solutions will hit you as an especially great idea, and one that you hadn't considered. *That will become your new goal.*

You're going to turn that goal into a plan of action, right now, by breaking it down into one small, doable step after another. And then you're going to do it. You'll probably need some ongoing support to keep you going if your courage should fail you— and it will fail you from time to time. But you'll have a ready-made support system after you've pulled a roomful of people in on your problem. After your potluck dinner, many people will be very interested in seeing you get to your goal, because they helped create it! Ask a few of them to act as phone buddies, buddies you can call for a brief pep talk when you have to do something especially hard, buddies who will call you to see if you're staying on top of your plan.

It's wonderful to have friends who will try to *make* you do what you *want* to do. Just remember, don't go into a long, tedious rehashing of the problem on the phone. That's taking too much from your buddy, and taking too much isn't fair. Even more to the point, *talking about something too much is often just another way of not doing it.*

Keep the buddy calls snappy and to the point. You say, "Tell me I'm not a fool for calling Eleanor to remind her how much she loves me"; your buddy says, "You're not a fool for calling Eleanor to remind her how much she loves you—you're a mensch. Go to it."

Then you'll be able to make that phone call. Or send a dozen roses.

ABOUT THAT CAREER OF YOURS

Next, I want you to find something you want to do—something that doesn't conflict with the goal you're now working on— and design a campaign to achieve that goal too! When you plant seeds in a garden, you're not supposed to stand there and stare at the ground waiting for them to sprout, you're supposed to get on with another task.

That's right, you must have a second project going. If you don't have one, start one—right away.

You can play two games at once. And being involved in a career goal will keep you from feeling empty or desperate. Having a second goal will make you patient too, and you need to be patient now, more than ever. Remember, when it comes to dealing with other people's resistance, timing is important.

If Lee had started working on getting back together with Steve and made that her only project, she would have lacked patience and timing. So she pursued her new career as a comedy writer at the same time she pursued Steve. Pursuing her career reminded her that, although her need for love was the most important thing in her life at that time, it wasn't the *only* thing. Working on both goals at the same time was essential to help her remember who she was.

Also, it's always so much easier to do something that's not charged with urgency. I know writers who have no trouble turning out a book they've been commissioned to do, but can't get anywhere on the novel they've been dying to write for years. This is a common ailment, and right now you can turn it to your advantage. Select a career goal, come up with a list of obstacles, get some fresh ideas, create a plan, and get a support team—just as you did with your "love goal."

Now you can get back to the work of living, and you can expect to feel much better because you know there's some hope of getting the love you need.

But what if you don't have a happy ending?

If your campaign works and you wind up with the person you want, you don't need any further advice from me. *But what if your campaign doesn't work?* What if the person you want really doesn't want you? You've done everything that could be done, and the final conclusion is that there's no more doubt. The party is over.

What happens then?

When you fail to get the love of the person you cared for, you put your beautiful, loving feelings back in your pocket and get on with your life.

With a heart like yours, you will love again.

Ralph Waldo Emerson's poem "Give All to Love" begins: "Give all to love; obey thy heart."

And if your love should leave you? Emerson knows exactly what will happen then:

> *Though thou loved her as thyself,*
> *As a self of purer clay,*
> *Though her parting dims the day,*
> *Stealing grace from all alive,*
> *Heartily know,*
> *When half-gods go,*
> *The gods arrive.*

When half-gods go, the gods arrive.

When you go after what you want with your whole heart, it's always worth it. It really is better to have loved and lost than never to have loved at all. Even if you don't get what you want, if you gave it your best try you'll find yourself mysteriously fulfilled and able to move on with the rest of your life. You may feel some hurt—although you may be surprised to find that you feel less hurt than you imagined possible.

The heart hates unfinished business.

You simply can't walk away from the game of love when you know deep down that all the cards haven't been played yet. When you've played out your hand, your heart will set you free.

So don't concern yourself with the outcome. If you get the love you want like Lee and Celia did, you'll be riding high. And if you don't, well, then the gods will arrive.

Epilogue

W ELL, if you've read every chapter (and I hope you have), you've been on a long and eventful journey, full of new feelings and realizations. I hope you now see through the mystery of why you've had trouble going after what you want—or even *knowing* what you want.

This whole book, of course, is about buried desire. With all the dangers our dearest dreams have had to survive—criticism, expectations, sorrow for the unhappiness of others, lack of support and information—it's no wonder we buried them for protection.

The good news is that you were remarkably successful at protecting your longings. And, as you now know, they survived, completely intact, and as beautiful as they ever were.

Understanding leads to action. That's what should have happened in every chapter—you found out what was stopping you, and you did the exercises to help you break through your block.

If you've made even one significant breakthrough while working your way through these pages, your wishes should already be making their presence known, reappearing timidly, or banging on the door of your memory, demanding their day.

But your job of facing inner blocks will never be entirely over.

Every time you begin pursuing a goal you really love, you can expect to hear loud complaints from all of your old defense mechanisms. They still think they're helping you; they *never* believe the old dangers are past.

Whenever those defense mechanisms act up, just go through this book again, even the chapters that don't seem to apply directly to you. Reading these pages, and reading your own pages, the ones you wrote while you were reading, will bring you back to clarity whenever you lose sight of your dream.

You need never be hopelessly stuck again; you can get moving now—start singing, see Alaska, start your own business, find someone to love, or all of the above—whatever makes your eyes light up. And you can do these things without settling, without sacrificing your security or hurting anyone else.

Langston Hughes said a dream deferred "dries up, like a raisin in the sun." It atrophies, in other words, just like an unused limb. A dream *lived,* however, a dream that gets daily workouts, becomes stronger with every passing day. More beautiful. More healthy from the exercise. More sustaining.

And who knows where such strength will carry you? Novalis, an eighteenth-century poet, said, "We are human and our lot is to learn and to be hurled into inconceivable new worlds."

Bon voyage.

INDEX